I dedicate this book to
my family, friends, and anyone who has dealt
with adversity, shame, or a dysfunctional past
and needs to know they're not alone.

Contents

Part I – Sunshine and Lollipops 1
Dad Left 1
The Good Ol' Days 2
Don't Outshine the Princess 4
Mom 7
Road trips, Popsicles, and Grandma Lou's House 9
Dad's Prospering, Mom's Not 11
Uncle John & Chance 14

Part II – Crap Sandwiches 19
Enter Eddy 19
Surprise! 22
Dropping Balls 25
More Roommates 27
All My World's A Stage 28
Thou Shall Not Commit Adultery or Clean Your House 33
Thou Shall Not Covet Other Kids' Clothes, Hair or Pizza 38
Entrepreneurial Spirit 41
Family Time 44
Discipline 48
Thou Shall Not Kill Yourself 50
Thou Shall Not Bear False Witness
   Unless Your Name is Summer 51
Honor Your Father and Leave Your Mother 55
Thou Shall Not Steal Candy Bars 56
Thou Shall Not Use Thy Lord's Name in Vain
   – Or Burn Down Dad's House 58
Paradise is in California 60
Surprise Dinner 65
Summer at Auntie Raven's 67
Grandpa Joe 74
Just Kill Me Already 76

Part III – Things Are Looking Up 79
Girlfriends 79
Thou Shall Have No Other Gods Before Me, Even Boys 83

Night Terrors 86
Planned Promiscuity 89
Working Girl 91
Dudley 93
Working for Dad 101
Girl Time 103
White Trash 104
I'm Fine, Really! 108
Pills, Thrills, and Guys Feeding Me Meals 109
I Got an Office Job! 117
Addicted 119
Kurt 127
Broken Promise 131

PART IV – CAN I GET SOME DESSERT WITH THESE CRAP SANDWICHES? 139

Marriage Material 139
Brad, Take #3? 146
The Happiest Year Ever! 147
Working It 149
Are You There Mary? It's Me, God 152
Somewhere-else-itis Relapse 156
Family Time 162
Disease to Please 165
Ritz Made me Too Big for my Britches 172
Mama's Helper 176
Heaven, Don't Make me Wait 182
Poolside Epiphany 185

PART V – TRYING OUT NEW PRESCRIPTIONS 193

Cheerleading Tryouts 196
Project from Heck Made Me Read the Bible 198
Finding My Passion 203
Pinky Promise 208
Actor's Studio 210
Auntie Raven Came Back 211
Job from Heck 215
Mom's Back in the Hospital 219
I Guess I'm a Thief 227
Auntie Raven Visits 229

PART VI – GROW UP ALREADY 233
    Thank God for Having to Show up to a Job 233
    Lionel 235
    Perspective 237
    Jailtime 239
    Auntie Raven's Back 241
    Codependent A Little Less 244
    From Helicoptering to Gallivanting 248
    Just Say Nope 251
    Cure for Somewhere-Else-Itis 254
    Mom Visits from the Grave 255
    That's it for Now 259
    One More Thing 260

    Acknowledgements 265
    About the Author 267

Part I – Sunshine and Lollipops

Dad Left

It was bedtime. Dad came home from Ireland a few weeks ago and forgot to bring us souvenirs. I heard Mom and Dad quietly talking in their bedroom. That was different. They were usually shouting at each other. Leah climbed down from her top bunk. I followed, rolling out from underneath my orange bedspread. Our baby brother slept in the next room.

It was 1977. Jimmy Carter was President, and the Bee Gees sang us songs on Dad's loud stereo. That means I was seven, Leah was nine and Chance was one. Leah and I tiptoed across the small hallway to our parents' bedroom to investigate. I looked up at the scary fishing landscape hanging above their bed. Fishermen with poles in hand and pointy straw hats were painted on the black velvet canvas. I think Dad got it while he served in Vietnam. I didn't like that painting because it was dark and sad. I preferred happier colors like pink and blue. On the opposite wall, I noticed Dad's hats hanging on hooks next to the belt rack. A couple were homemade hats Mom stitched together using slices of old beer cans and red yarn. Dad's suitcase sat open on the fake fur bedspread that looked soft but was as rough as his red beard. Mom was in the background, begging Dad to stay.

In my squeaky seven-year-old voice I asked Dad, "Where ya going?"

"I want to be free," Dad said as he stuffed his fancy work clothes into his suitcase. The word "free" conjured up an image of deer and antelope playing in amber waves of grain from songs we sang at school, like "Home on the Range" or "America the Beautiful." I thought Dad must be headed on another trip, and this time he was going to hang out with deer. Maybe camping. He walked out the front door, carrying his suitcase. I don't remember a hug goodbye or, "I'll see you kids later." But Leah tells me she remembers crying, begging Dad to stay. Chance slept through everything.

At the time, that day didn't seem out of the ordinary. But it was. That day burned an indelible thought pattern on my brain that still lingers, like an ill-conceived spring break tattoo. It taught me that when life's good, it's about to get bad. When the pantry and fridge are full of food, and the closets are full of toys and pretty dresses, things are about to change.

The Good Ol' Days

IN OUR SMALL neighborhood in Northern California, Leah and I played on the green grass and swing set in our backyard, with me obeying her every command. By the time I arrived, our backyard had fruitful plum, pomegranate, and apple trees, and raspberry and grapevines. There was a sturdy wooden trellis Mom and Grandpa built where my sister and I climbed. Leah and I loved to pick the juicy raspberries and grapes. We built forts out of sheets and chairs and hunkered down to enjoy our harvest.

Mom was always busy folding clothes, cooking, crocheting, washing dishes, doing yardwork, or watching *Phil Donahue*. She kept a long strip of packaged lollipops on the inside of our pantry door. We helped ourselves to snacks anytime we wanted, even the lollipops.

At dinner, Mom cooked juicy bone-in steaks, Rice-A-Roni, and canned vegetables—usually slimy spinach because it made Popeye strong. If we were lucky, we'd get TV dinners. My favorite was Salisbury Steak with the hot chocolate pudding. For drinks, she poured us cups of Hi-C juice from the large tin can. Mom dressed Leah and me in matching clothes and tied colorful hair ribbons in our thick ponytails. The only difference was Leah had white-blonde hair and mine was strawberry, just like Dad's. I liked it when strangers asked if Leah and I were twins. Sometimes Mom dressed baby Chance in my old blue dress, tied ribbons in his brown hair, and called him, "Christina."

I looked up to Leah and followed closely behind as her adoring shadow. Leah loved her time as an only child until I came along two years later. She often said, "I wish I was the only child!"

Dad called her "Princess." Everybody called me Mary Kay.

My earliest memories are when I was around three and Leah was five. Mom put her ice-cold Pepsi can on top of the air-conditioning unit that sat on a slab of concrete in our backyard. Leah and I pushed our handprints into that slab of concrete right after it was poured. We often placed our hands in our imprints to see how much we grew.

When Mom rolled the lawnmower from the front yard to the back, that was our cue to run and get our own Pepsi cans and place them next to hers. Our chubby fingers clumsily pried the aluminum tabs to open our sodas. We sipped our bubbly drinks as fast as we could and danced around and giggled in the yard as she mowed, with the smell of freshly cut grass in the air. With our bellies full of bubbles and sugar, we splashed around in our blue wading pool near the grapevines.

As I stood in a few inches of cool water, Leah's mouth suddenly spewed Pepsi-laced vomit on top of the water. She pushed it towards me, laughing and thinking it was funny.

"If you don't stop, I'm gonna get out!" I surprised myself when I stood up to Leah. Nothing like floating vomit to give me some courage. My surprise continued when she *actually* listened and stopped. We continued to play, doing our best to avoid the chunks.

Moments later we had to pee. Somehow, we knew better than to relieve ourselves in the pool.

"Let's pee over here—it'll be quicker," Leah said as she ran to the side yard. I didn't want to get in trouble but was easily hoodwinked by my big sister. I climbed out of the pool and ran to the side of the house where Mom couldn't see us. I copped a squat and peed on the grass and my feet. Leah didn't join me. Instead, she yelled, "MOOOOOMMM!!"

Mom came lightning fast, and I got caught in the act. Mom spanked me hard. Leah smiled as she watched me get in trouble.

Don't Outshine the Princess

MOM'S SISTER, AUNTIE Raven came over to visit often. It was exciting when she showed up. She was the youngest of Mom's five siblings, and only eight years older than me, so she didn't mind hanging out with us. She had long hair like Marsha from *The Brady Bunch*, a loud voice, and tons of friends. Mostly boys.

On one visit, she grabbed me by the hand and said, "Mary Kay, come on, let's curl your hair!" She worked hard taking small sections of my hair and made spiral curls all over my head, just like Shirley Temple. I felt pampered and I liked that she didn't pull my hair like Mom did. Auntie grabbed Mom's Final Net pump hairspray from the bathroom shelf and sprayed my hair. I loved that smell; it reminded me of Mom when she was in a good mood, getting ready to go out to dinner with Dad.

Auntie held me up so I could see myself in the bathroom mirror above the sink. I couldn't believe my eyes and wondered, "Who is that pretty girl looking back at me in the mirror. Is that me?!"

I carefully walked from the bathroom and down the hall extra slow, not moving my arms or my head, so my new hairdo wouldn't get ruined. I wanted to look this way forever. I walked through the door to the garage and out to the front yard and found Leah. She was playing with our bright orange Barbie automobile. It used to be Auntie Raven's and was big enough to have us take turns sitting on top of it and coast down our driveway. Leah looked up at me and stared with her mouth wide open. I could tell she was impressed with my hair. I smiled at her and felt pretty, just like Leah.

Suddenly, Leah pushed her bottom lip out, ran inside the house and cried, "Mom! Mary's acting tough because of her hair!" Acting "tough" meant I was acting too big for my britches and not being kind. I did neither. Shocked at Leah's accusations, I could find no words to tell Mom that it wasn't true. Mom believed Leah. Mom grabbed my arm and marched me inside the house. She took her rubber Goody hairbrush and dunked it into a Tupperware cup and flattened my curls with a few strokes as I stood barefoot on the linoleum floor, my chubby cheeks soaked with tears and water from Mom's brush.

Leah's frown turned upside down. I learned I had better not try to be as pretty as Leah. It wasn't worth the trouble.

In preschool, I wore an orange felt name tag in the shape of a caterpillar pinned to my pink dress. I was in the Caterpillar class at the local church preschool less than a mile from my house. I was baptized at Saint John's Catholic Church down the street. We didn't go to church, but Mom said I would attend catechism class when I was old enough, so I would be a full Catholic like her family; whatever that meant. We didn't pray as a family or talk about God. Mom once took Leah and me to a church wedding. It was horribly long, and Mom grew impatient. We left way before the groom kissed the bride. I cried because I didn't get the piece of wedding cake mom promised.

I waited in line for my turn to color on a sheet of heated aluminum foil with a crayon. I wondered why the line was taking so long and thought the other preschoolers should hurry up. It was finally my turn, and I chose red. I liked how the crayon glided on the foil, with the smell of melted crayon drifting towards my nostrils.

I was hyper-aware that there were people waiting behind me and I didn't want to keep them waiting. I felt nervous and thought it was my job to keep the line moving. Instead of taking my time to draw a picture of my family, I quickly scribbled a three-second, jagged mess of lines on the foil and dropped my crayon in the metal tray. There was no time for a stick figure with the arms and legs coming out of the head. I could tell the teacher was surprised by my fast finish when she asked, "Is *that* all?"

Wanting to do more, but not wanting to make others wait, I said, "Yes." I felt relieved that I finished fast so others could take their turn. But I also wished I could take my time like the other kids. I knew I had to hurry so others could go. For some reason, I was born in a hurry.

After school, I ran from class toward Mom, who was waiting for me in her white Datsun hatchback wagon. Sometimes Mom's face lit up, and she smiled when she saw me. But most days, she looked mad and preoccupied. I felt like I'd done something wrong to make her feel that way. I thought to myself, "I'll be extra good, so Mom won't be mad."

I got that same feeling of anxiousness when I watched the lady on TV who told us the news. For some reason, I felt her feelings. If she was nervous about being on TV, I felt nervous too. I didn't understand it, but somehow, I took on whatever everyone else was feeling and wore it like one of Mom's crocheted blankets.

Leah and I were both home from school, and she told me to follow her. We walked down the short hallway to the bathroom to do our business. She took several squares from the toilet paper roll, turned on the faucet and got the toilet paper wet. She turned to me and said, "Mary, all the kids at school do this," as she underhandedly threw the wet wad of toilet paper. It stuck to the ceiling like glue. "C'mon Mary—all the cool kids do it!"

"No, I'll get in trouble."

"C'mon Mary, I swear I won't tell!" Knowing better, and hoping for the best, I followed her instructions and wet my own wad and threw it on the ceiling. As soon as it stuck, she yelled, "MOOOOOMMM!" I heard the familiar jangling sound of Mom removing one of the leather belts from her belt rack.

I knew I had to lay belly down on my bottom bunk. I'm the only one walloped that day as Mom said, "It hurts me more than it hurts you!" I never understood why she said that.

Because I loved my sister so much and wanted her approval, I would do whatever she said, even when I knew it would get me in trouble. You'd think I would have learned my lesson.

Mom

I DIPPED MY palms in red paint. The kindergarten teacher helped me place my painted hands on a white sheet of paper. My handprints were an art project that would become a Mother's Day gift. The teacher asked questions like, "What's your mom's favorite food?" "What's your mom's favorite thing?"

I told the teacher Mom's favorite food was "red juicy meat." I knew this because at dinner, Mom sucked on the bones of her red juicy steaks. Mom's favorite thing was, "peace and quiet." When there was too much noise in the house, Mom shouted, "I just want a little peace and quiet!" The teacher wrote my answers down in her cursive handwriting. I pasted the piece of paper with the questions and my answers on the left side of the green construction paper and my handprints on the right. I loved the smell of that grainy paste, but I didn't eat it like some of the kids.

On Mother's Day, Mom loved her gift and placed it inside my scrapbook, just like she did when Leah did the same exact project in her kindergarten class. Mom compared my answers to Leah's and laughed when she realized they were identical.

We'd often watch *The Six Million Dollar Man, Happy Days, The Carol Burnett Show, Quincy, Laverne and Shirley,* or *Emergency,* the show about firefighters. When the theme song for *Laverne and Shirley* came on, Leah and I held hands, singing it incorrectly while running around the coffee table, "We're gonna do it!"

After the theme song, we sat crisscrossed applesauce close to the TV to watch the show. I loved how Laverne had the letter "L" stitched on all her shirts. We begged Mom to make us Laverne's favorite drink, Pepsi with milk. Mom wouldn't allow it, telling us, "You won't like it."

My hero from all the shows was Pinky Tuscadero, Fonzi's girlfriend. She was tough and pretty with her pink clothes and matching motorcycle.

Mom was the one who took us to our doctor's appointments. I sat in the waiting room, turning the pages of a Dr. Seuss book, hoping the other kids would be impressed when they saw my lips moving as I pretended to know how to read. After our shots, the doctor gave us a lollipop and stickers. Shots never made us cry.

Mom read books to us. There were plenty of nursery rhymes and stories I learned. I loved Mary Quite Contrary and her garden. I was so sad for Cinderella until she found her handsome prince. I wondered why her stepsisters were so mean. I also wondered why only one of the three little pigs built a sturdy house, while the other two built their house out of sticks. What were they thinking? Those houses could easily be blown down by the big bad wolf. I told Mom, "I'm gonna build my house out of bricks!" I just knew my sister would do the same.

Mom shopped for us and hung colorful ruffled dresses in our closet and placed folded socks and underwear in our dresser drawers. On some nights, she'd hold me on her lap while delicately taking a bobby pin and Q-tip to clean out my ears. That was my favorite memory of Mom. That was when I felt like she was giving me a big hug and loved me. She wasn't the type to give smiles, hugs, or kisses, and this was almost as good as a hug from Grandma Lou.

When Leah and I heard Dad's shoes make the click noise in the front doorway, we knew he was home from work. We'd run toward Dad at lightning speed yelling, "Daddy's home, Daddy's home!" He picked us up one at a time and gave us big hugs and kisses on our cheeks. He was as affectionate as his mom, Grandma Penny. Except Grandma Penny's lips were wet with lipstick, and she kissed us smack dab on the lips. Grandma Penny lived near San Francisco, so we didn't see her as much as Grandma Lou.

Sometimes we yelled, "foot ride!" at Dad. That was when Leah and I sat on Dad's shiny shoes, wrapping our arms and legs around his legs. We giggled as Dad walked fast around the house, with us hanging on for dear life. Sometimes Dad yelled, "tickle monster!" and started chasing us around the house to tickle us.

When Dad made us laugh, it annoyed Mom. She'd yell, "cut it out!" Dad always seemed happy when we got to see him.

I had no clue Dad was experiencing panic attacks because of the amount of responsibility he had at such a young age. Dad later shared, "The doctor told me people like you are the doers of the world, but they pay a hefty price." By then, Dad began his own photography business at the local military base, despite Mom and Grandma Lou telling him he wouldn't succeed. He took his $500 life savings and worked hard to prove them wrong.

Road trips, Popsicles, and Grandma Lou's House

WE HEARD THE ice cream truck coming from miles away and begged Mom for money. Coins in hand, we ran down the bleached-white sidewalks brightly lit by the sun, since the neighborhood's shade trees weren't fully grown yet. I got a "fruity missile" that melted down my arm quicker than I could eat it.

After eating our treats, Leah and I raced our popsicle sticks in the gutter's steady stream of water, fueled by the neighbor's sprinklers. Mom yelled for us to get in the car to go to Grandma Lou and Grandpa's house. We loved visiting our grandparents and swimming in their pool. Like most sunny days, we loaded up in the Datsun hatchback; no seatbelts required.

Grandma Lou and Grandpa Joe lived with Mom's siblings a mile down the road from our house. Grandpa was in the military and worked at the local base. He's an efficient guy who refused to install toilet paper holders, since the TP was easier to access and replace without them. He was quiet and wore a baseball cap balanced high on top of his bald head. I thought it might fall off at any moment. Maybe Grandpa thought it made him look taller, since he was short in stature. His almond eyes were always smiling, and they looked extra blue against his reddish-brown skin, just like Mom's. He didn't say much, but I loved being near him. Grandma Lou had a scruffy dog named Oly, after Grandpa's favorite beer. Grandma taught Oly how to say, "MaaaaahMaaaaaaaaah." Grandma Lou could teach anybody anything.

Grandma Lou was the opposite of Grandpa. Her voice was loud and joyful, like she had a built-in Mr. Microphone. She smiled all the time and said, "dammit Joe!" an awful lot to Grandpa. She told me she loved me and meant it. Her eyebrows were the shape of boomerangs, and it made her seem permanently surprised. She was usually in the kitchen making cookies and cakes from scratch. She made us plates of sandwiches, desserts, chips, and chocolate milk. I loved how it felt when she hugged me with her large, squishy, crepe paper arms. And I loved how she smelled like roses. My happiness meter was at its highest when I was with Grandma Lou.

Grandma Lou married Grandpa Joe after knowing him only

three days. When they married, she already had a son, Larry, from her first husband, George, who was killed at Pearl Harbor on December 7, 1941, while serving on the USS Oklahoma. I never got to meet Uncle Larry, since he died in a car crash when he was 18.

Grandma Lou and Grandpa Joe's first child together was my Aunt Darlene. She was disabled at birth thanks to a doctor who aggressively used forceps to yank precious Darlene out of Grandma's body. Grandma told me the story of the doctor having one foot on the ground and the other on the hospital bed for leverage, with both hands on the forceps, while trying to pry Darlene out from Grandma's nether regions like a stubborn champagne cork. This caused Darlene to be born blind in one eye and mentally impaired. Despite her disabilities and the doctors telling Grandma that Darlene would never walk or talk, she did. That was due to Grandma's love, patience, and persistence. Darlene was smarter than most people and could answer any random question you threw at her about sports, music, or history. Darlene and Grandma Lou were the happiest people I have ever known.

Mom was the next oldest behind Darlene. Mom later told me she helped raise Darlene and her younger siblings, Uncle Bruce, Uncle John, and Auntie Raven. Mom told me stories about how Grandpa often made her do a ridiculous number of chores as prepayment for allowing her to go out with friends. By the time she finished, Grandpa was already drunk and wouldn't let her go. It's no wonder Mom happily married Dad when she was 19. She couldn't wait to leave home.

Dad's Prospering, Mom's Not

I WAS IN the second grade. Dad's photography business was taking off due to his likeability and workaholism. He was sort of a celebrity around town and had a way of making people feel like they were the most important person on the planet. Everyone thought he or she was Dad's best friend and wanted to spend time with him. Everyone except Mom. She preferred peace and quiet.

Everybody seemed to love me too. I was adopted by three older girls who gave me presents each week and played with me on the playground during recess. One day, they gave me a stuffed koala bear. I was so happy to see them, and they were happy to see me. Maybe I was like a living doll they could play with. I had chubby, freckled cheeks and was much shorter than most kids in school. Because of my size, Leah teased and called me, "Midget" or "Mary Hartman Midget" after the *Mary Hartman, Mary Hartman* TV show. Mary Hartman also had red hair.

One evening, Mom and Dad were going out to dinner. The pleasant smell of Mom's blow-dried hair and Final Net hairspray permeated the house, like the best smelling candle ever. That smell, along with mom singing Lesley Gore's, "It's My Party" song meant she was in a good mood. Mom teased her hair into a bouffant and drew winged eyeliner on her eyelids. Barbara, our babysitter, was there to watch us. Barbara was Auntie Raven's best friend. She looked like Cinderella and radiated love and goodness. When Mom and Dad left, Barbara excitedly asked, "What do you guys wanna do!?" Weird. She seemed genuinely interested in playing with us. No babysitter ever did that.

I squeaked, "Can we play soda shop!?" Leah and I had a brand new, unused toy that you poured real soda into and pretended that you were at a soda shop. Mom never let us play it, because she said it would make too much of a mess. Barbara happily got the box out of the hall closet and set it up on the kitchen table. The night went by fast. We had a blast playing soda shop, sipping tiny glasses of Pepsi and giggling. Barbara cleaned it up without complaining. She was our favorite babysitter. I could tell she liked my sister and me, and we adored her. She had that effect on everyone.

Auntie Raven babysat us too, but I preferred Barbara. One evening, Raven taught us how to smoke. She was excited and announced, "Mary, Leah, come here, I want to show you something cool!" Excited, we did as she asked. She walked us outside the front door, removed a cigarette from her package of Virginia Slims which she called, "Vagina Slimes." She took her lighter to her cigarette and taught us how to make a V with our two fingers and place the cigarette in between, like so. Being the oldest, Leah went first. Leah put the lit cigarette to her lips and pretended to smoke like Mom and Auntie Raven. Auntie cracked up. It was my turn. I put the cigarette to my lips and blew on it. Auntie Raven laughed again. I was happy to entertain.

Auntie Raven picked up the rotary phone hanging from the wall and called the neighborhood boys who were her age. She told them to come over and make it snappy!

Auntie Raven made us do it again, and the group of boys laughed. After our performance, all the boys and Auntie Raven went into our garage, while Leah and I stayed inside wondering what to do next.

Leah and I grew curious and bored. Leah opened the garage door. I was right behind her. It was smoky inside the garage, and it smelled like a skunk. One teenager had his mouth on a colorful tube, and his eyes got big when he saw us. Auntie Raven yelled, "Go back inside!"

The next day Dad drove us to a park, so his friend could take our family photo. Leah and I wore matching dresses. We giggled as we jumped around on the floorboards behind Mom and Dad's seats, holding onto their headrests, causing Mom to yell, "Stop pulling my hair!"

Since we giggled so much, she yelled, "If you don't knock it off, Dad's pulling over, and I'm spanking you!" Soon Mom turned her attention back to Dad and screamed, "I'm leaving!" Mom reached for the door handle of our moving car, so she could leave us right then and there. I thought she wanted Dad to beg her to not jump out of the car. I was convinced Mom would leave us forever once the car door opened.

Dad yelled back, "Go ahead, nobody's stopping you!"

It was up to Leah and me to make sure it didn't happen so we both cried, "Mooommmm! Please! No! Stop! Don't!" This was more frightening than watching *The Blob* movie or being with Auntie Raven. Somehow, we made it to the park with Mom still in the car. We all smiled for the photo, as if we were a happy family.

Mom and Dad were always mad at each other for some reason. Weeks later, Mom tried to run Dad over with the car after they came back from a party. I tried to be extra good and not bother anyone.

Uncle John & Chance

"Leah! Mary Kay!" Mom called for us from the living room. We ran down the hallway from our room where we were playing quietly, trying to delay bedtime. The house was dimly lit with a yellow glow from a pair of barrel-sized lampshades. The TV wasn't on, which was different. Mom loved her programs. Mom, Leah, and I were in our jammies. Mom was lying on the couch covered by a crocheted blanket. I thought it seemed strange. She never rests. Dad wasn't home from work yet, since he usually got home after bedtime, or lately not at all.

Mom was pregnant with our brother and her belly was getting big. She asked Leah and me to come closer. Her voice was quieter than normal. She whispered, "I'm really sick and the doctor thinks I have cancer." We didn't know what it meant but thought Mom must be sick. We didn't cry, not able to process her message, but

Mom seemed sad. Mom's usual mood is mad, not sad. Leah and I walked back to our bedroom.

Good news. Dad called a couple nights later, and Mom found out she didn't have cancer. She had something else. And Dad gave it to her. This upset my Uncle Bruce and Uncle John. They went searching for Dad that same night.

Dad gave Mom gonorrhea. He got it from one of his affairs. Dad didn't have the nerve to tell her in person or come home that night.

Uncle Bruce, born after Mom, was a hippie with an authoritative laugh. He looked like Grandpa, but with more hair. Uncle Bruce's favorite outfit was his tight denim overalls with no shirt underneath. He said funny things that made people laugh like, "Nothing's better than a healthy shit." He laughed so hard at his jokes, he made other people laugh along too.

After Uncle Bruce, came Uncle John. He seemed to be everyone's favorite. Uncle John could make his voice sound like other people, like Wolfman Jack from the radio. He'd sing me silly songs like, "Mary is a canary, and she smells like gasoline...." When Uncle John was around, he had a way of making any room happier and brighter. I remember standing on a stool in Grandma Lou's kitchen watching him mix up mayonnaise and something in a bowl that smelled like fish. He asked, "Mary, it's bumble bee stingers, you want some?"

"No!" I didn't want to get stung.

I woke up the next morning after my uncles searched for Dad. I thought Dad was probably working somewhere where my uncles couldn't find him. Maybe he had another wedding to photograph. This morning Mom was sad and crying. "What's wrong?" I asked.

"Uncle John crashed his motorcycle last night. Now he can't walk." I loved my Uncle John, and I knew he loved me too. I just knew he would get better. I wanted to hug him. My sister and

I weren't allowed to go to the hospital to visit. Mom said only grown-ups could go.

A few days later, my sister and I sat on the floor in front of the TV watching Popeye eat spinach and fight Brutus. Mom wasn't home, but Dad was at home sleeping in. Mom walked through the front door, put her leather purse on the kitchen table, and said, "Uncle John's dead." Leah and I looked at each other. Time stood still for a moment. We both started crying hard and loud. Mom knelt and cried with us too. "The hospital killed him," she said, "He choked, and nobody was there to help."

Uncle John choked on a McDonald's French fry and the hospital staff didn't get to him in time. Leah and I weren't allowed to go to the funeral. Mom said that Uncle John was sad and didn't want to go on living if he was paralyzed. Our family was no longer joyful, and things were about to get worse.

Dad later told me the family blamed him for Uncle John's death since the wreck occurred the night the family learned Dad gave mom the clap.

Mom's belly kept getting bigger. She worked to get our brother's room ready. I watched her place a mobile over his crib, hang curtains, and paint a ceramic teddy bear for his room. Our brother Chance arrived earlier than he should have, weighing three pounds and two ounces. Grandma Lou repeated many times, "Three pounds, two ounces." Mom and Chance had a tough time during labor, so they stayed in the hospital for a while.

Dad later shared what happened, "The doctor told me your brother wouldn't live through the night. I was devastated. I prayed so hard that night and asked God to take my strength and give it to Chance. I actually visualized all my strength going into your brother. I'm convinced my prayers helped save your brother."

Baby Chance was so tiny when we finally got to see him, even the newborn diapers were too big for his bottom. Grandma Lou came over to help. She bathed Chance in the kitchen sink and fed him his bottles. I could tell Chance was now Grandma Lou's favorite. I didn't mind. She was still the best grandma, even if Leah and I were dethroned.

Leah started getting boy crazy. She hung a Shaun Cassidy poster on the inside of our bedroom door saying, "Isn't he dreamy?" I didn't think so. We speed prayed every night and ended with, "Good night. Sweet dreams. God bless you. I love you." The other responded, "Same to you, but more of it!" We must have got the idea to pray from our preschool or TV. As usual, Leah and I waited to hear the sound of Dad's shoes click on the entryway floor so we could run and hug him. That night, Mom asked us to stay in bed and ignore Dad.

Mom and Dad drifted further apart each day, until Dad left for good.

Dad later shared, "Your mom treated me like shit. She held my hand when your grandma was around, but she was a different person at home—constantly nitpicking and withholding sex. She said that was all I cared about. I had all these girls treating me like a celebrity and was a young man. I'm not making excuses. I'm telling you the truth. I asked her to go on trips with me, including Ireland. She never wanted to do anything. After your sister was born, she went from happy to angry and mean all the time. Your mother realized I was going to leave and tried to be nice, but it was too late. I was done being treated like shit at home."

I didn't realize these were the "Good Ol' Days" until I had some bad ones to compare. I'm grateful I had a good seven-year pour of a sturdy foundation before the big bad wolf blew my house down.

Part II – Crap Sandwiches

*When life gives you crap sandwiches, God brings the dessert...
but it might take a while.* – M.K. Hughes

Enter Eddy

IT WAS ONE week after Dad left to be free like the deer. Leah and I walked ourselves to and from school, since Mom said we were old enough. After another day in school, something weird happened. I stepped inside our house, and Mom was actually smiling and happy to see me. She was usually irritated and didn't notice Leah or me much. I surveyed the situation. Chance was on the backyard swing getting pushed by a strange man. They were both smiling. Mom proudly beamed, "They played so hard... *all day*!" It was as if playing hard were an official assignment, and they were given an A+. The man walked from the backyard and opened our sliding glass door. Mom said, "This is Eddy."

He seemed OK, but there was no way I was calling him Dad. He had a large nose and wide-set droopy eyes like a basset hound. He wore a trucker's hat that said "CAT" on his red curly hair, faded jeans, a T-shirt, and dirty boots. He kind of looked like the Marlboro man from the commercials, but without a horse or car.

Once Dad left, Mom joined a drinking team that also played softball. After games, she went to Peggy's Bar with her girlfriends. There, she found a "real man," as she called him. Eddy moved into our house that day and slept on Dad's side of the bed. Sometimes he'd take off his shirt and make his two pectoral bird tattoos dance, one at a time. I wished Mom and Dad would get back together and this man with wild hair would go away.

At school, it was easy to make friends and I had many. Fay was my best. We were inseparable. We played dodgeball, handball, and swung on the monkey bars. She had black freckles, tiny features and snorted after her corny jokes. I didn't realize it at the time, but she was the most popular girl in school. Most days we walked to her house after school. She asked, "Who should we invite to my slumber party?"

I was happy to tell her, "Let's invite all the girls from our class," thinking we should include the girls who didn't have best friends. She didn't seem happy about my suggestion but still invited everyone.

Her slumber party was a blast. We ate pizza and chips, slurped root beer through Krazy Straws, and played "Light as a Feather, Stiff as a Board." I was surprised that people complimented me on my outfit. I didn't think my Ditto jeans were anything special.

On another day after school, I noticed Fay's dad looking in the yellow pages while sitting at his kitchen table. Fay asked, "Whatcha doing, Dad?"

"Looking for an attorney," Fay's dad said. Fay's parents were divorcing too, and she seemed fine with it.

Months went by, and it still hadn't dawned on me that my world shifted. My self-esteem was fine, even though Dad left and Eddy moved in. I sat at my classroom table with a kind, dark-haired beauty named Stacy and a few others. A boy in our class said something unkind about me. I didn't hear it. Stacy took it upon herself to report to me, "Donny said you have a freckled face."

I said to Stacy, "So?" And I meant it.

Fay was impressed by my unaffected response and proudly told our friend, "At least *she* doesn't care what people think, Stacy!"

My solid childhood kept me strong for that first year after Dad left. Things didn't seem too different. My abundant clothes still fit, and we had plenty of food in the cupboards.

While Leah and I were at school, Eddy usually played with Chance. Sometimes he went to work as a construction worker. Eddy usually had a Coors can in one hand and took intermittent swigs from his whiskey bottle he tucked in between our sofa cushions. The label said, "Smooth as Silk." It was the same kind Grandpa drank.

I heard Mom phone Dad and say, "Now I have a real man, a man that has calluses on his hands, unlike you!" Maybe Mom watched western movies with John Wayne or saw images of the Marlboro man and thought only real men had dirt under their fingernails. Dad was the opposite of the Marlboro man. His clothes, fingernails, and hands were clean. He didn't have tattoos. Mom continued, "And by the way, Tom—you have short man's disease!" At the other end of the phone, I could hear Dad howling with laughter. Mom's words didn't have the intended effect. Dad was happy with his new bachelor status, dating several ladies, all younger than him. I liked the short-haired one. She bought us snacks and reminded me of a brunette Olivia Newton-John.

Mom didn't vacuum or clean the house anymore. Sometimes she mowed the lawn, and she drank Coors instead of Pepsi. Every morning, she called Eddy's brother Harvey on the phone, and they worked together to solve the newspaper's daily puzzles. I liked Harvey. He was nice to me and my siblings. He showed up to his job every day, unlike Eddy.

Chance started calling Eddy "Dad." Leah and I didn't. Normally we did whatever Mom told us, but not this. She didn't force it, although she asked us a few times.

While I was at school, Mom watched Jayne Pauley on the *Today Show*, *All My Children* with Jenny and Tad, and *General Hospital* with Luke and Laura. By the time Leah and I got home,

Phil Donahue or *The Mike Douglas Show* was on. Mom cooked dinner and was a great cook. Pepsi and lollipops were no longer on her shopping list. Coors, Kessler, and cigarettes took their place. Mom switched from smoking Salem cigarettes to Eddy's favorite, Marlboro Reds.

We didn't see any of our babysitters anymore. Instead, several of the softball team members and neighbors came to our house every day. Mom was the scorekeeper for Eddy's team, and she was friends with everyone. Mom was on an all-girls team, named after the insurance company who sponsored them. Her jersey was black with white lettering. Eddy's team was named, "Stoners." His team jersey had a cartoon drawing of a softball player with a joint in his mouth.

Mom's male softball friends were nice. I got to watch them expertly roll and smoke joints at the kitchen table while I did my homework. Some could do it one-handed. They said it came in handy when they were driving. They guzzled beer and chain smoked, filling up ashtrays and turning our white walls nicotine yellow. With the massive quantity of empty beer cans, Leah and I started collecting them for money, so we could buy luxuries like candy bars, three-cent Bazooka gum, and bottles of soda. The houseguests caused a steady stream of noise at the house, making it the opposite of peaceful and quiet.

Mom cooked large dinners for everyone, including on Thanksgiving. I'm not sure if the houseguests had full or part-time jobs. It was like she adopted them as her new children and focused on giving them her beer-induced conversation, laughter, and attention. Chance, Leah, and I faded into the background, like extras in a movie.

Surprise!

I HAD MY ninth birthday coming up, and I knew Mom had to have something planned. Maybe it was going to be a surprise party since I hadn't heard her say anything. I could always count on a cake and a present at a minimum. I didn't ask to have a slumber party like Fay because my house was too full of people.

Leah and I continued to get ready for school while Mom slept. We no longer got our Holly Hobby lunch pails filled with sandwiches, chips, and foil-wrapped Ding Dongs. We now got free lunches at school.

My birthday fell on a school day. As I walked towards the front door to leave, I glanced towards the kitchen and noticed a pink box sitting on top of the refrigerator.

I thought, "That must be my birthday cake. Mom remembered! I bet when I come home, she'll have some of my classmates hiding, and they will all yell, SURPRISE!" I was excited about that all day. I had a smile on my face as I walked home.

I slowly opened the dusty screen door to make sure everybody could get ready to yell, "SURPRISE!!!!! HAPPY BIRTHDAY!!!" I tiptoed across the threshold. As I stepped inside the house, I noticed it was quiet. The only voice I heard was Phil Donahue's. Mom was on the loveseat watching her program, Coors in one hand, cigarette in the other. I thought, "Hmmmm. That's strange. Where are my friends? Where's the cake that was on the fridge?" The house didn't have any of my schoolmates inside. I realized there wasn't a cake in the pink box. She probably forgot. I was bummed but knew better than to bother Mom with questions and make her mad.

I saw the stack of mail on the kitchen table. Grandma Lou had sent a birthday card with $5. She never forgets birthdays. With that five-spot, I walked to the grocery store and bought my favorite snacks. A glass bottle of ice-cold Coca Cola, a Snicker's bar, a bag of pumpkin seeds, and a chocolate Home Run pie. Who needs a birthday cake or party when you have your favorite snacks?

By now Grandma and Grandpa had moved a few hours away

to the new retirement community in Paradise. I wished they still lived close by.

Every summer, my brother, sister, and I visited them for a couple of blissful weeks. It was like old times when we were a happy family. I wondered if Eddy would be nicer if Grandma and Grandpa still lived nearby.

Eddy's default mood was crangry. A cross between cranky and angry. He pretended to be a nice person when he first showed up. But after a while, he was only nice when certain people were around, especially when Dad came to pick us up. The changes in Eddy and Mom happened so gradually that I accepted it as normal and didn't think to tell Grandma Lou or Dad about it.

Eddy wouldn't allow us kids to help ourselves to food in the pantry or fridge. I learned this when I opened the bread drawer to take a slice of bread to make toast after school. "You didn't ask!" Eddy yelled at me. I stiffened and slowly put the bread back. I didn't think I could talk back or ask, "May I please have a piece of toast?" It was easier to keep a low profile. I told myself, "You'd better eat more of your free lunch."

I didn't mind the free lunches at school, it was usually an ice-cream scoop pile of rice or instant mashed potatoes smothered in brown gravy with a vegetable and bread roll. Sometimes it was a premade subway sandwich that took on the flavor of the green plastic wrap. I ate as much as I could and dumped the leftovers in the big garbage can so I could get in line to play handball. As I dumped my lunch tray, the lunch lady and recess guard blew her whistle and announced to the quieted cafeteria, "I see many of you throwing away good lunches, especially those of you who get them for free. It's not right. Don't waste food, especially if it is free!" I didn't make eye contact, knowing her comment was directed at me. As I walked towards the exit, I snuck sideways glances at the lunch tables full of kids who had homemade sandwiches and Hostess desserts.

Dropping Balls

MY FIFTH-GRADE TEACHER, Mrs. Sullivan, had us rehearsing lines for a play. I sat across from my classmate acting out a scene. The words surprised me when they effortlessly flew out of my mouth. I wasn't really acting. I was just being myself. I felt like the character and the lines were something I'd say anyway. It was fun and I fell in love with acting.

I got the idea to direct a play with some of my classmates. All I needed was someone to take the play I chose from our schoolbook and copy the lines for everyone's part so we could rehearse. Brenda volunteered. We were going to do a play and I would be in charge.

After school that day, I walked home with Fay. I liked it at her house more than mine, plus Mom didn't mind if I didn't come straight home. Mick Jagger was prancing around on her TV, singing, "Start me Up." I fell in love at first sight. It was something about the way he danced that captivated my attention. Mick was now my second crush. My first crush was on the cigarette-smoking baseball player from the *Bad News Bears* movie.

Fay snatched me from my Mick trance when she matter-of-factly said, "Your house is scummy." I didn't have a response and kept quiet. Instantly I felt hot all over, and I'm sure my face turned red. I kept watching Mick, hoping she wouldn't notice my reaction. I decided in that moment I was not worthy of having her as my friend. If my house was scummy to her, that meant I must be scummy too.

I stopped talking to Fay, and no longer had a swarm of girls next to me at recess. Instead, I wandered around aimlessly, feeling lonely, sad, and worthless. I understood why people no longer commented on my pretty hair and nice clothes or gave me stuffed animals. I didn't have any new clothes that magically appeared in my closet and my shoes were getting holes in them.

A few weeks later, Brenda walked up to me as I waited in line to head into Mrs. Sullivan's class. She handed me all the scripts, in her neat cursive handwriting, stapled to colorful construction paper announcing, "I finished our scripts!"

I took the scripts and said, "Thank you."

Part of me was happy she still thought we were doing the play. Another part of me knew the play wouldn't happen. I felt unworthy. Nobody would listen to someone who was scummy. I didn't step up and follow through on my commitment, and I felt horrible every time I saw Brenda. She worked hard writing all those words in cursive.

I thought that because I wanted to be an actor, everyone else must want to be one too. With all that competition, there was no way I would succeed. I put that dream aside, like my ballerina dream. Maybe someday I could work at a grocery store, and I could buy all the clothes and sodas I wanted. They seemed happy, and I overheard Eddy say, "They make good money."

I decided to stop doing homework. My mind drifted in class. I noticed a girl who got to sit in the back of class and do nothing. I thought she had a good plan. I was transferred out of the gifted math group. I got to sit next to the girl in the back of the class. She smelled like a fresh sneeze, even when she wasn't sneezing.

After a month or so, doing nothing didn't feel right, plus I don't like the smell of air-born spit. I decided I would keep doing my schoolwork.

I realized not following through on my homework or the play was more painful than feeling scummy. I never wanted to feel that way again, but I felt like too much time had passed, so I didn't try to organize the play. I began doing my homework again and was back with the kids who were good at math.

I stopped my pity party. I wanted to join all the girls playing at recess, giggling about something, while searching for four-leaf clovers in the field. I tried to blend in and pretend I knew what they're giggling about. I giggled too. This kind of pretending was much harder than acting in a play.

At recess, I occasionally saw my sister and her best friend, Tosha. They gave me attention and boosted my social stock price. Tosha was tall, with big shoulders, milk chocolate skin and attitude. She lived around the corner from our house and was still Leah's best friend even after our house became scummy. Tosha protected Leah from all the mean girls. When Tosha was around, nobody dared to tease Leah about her hair or clothes. Tosha would pop them in the mouth.

More Roommates

MORE PEOPLE STARTED living in my house. They showed up a couple years after Eddy arrived. That made me around nine, Leah eleven and Chance three. Leah and I walked outside the front door with Mom and saw two short girls nervously smiling, shoulders hunched, standing near Eddy and our perpetually open garage. Instantly I thought they looked strange, something about their faces seemed different than any other face I had seen. They were twins but not identical. They had unusually large wide-set eyes and long eyelashes that took me a moment to process. Misty was slightly taller than Summer and had Eddy's features and complexion. Summer, the nicer one, had darker hair and a flair for the dramatics.

Their mom's name was Trish. She drove a motorcycle and worked as a part-time escort. She was cool like Pinky Tuscadero. I didn't know what the word "escort" meant. Misty explained it meant she got paid to go on dates. It sounded like a cool job and better paying than the grocery store.

Trish bounced when she walked and spoke loudly, using her

hands, and no end of curse words. Trish was no more than five feet tall with the help of her high-heeled leather boots. She carried a small spray bottle full of water to tame her wild mane of windblown hair from her motorcycle rides. She smelled delicious when she walked past me. Misty told me it was Ciara perfume. I thought someday maybe I could save up for a bottle and smell that good.

Summer and Misty moved into our room that day without much. I shared my bed with Misty. Leah with Summer.

Mom enrolled Summer and Misty at the other elementary school down the street, since ours was too full. Misty and Summer helped themselves to my underwear, socks, and clothes. I wished they wouldn't do that, or at least ask permission, but I was too afraid to speak up. Summer was occasionally polite and asked to wear the jeans Dad had bought for me. These were unfamiliar circumstances, and I didn't want to get in trouble.

All My World's A Stage

All cruelty springs from weakness. – Seneca

EDDY, MISTY, AND Summer made themselves at home while Leah and I became unwelcome houseguests. Misty joined Eddy in scrutinizing Leah's and my every move. They often shook their heads in disgust saying things like, "Hmph, look at her pimply face." "Tsk, her neck is dirty." "You're stupid!" "Your feet stink." "You look like a clown, where's the circus?" Leah and I were on stage for the devoted audience.

I didn't speak up or fight back. It didn't occur to me that I had choices. With fight, flight, or freeze as coping options, my instincts chose the latter until it became rote. Misty and Eddy were committed to their bullying and treated it like a full-time job. I now think their brains must've received a chemical reward for their efforts.

Any remaining crumbs of confidence built during my first seven years were now crushed. As I went about my days, doing homework, watching *Gilligan's Island* or *The Brady Bunch*, I felt their laser stares burning cuts into my flesh and soul. I guessed Misty felt she had to follow suit with her dad's example. It kept Eddy's anger focused away from her and her sister. Misty was like the mean stepsisters from Cinderella, all wrapped in one person. I wished a handsome prince would come save me.

Leah was more courageous. She talked back and made things worse for herself, saying things to Mom and Eddy like, "Have another beer!" Because of her courage, Mom gave Leah a new nickname, "Mouth" and often smacked her upside the head or made her take a bite of soap.

Eddy and Misty didn't like it when Leah talked back. But I liked it and wished I were that brave. Thankfully, Chance's adorability factor kept him off the radar.

With each stare-down, headshake, and unkind comment, I learned my existence on this planet was unacceptable and offensive. Like in Eddy's favorite show, *Wild Kingdom*. I was the weakest and most vulnerable antelope in the pack. Eddy and Misty knew I wouldn't put up a fight like courageous Leah. I submitted to my hungry predators and let them make a meal out of me without a fight. It was easier that way. As they wounded me with their words and stares, their thin lips wore perpetual smirks of victory matching their hateful eyes.

I became super self-conscious, as if everyone in the world was watching me, ready to pounce and accuse me of being a piece of shit. I learned to not make eye contact with any human so I wouldn't provoke an attack. I tuned out my surroundings and retreated inside myself where it was safe. I distracted my attackers with humor or changed the subject as a preemptive measure. Sometimes it worked. If I cracked a good joke, or danced around,

I got a little reprieve, and the attack was diverted. This constant stream of criticism sliced and diced like a Ginsu knife, wounding and tenderizing my fragile spirit. But wait, there is more.

I became uncomfortable in my own skin and hyper-aware of other people's moods, thinking I must be the cause for anyone's discontent. I was born an empathetic person, and now I was being programmed to float around life trying to seek some version of approval from others and make them happier. It was my custom People Pleasing 101 class and I would earn my A+ no matter the audience or consequence.

Mom didn't stand up for my sister or me. She went out of her way to be extra nice to Summer and Misty, leaving us starved for her maternal protection and wondering why we were treated worse than these strangers. If we complained, Mom told us, "Kill 'em with kindness" or, "If this is the worst thing that happens to you, you're doing good!"

Mom took the enemy's side as if she were trying to earn Chuck E. Cheese tickets from Eddy. Maybe she was hoping to get enough to buy a top-shelf prize, a 12 pack of Coors, case of cigarettes, or a man that didn't leave. The feeling of unconditional love and acceptance became a faded memory for my sister and me. And probably Mom too. Maybe Mom thought the adversity would make us tougher. Maybe she was right.

Our new family culture didn't help with my sister's tendency to pick on me. Being the sissy of the bunch and not street smart, just book smart like everyone says, I was usually the odd man out of the foursome of girls. Three against one. When they hit or kick me, I didn't hit back. I thought about it, but I was actually scared I might hurt someone if I unleashed my anger.

Every so often, I got kernels of kindness from Eddy. I sometimes danced in front of the TV, copying moves I saw on *American Bandstand* or *Soul Train*. Eddy commented, "She's got rhythm."

These positive words were music to my thirsty ears. Or he'd say, "Your so skinny, if I held you up to the sun, I could count the turds in ya." That was much better than his anger or him calling me "clown face" or "fat" like he did to Leah. I was happy to have those kinder comments, even if it was dog scraps.

Another nice thing about him was when we were invited to swim in the neighbor's pool on a hot summer day, he'd put me on his back, like a piggy-back ride as he dove into their pool. I was scared to do it, but I jumped at the chance to receive positive attention.

School reminded me that life sucked. I sat at my desk and looked around the classroom. There was Anne to my left who curled her hair every day and wore colorful outfits. There was super smart Karla at the front of the class. She must have had twelve pairs of shoes. I thought everyone else must be happier. They had normal homes, parents with real jobs, clothes in their closets, and plenty of groceries. I was envious, sad, and angry. I felt like they were all looking down on me, just like at home. Well, some of that was true. I got teased about my shoes, freckles, and free lunches.

One day I mentally polled the classroom thinking about shooting a laser gun that would make them all go away. "Pew, pew, there goes Anne. Pew, bye-bye Karla." I shot anyone who teased me or seemed happy. Just a handful of kids were left. Kids like me. The teacher interrupted my mental exercise, placing a Scholastic book order form on my desk. I looked at the handout, thumbing through it pretending that purchasing a book was an option for me. "Hmmm, let me see, yes, I'll circle that book," I said, as if I were able to place an order, hoping to not draw more attention to myself.

There was no money for ordinary stuff like school clothes or toiletries, and I knew better than to ask. The last time I asked Mom for a chocolate bar, she said, "Want in one hand and shit in the other and see what you get." It was a safe bet that books, like Judy Blume's, *Are You There, God? It's Me, Margaret* was not an option.

Please don't send me to the funny farm just yet, and in no way do I condone this, but much later it did make me realize how the seeds for school shootings can germinate. Take someone who is bullied, feeling hopeless and watching others who seem to enjoy life and chocolate bars. Add easy access to weapons, a breaking point with no outlet, a grown-up to confide in, or coping mechanisms, and I could see how some poor kid would implode, nursing his or her wounds and do something horrible. I imagined it myself. I'm thankful I had some adults in my life that brightened my days, and that I was incapable of hurting others no matter how badly I hurt.

During this time, there was this one softball player who was a good friend to Mom first, then Eddy. His name was Jimmy. He was a shining beacon of light in the darkness. He'd often show up to our house on weekdays and weekends like the rest of the softball players, but there was something much kinder and generous about him. He was tall, with a head of thick, curly hair, darker skin, and a cheek mole. He spoke wise words like a Stoner prophet, teaching us kids things along the way, like, "Save your money" "Go for the gold!" and "Do your homework."

He made us all laugh with his one-liners and contagious belly laughter. Jimmy often helped me with my math homework, especially when it got hard. Jimmy was a positive male figure in our lives and more of a dad to my siblings and me.

The house mood instantly shifted when Jimmy walked through the door. Even Eddy was nicer when Jimmy was around. Chance knew it too. He'd ask, "Jimmy, you want another beer?" Everyone knew the longer Jimmy stayed at our house, the happier and safer our home would be.

Chance was in kindergarten, and it was his turn to do the Mother's Day project. He too got to place his painted hands on a piece of paper and answer the same questions as Leah and me. His answers were much different.

On Mother's Day, Chance grinned ear to ear and handed Mom a large piece of red construction paper folded in half. Mom was sitting at the kitchen table smoking a cigarette and drinking black coffee. She opened his gift. On one side were Chance's small handprints. On the other, were his answers to the same old questions. "What's your mother's favorite food?" The teacher's handwriting recorded, "beer." "What's your mother's favorite thing?" Instead of "peace and quiet," Chance answered, "Coors." Mom read it too. She didn't smile or frown. I felt embarrassed and wondered what the teacher must've thought when Chance gave his answers. Maybe she shared it with the other teachers in their lunch lounge. I hoped Chance's answers might make Mom stop drinking right then and there and switch back to Pepsi. Instead, Mom folded Chance's gift, and got up from the table with it in her hand.

Chance didn't have a scrapbook for her to store the artwork. Mom stopped making crafty things like scrapbooks and crocheted blankets after Dad left. She also stopped taking Leah and me to our catechism classes. And now we were getting a different kind of religious instruction where we learned all about breaking the ten commandments and other life lessons.

Thou Shall Not Commit Adultery or Clean Your House

OUR ONCE PERFECTLY tidy and sanitary house was downright dirty. It was party-central for all the softball players. Inside, the kitchen counter's grout had so much grease and dirt built up that the grout was black and gooey. Sometimes I got bored enough to scrape it clean with a butter knife. The avocado green carpet was rarely vacuumed so the decorative pattern was barely discernible and matted from heavy traffic.

The formerly pristine white walls were yellowish brown from

cigarette and marijuana smoke. The orange and brown striped couch and loveseat were worn and stained with spilled beer. Instead of glitter popcorn ceilings, like in the neighbor's house, our non-glitter asbestos ceilings were caked with dirt and cobwebs. The bathroom was abused like a construction-site porta-potty. It's hard to aim when you're drunk. One night, a softball player mistook the dishwasher for a toilet. The single shower in the house had mold and caked-on soap scum. My bedroom's orange shag carpet lost its shag and was matted with pancakes of chewed bubble gum.

The four of us girls took turns loading and unloading the dishwasher. We'd sometimes decide to write chores on strips of paper and draw them out of one of Eddy's trucker hats. We worked together to make things more presentable by vacuuming, scrubbing, and dusting, especially when there was a threat of a schoolmate visit. Those were the times when we all got along, working towards a common goal.

One thing that was regularly cleaned by Eddy was the fish tank. He loved animals and bought two piranhas from a friend of a friend. He fed them regularly with goldfish. But sometimes he forgot, or we ran out of feeder fish. One extra hungry piranha took a bite out of the beloved Arowana fish and that was the end of that poor fella.

Our backyard trees were unpruned, dropping loads of ripened plums and apples on the ground. It created a fermented sweet scent that permeated the backyard. The plums and apples tasted too sour for me, but if I took the skin off with a potato peeler, they were edible. The grapevine structure had plywood and chicken wire haphazardly nailed around it so it could house the red-tailed hawk Eddy found injured on a construction site. He fed the hawk plenty of beef hearts purchased with Mom's Food Stamps from the corner grocery store. He named the hawk Baldy.

Each of us girls had our own pet rabbits. There was a large

mound of rabbit poop under their cages that looked like Cocoa Puff cereal. I named mine Snowflake, since she was white. She had red eyes and sometimes let me pet her. She was usually unfriendly and tried to bite everyone's fingers, so Eddy shot her in the head one morning. I don't remember crying over Snowflake.

I'd sometimes get inspired to make things look better outside rather than watching another rerun of *Three's Company*. I calculated it would take me thirty minutes to either mow the lawn or watch another episode. I knew what choice would make me feel better in the long run. Work felt better than laziness. And maybe I'd earn some love. So, I pushed the heavy lawnmower over the dried grass. It made loud gulp sounds as it sliced through piles of dehydrated dog poop and rotten fruit. It made me proud when someone asked, "Who mowed?" I was able to nonchalantly reply, "Me," beaming inside that my work was noticed, but playing it off like it was nothing. Like doing well in school, I found comfort in working hard, instead of watching TV.

The front yard looked different too. Instead of lush green grass, we had patches of dirt sprinkled with dead grass. There was a nonstop yard sale hosted on our front lawn with mountains of clothes, shoes, and miscellaneous household items placed on tarps. It's not that we lived in abundance. One of the softball players happened to drive a truck that picked up curbside donations. The donations were intended for a non-profit thrift store that helped veterans, but instead of dropping off all the donations to the thrift store, he gave most of them to Mom so she could sell the items. It must have been his way of thanking Mom for her hospitality, since she provided lots of cold beer and a place to crash for her friends. I think Eddy was a veteran, so maybe it was legit.

The donations were fun to rifle through, and I pilfered a couple of things for school. A peasant skirt that was too long, and white go-go boots I wished I could find the nerve to wear. I did wear the skirt to school one day, and discreetly held it up with my left hand hoping nobody would notice it didn't fit. A classmate asked me why I held onto my skirt. I was mortified by his question, thinking he knew my secret, or worse, saw my house. I didn't respond. I never wore it again and returned it back to the pile.

Mom manned the front-yard store, wearing her faded daisy duke shorts, pink tank top (braless), and her hair tied back with a navy-blue bandana folded in a triangle. Mom had a thin frame, dark skin, and athletic arms without doing a single push up. In her mouth was a lit cigarette, and in her hand, a Styrofoam beer holder with a Coors can. You could hear the house stereo playing something in the background like Waylon Jennings or Ronnie Milsap songs.

One Saturday, Leah watched Mom sell a vacuum cleaner to one of her schoolmate's older sisters for a dollar. "Does this work?" the customer asked.

"Yes," Mom lied. Leah's face flushed red realizing her schoolmate would soon learn that her mom is a liar.

In addition to the Stoner guests, there were friends from the neighborhood who liked to hang out. Most were regulars, but there were some I hadn't seen before. They all seemed happiest when they were drinking and smoking. It made me think all happy people drink and smoke.

Eddy joined the club where the record company mails you an eight-track tape every month for super cheap. You had to end up buying a certain number of tapes over two years. He was a connoisseur of great music. He'd play Hank Williams, Fleetwood Mac, Eric Clapton, Kenny Rogers, The Statler Brothers, and others. The only thing was, he played his music so friggin' loud, it was hard to think about anything other than the songs. Eric Clapton's "Cocaine" was not just a song playing in the background, it was also part of the adult recreation. During the '70s and '80s it seemed normal for people to get a divorce and use lots of alcohol and other drugs. At least that's what happened in my world.

The endless party centered around the dining area's white Formica kitchen table, with both leaves in to make it big. Eddy sat at the head, like honkytonk royalty. The adults drank, rolled joints, and smoked weed. I didn't see Mom smoke weed or snort cocaine, but most everyone else did. Sometimes they didn't mind that I was there being nosy. On those occasions, I sat quiet, trying to be invisible and take it all in. When they did shoo me away, I watched the *Solid Gold* TV show and dreamt of being one of the dancers someday. *Sold Gold* and *American Bandstand* transported me to a happier place. Seeing Prince for the first time, or watching Hall and Oates, was mesmerizing. Later Prince became my long-term imaginary boyfriend.

A cacophony of loud music, TV, and voices filled the house until houseguests passed out or left. A Stoner decided to write the number "69" on Chance's Fisher Price dog toy. I put myself to bed and pulled a pillow over my head to try and sleep as best as I could. After a long night of partying, before the sun came up, I heard Eddy playing Leah's old acoustic guitar. He strummed away, soulfully singing about some girl, "Charlene, Oooohhh Charlene." Maybe he dreamt of being in a band instead of terrorizing my siblings and me.

During a noontime party, it was an all-female conversation, like a talk show. The question of the day was, "Should one of the ladies go for it and cheat on her husband with this mysterious drifter who's been hanging around the softball team?" He had stringy hair and wore wire-rimmed glasses like math teachers wore. She thought he was cute. I disagreed but kept my opinions to myself. She and her chubby, jokester husband had a young son, and she was mulling over whether or not to have an affair, like deciding what tube top to wear. Mom and the other ladies urged her to go through with it. They didn't see anything wrong with it, saying, "Hey, why not? Life's short!"

She ended up taking their advice, committing adultery and the outcome was not positive. She realized the drifter was not an upgrade and neither relationship lasted.

Thou Shall Not Covet Other Kids' Clothes, Hair or Pizza

THE HOUSE WAS full of excitement on softball game days. Leah, Summer, and Misty primped for hours, taking turns with the community curling iron and the same tube of Covergirl mascara we all pitched in to buy. I didn't understand the fuss and preferred to use my time doing more important things, like anything else. I sometimes wore my shirts inside out to save the precious time it took to turn them right side in. People pointed it out to me as if I cared. I don't know why I tried so hard to save all those seconds, but time was always something I didn't want to waste.

Leah, Summer, and Misty talked about the sons who might show up. "Isn't Shane so cute! I hope he wears his muscle shirt! Do you think Jason will play catch with me?" Ok, I thought they were cute too, but I didn't think I was worth noticing, so why bother to curl my hair.

Eddy was fresh from a shower, smelling of his favorite Brut aftershave, and had his hair slicked back with Vitalis hair cream. He wore his softball jersey with white softball pants and matching stirrup socks. Eddy had plenty of his favorite toiletries while I rationed the sacred bottle of generic shampoo Grandma bought me for Christmas. I don't think my hair was ever clean back then.

Eddy spent his pregame time sitting on his throne at the head of the kitchen table preparing the large ice chest with plenty of Coors. The chest of beer also served as Mom's fridge and chair during games. Eddy used his pocketknife to break open the solid gallon block of ice from a repurposed milk jug. He stabbed the block and created ice chunks and shards for the ice chest. It was a treat when there was a six pack of sodas for us kids.

It was rare to stop for McDonalds on the way. When we did, I ordered my favorite, a Happy Meal with chicken McNuggets and fries. On this night, I couldn't wait to get to the softball field so I could eat.

I was so thrilled to sit on the grass and dig into my deep-fried goodness. My happiness was crushed when one of the softball wives asked for a nugget. I wanted to say, "NOOOOOOOOOOO!" because I wanted them all. Instead, I handed her a precious nugget. I wondered what my face looked like. Didn't she know I wanted all my friggin' nuggets?! I should have sat far away by myself and had a little peace and quiet as I nugged out. "No" was a word I couldn't pronounce.

During the game, many of the Stoners asked Mom for beers. Her cutoff-jeaned bottom protected the ice chest like a mother hen. She obliged, but later bitched to Eddy about it. I didn't watch Eddy's or my mom's games. Instead, I stared at the pretty girls on the sidelines of a different field. I imagined they had much nicer homes and lives. I saw them wearing the latest clothes, like the Dolphin short shorts, red on one side, white on the other. They wore fashionable designer sneakers. Their hair was bouncy and behaved, feathered perfectly, and glued in place with Aqua Net or Breck. They wore blue eye shadow like all the pretty girls did.

The happy girls were cheering for their mom's team, "Ballbusters." Their team color was hot pink which was my favorite color and way prettier than Mom's boring black and white uniform. I wished I had a pair of those Dolphin shorts. I was wearing the ones Grandma Lou made for me. Leah and I begged her to make us some clothes and told her the styles right before Summer and Misty showed up. A gifted seamstress, Grandma made Leah and me several pairs of shorts and tank tops. My favorite pair were the pink satin ones, but I was too scared to wear something so nice, thinking I might ruin them. Or worse, people might make fun of me wearing something so pretty and out of the ordinary.

I walked to the other side of the park to watch a group of cheerleaders practicing their routines. Man, I wished I could be them. I knew I could learn the moves. This routine's song was performed to Hall & Oats' "You Make My Dreams Come True." What I wouldn't give to be them. I thought they wouldn't be scared to wear pink satin shorts if they had them.

After every softball game, win or lose, everyone drove over to the Red Dragon pizza parlor so all the parents could drink beer and hang out. The five of us kids tried not to stare at the other families sitting at the indoor picnic tables enjoying pizza, hamburgers, fries, and cold soda. We sipped cups of water since they were free. I saw Fred and Sherry from our neighborhood enjoying their burgers and salty fries. Our moms were on the same team.

The five of us kids didn't acknowledge our desires, and more importantly, we didn't want people to notice we didn't have food. I was embarrassed enough to be alive and ugly, plus I didn't want to make Mom upset and get in big trouble. Game days didn't bring me excitement, it made me covet the lives of the cheerleaders and kids who had ample clothes and food. It made me more miserable.

Mom and Eddy sat at the table laughing and smiling, pouring another mug from their pitcher of beer. I pulled up a chair next to Eddy's brother who sat at the bar and quietly watched him drink his beer, staring off into space. He asked the bartender for a Snickers bar and handed it to me without saying a word. I was so happy to have a Snickers!

Queen's "Another One Bites the Dust" played over and over on the jukebox. After the other kids ate their meals, we all stepped outside to the gravel parking lot. It was dark and we were near a busy street. We were bored and started throwing some of the larger rocks towards the street. We heard a smash and ran back inside.

Days later, the police showed up to our houses to question us. One of us cracked open a lady's windshield and hurt her. I think they took one look at our arms and decided that Fred and Sherry were more plausible suspects.

Entrepreneurial Spirit

During some weekends, we attended softball tournaments to watch the Stoners play. Mom kept score and drank beer with the rest of the fans. Us kids played on the available playgrounds to pass the time.

At this dusty park with multiple fields, I hit the jackpot. Big time. I learned that if you track down a wayward foul or out-of-bounds ball, you could turn it in at the snack bar for a free cup of soda. I parked my carcass on a field sideline and waited for the balls to come my way. When it happened, I never ran so fast in my life. I had all the sodas I wanted that weekend.

I had many odd jobs and knew how to work hard. My initial motivation was to buy candy and shampoo. Man, how cool would it have been to have the Dollar Tree back then with shampoo and deodorant for only a dollar?! My first paid gig was collecting cans at softball games and at home when I was around eight. Leah and I stomped on the cans and smooshed them into a disc so more could fit in a plastic bag. We got skilled at that. One stomp at just the right angle did the trick.

Sometimes we got to keep our recycling money, but oftentimes Eddy would take it without saying a word. Around ten to thirteen, I babysat for many neighbors and softball players. I mowed lawns. I delivered newspapers. Delivering was the easy part. The hardest part was collecting the money. Sometimes I was too scared to knock on certain doors. And many of the houses wouldn't even answer, even though they were home. Naturally, I was not successful at the paper route job. I buckled under the pressure of confrontation.

Some of the players were thoughtful and asked me to babysit or clean their houses. Babysitting usually fetched fifty cents to a buck an hour depending on the number of kids and generosity. One Stoner, Nathan, hired me to watch his three kids. They were all under five and wild. I feel bad for writing this, but they were not your ordinary cute kids and sort of looked like cartoon characters with pointy teeth.

Nathan asked me to stay the night so the kids could be home, and he could party all night and into the next day. I slept poorly on his sofa bed with the mattress springs poking at me. I tossed and turned, calculating what I might get paid. At fifty cents an hour per kid, I hoped to get $1.50 each hour. Surely, I would get at least $10.00. I thought of all the shampoo and conditioner I could buy, plus have enough left over for candy bars and soda. I planned to hide everything to keep it safe and make it last.

My terms of employment were never discussed, I didn't have that kind of courage. Nathan staggered through the front door the next morning. He drove me home and promised he would pay me later. I saw him several times afterwards and didn't have the nerve to ask him for payment.

Nathan had a brother on the team as well. His brother, Curtis, was more of a stand-up guy. I think he had a clue about our unawesome situation. Curtis took a few of us out to see the new Indiana Jones movie. Near one Christmas, he showed up in the morning and asked all of us girls to pick a number. We were all excited. Curtis had one prize to give and wanted to make it fair. I guessed the correct number and it was a green and red beaded elastic Christmas bracelet. I loved it!

Later, I wondered if he fixed it so I could win. Usually I got the leftovers, but not that time. Like when we played Monopoly,

I picked the thimble since nobody else wanted it. Or like when us girls watched *Charlie's Angels*; they chose who they wanted to be first. Leah was Farrah. Summer was Jaclyn Smith. Misty was Cheryl Ladd. I got to be Kate Jackson.

I had a sort of regular cleaning job, working for a Stoner to clean up his place inside and out. I scrubbed Sherman's toilets, tub, and sink with Comet. His girlfriend taught me how to take a paper towel and put some ammonia on it and clean the bottom of the toilet that collects dust and hair. That was a whole new level of clean to me. I vacuumed the floors, dusted the bookshelves littered with her knick-knack paddywhacks, and changed the sheets on their waterbed. Next, I hit the backyard. I skimmed the pool with a net and scrubbed the sides of the pool with a brush. Sherman had me rake the leaves in between the bushes and mow the front and back lawns. Finally, I shampooed his golden retriever. When it was time to pay me, he'd reach in his wallet, thumbing through a thick wad of tens and twenties. Sherman pulled out a five-dollar bill and handed it to me, asking, "Is that good?"

People-pleasing, non-confrontational me lied through her cavity-infested teeth and enthusiastically said, "Oh yes, thank you!"

Sherman later married a kind woman with beautiful curly brown hair and large teeth. Her teeth were visible even when she wasn't smiling or talking. I noticed little black spots in many of her teeth, including behind her front teeth. Thanks to her, I decided to brush my teeth better, so my teeth wouldn't get black polka dots.

By now, Sherman must have a few million in the bank account. At least Mrs. Marriot, the senior citizen across the street, would pay me a couple of dollars to mow her front and back lawn.

I also cleaned my dad's house and he paid me five dollars. That was a decent gig, but when one of his girlfriends moved in, the job was worth more than what he paid me. I couldn't wait to get more lucrative jobs once I was a bit older and could get a work permit.

Maybe I would get to work at McDonalds and have unlimited McNuggets with barbeque sauce.

My best paying job happened one summer. Eddy was working as a bricklayer for an old friend of his. Misty and I were invited to help as hod carriers. We scored! Hod carriers are the people who move the bricks close to the people who are laying them. We used wheelbarrows instead of a hod which is a box that is carried on a shoulder. I couldn't put too many bricks in my wheelbarrow or else it would tip over. But I worked hard on that dusty job site, and I was fast. Eddy's boss paid us well, and we worked up a good sweat. I think we got at least $20.00 each day. Back then $20.00 was a fortune.

Family Time

FOR FAMILY VACATIONS, we camped at this shithole called North Park Reservoir with many of the Stoners and their families. This location was probably selected because it had a lake and there was no entry fee. The lake was so muddy, it looked like Willy Wonka's chocolate river. I wondered what kind of scary creatures lurked in the lake. At night, the sky rained swarms of gnats as we tried to eat food in the dark using flimsy paper plates.

Jimmy, my favorite softball player brought his beige van and ski boat to the campsite. Our living-room loveseat was transported in Jimmy's van each trip and placed on the dirt for general seating.

Emma, Jimmy's gorgeous girlfriend, held court inside the van, with the sliding door wide open. It was the VIP suite of the campsite. She wore a bikini and a cowgirl hat with a feather roach clip pinned to the back. I overheard someone say that an eight ball of cocaine helped convince Emma to go camping. Misty and I bathed with Emma in the muddy lake using her high-quality shampoo and conditioner. That was my favorite part of camping. I was grossed out by the slimy muddy and grassy bottom of the lake squishing between my toes. I wasn't sure I was getting clean with this bathing method, but I loved the smell of Emma's high-quality products. At night, we slept in a large canvas tent Mom borrowed from Grandpa.

While boating in the reservoir, Misty got up on one ski. "Way to go Misty!" the softball players said. I felt like there wasn't a lot of patience for each kid to get prepped and try to get up on a ski, so I passed, not wanting to take up precious time. I knew the adults wanted to ski too. My need for efficiency always trumped my desires.

I was in charge of holding up the orange flag when someone was in the water. I noticed how Misty got compliments while the rest of us kids didn't. Not sure why, but it was obvious Misty was the golden child. When Misty played catch with softball players, they said, "What an arm Misty has! Get her in little league!" The rest of us were red-headed stepchildren. Our comments were usually something like, "Mary, Summer, get me a beer, will ya?" or "Chance, go get some firewood!" and "Leah, you sure you want to eat that?"

Some of the softball players had dune buggies, and they let us drive them while they took a break. I got behind the wheel and thought, here's my chance to show off. I drove straight towards a mud puddle and gunned it. I didn't like getting dirty, but thought, hey, this might get me some attention. The dune buggy and I got drenched with mud. "Look at that!" the crowd of softball players said. I smiled as I climbed out of the dune buggy. Misty took her turn and also drove straight through the puddle. "Way to go Misty! Man, she's fearless," they said.

Days later, we drove home without air conditioning in 100-degree weather. Chance got car sick as usual, and this time sprayed barbeque-chip orange vomit all over the side of Mom's hatchback. Misty and I were directed to wash it off. We obeyed and tormented poor Chance later for him causing this disgusting chore.

Other family and softball events were at the sprint car racetrack. Eddy's nicer brother Harvey was always there, since sprint car racing was his favorite sport. I never understood why anyone would want to watch cars going around in a circle while getting sprayed with chunks of mud.

One night, Harvey splurged and bought us kids sprint car souvenirs. I got a pair of earrings for my newly pierced ears. Chance got a t-shirt. I stared at those dangly sprint car earrings and felt special, like someone cared enough to buy me something fancy.

After the races, we went to a nearby bar. Mom and the rest of the adults drank beers as us kids sat nearby and played with the salt and pepper shakers and ate free crackers and jelly. I watched Eddy sprinkle salt in his beer to reduce the foam. Like all the bars we visited, this place was super dark except for the illuminated beer signs. I liked the Olympia one best. It looked like actual water was flowing from the sign's waterfall.

One night after the races, Chance was driven home by a random Stoner. It was dark and Chance's driver kept falling asleep and the tires rapidly made the "thump-thump-thump-thump" sound as the car weaved in and out of its lane. Chance, around six, tells me he had to shove the driver's body with both of his hands yelling, "Wake up, wake up!" every two seconds so they made it home alive. Chance was scared to death long after we got home. Our guardian angels worked overtime back then.

That spring, Mom signed Misty up for Little League. Misty played first base and was as good as the boys. It was fun to watch the games, and the boys she played with were cute. Weekly, I sat on the aluminum bleachers which caused my butt cheeks to tickle for some reason. I really wanted to go to town and scratch my bottom, but someone might see, so I slyly wiggled my rump. I was entertained by watching one of the player's sisters enjoy her snack bar nachos with liquid cheese. I knew better than to ask for my own nachos. It would be a "Hell no, you know better to ask!" I was so impressed that her family was rich enough to buy nachos and a soda every single game. I wished I had her parents, or a few bucks from their wallet.

During the long games and practices, I daydreamed about playing a sport, especially cheerleading. I may not have gotten to play a sport or weekly nachos, but at home, we usually had bread, a block of cheese, and butter. Mom got the free cheese and butter from the church down the street. It was like the Velveeta cheese I once ate at Fay's house, but firmer and yummier. It was called Government Cheese, donated by the U.S. Department of Agriculture. Government Cheese was used in military kitchens and helped feed families while depleting the excess dairy supply. It was a win-win. Government Cheese melted perfectly and made the best grilled cheese sandwiches. It was a perfect addition to a fried egg sandwich, my personal favorite after a happy day of swimming in the neighborhood pool.

I genuinely believe it's smarter for the government to give needy families actual food since the money we got was usually spent on beer, cigarettes, and Eddy's preferences. I heard it somewhere that international charities learned to airdrop donations directly to those in need, rather than to third-parties who aren't trustworthy.

When it was halfway through the month, we ate from the same pot of pinto beans until payday. The large pot sat on the cold stove top until all the gross beans were gone. I couldn't stand the taste of those beans, no matter how much salt I put on them. Eddy loved them saying, "Nothing's better than a pot of beans," trying to persuade the household ears that nothing was wrong with the way the adults managed finances.

The gas got turned off and we couldn't heat up the beans

for days until Uncle Bruce showed up. Uncle Bruce's talents as a construction worker included finding a way to help us bypass the gas company. Thanks to Uncle Bruce, we had gas and Mom didn't have to pay the pesky utility bill.

Uncle Bruce brought even more happiness to the house when he bought a gaming system. He and Leah played Asteroids and Missile Command. I loved Pong best. When Leah beat Uncle Bruce at any game, he'd get so mad that he yelled bad words, threw the game controllers, and stormed outside. I'm also thankful we had unlimited cable TV, thanks to the illegal antenna Eddy installed on the roof.

Suddenly Uncle Bruce stopped visiting. It was right after Uncle Bruce punched Eddy in the face. I peeked from inside the house, watching Uncle Bruce and Eddy yell at each other near the mulberry tree. I saw Uncle Bruce pointing his finger in Eddy's face and suddenly there was pushing and punching. I didn't like fighting or yelling, and I wasn't sure what the fight was about anyway. But that day, I relished seeing Uncle Bruce get the best of Eddy's face. Now Eddy was bruised and a little bloody. It was a nice change to see Eddy on the receiving end rather than one of us kids.

Later, Uncle Bruce explained he was mad that Mom was prioritizing Eddy over her children and, "Eddy was an asshole who deserved it."

Discipline

EDDY HAD A prized tequila bottle a softball player gave him as a souvenir from Mexico. It had a worm in it, so it was extra special. He said eating the worm would get you extra high. Eddy kept it prominently displayed on top of our yellow refrigerator. One day, I opened the fridge and the bottle fell and crashed on the linoleum floor. Tequila and glass splashed everywhere. The bottle must have moved ever so slightly each time the fridge was opened, and I was the lucky one to trigger its fatal tipping point.

"What the fuck do you think you're doing? You fucking idiot!" Eddy screamed.

I knew I was in for big trouble. I don't recall the sequence of my punishment, but I remember falling to the ground and being kicked by Eddy.

Leah was called "clown face" most days, with her blue eye shadow, black eyeliner, mascara, and blush getting heavier so she could hide from the world. Eddy called her "fat" when she was just healthy sized and in no way overweight. Eddy regularly slapped Summer upside the head numerous times, especially as she sat at the dinner table not wanting to eat a crappy dinner. After the hard slap, crocodile tears welled up in her large eyes and I felt so sad for her. When dinner wasn't a pot of beans, around the first of the month Mom made hamburgers, chipped beef gravy, pork chops, and chicken enchiladas. I loved the pork chops with fried potatoes the best. Eddy's taste in food was horrible. He ate raw hamburger. Enchiladas were Eddy's favorite and nobody else's. Most of us kids fought vomiting urges as we cleaned our plates, otherwise we too would be slapped upside the head.

Eddy routinely punched Chance in the stomach and arm, to help make him tougher. Chance wasn't in trouble; these punches were Eddy's way of showing affection.

Mom and Eddy fought too. On one night, Mom was so mad at Eddy she tried to cuss him out. She got so flustered, her words wouldn't flow, so she took a stack of dinner plates and began to throw them on the kitchen floor—one at a time. The pretty plates with tiny olive-green flowers shattered around her feet. Misty and I snuck in the kitchen and grabbed the rest of the plates to hide them, so we'd have something to eat our Government Cheese sandwiches on. Mom stuttered and stammered, still not able to find words, and yelled at Eddy, "YOU...YOU, YOU, YOU ASSHOLE EYES!"

I thought, "Well said, Mom! As a matter of fact, he DOES have asshole eyes and an asshole face." I never laughed so hard on the inside. Her word choice was perfect.

Thou Shall Not Kill Yourself

CHRISTMASES WERE NO longer merry. Since Dad left, Santa was a hit or miss. Usually a miss. If Dad's business was doing well with the economic twists, he would come through for us. One time I got the popular Dancerella ballerina doll I saw advertised during Saturday morning cartoons. I always dreamed of being a ballerina.

On that Christmas Eve, Mom took us to Eddy's Aunt Jan's house. We were allowed to take our present from Dad. There were about thirty kids and adults at the party. When I opened my gift, I noticed Dad got me the black-haired version of Dancerella. I was hoping I'd get the one that looked more like me. As I pulled the doll out of her box, Eddy and his crew pointed and laughed hysterically, saying, "Tom got her the n****r doll!" I cried and ran out of the room, carrying my Dancerella.

The next Christmas, I got the best present ever from Dad. A blue ten-speed bike I rode everywhere. The bike was my favorite, next to the bottle of shampoo and conditioner Grandma and Grandpa mailed one year. A couple of years later, Dad even got us a pinball machine! He'd often barter his photography services in exchange for random things like that. Mom ended up selling it and keeping the money. Dad also bought inappropriate gifts for Christmas, but I was happy to get anything. One time it was much-needed underwear. It was very lacy and not age appropriate. Summer loved wearing them when she had a sleepover. Dad also bought me a chemistry set. It came with dozens of bottles of chemicals that had warning signs that if ingested, it would be fatal.

I got an idea on an especially tough day of being teased by Misty and smacked by Mom. I stormed to my room and found the chemistry set. I figured I would try to pry open one of those bottles with the safety key and drink it to end my misery, or at least get some quality time from Mom. I'm honestly not sure which. Leah walked in as I was frantically trying to open a bottle and yelled, "Moooommm!" I got attention alright. I got my ass beat and the chemistry set was thrown away. That wasn't the outcome I had hoped for, or maybe it was. I knew Mom must have loved me since she threw out the chemistry set. Leah started using a new nickname for me after that incident, and called me, "Psycho Mary."

When Dad's business wasn't doing well, and that seemed often, Christmases were rougher. On many Christmas Eves I went to bed knowing I would wake up to zero presents and nothing in my stocking other than an orange or an apple. I would have loved to get one of those Lifesaver Story Books that contained a bunch of candies in my stocking. The Christmas TV commercials had the nerve to rub in what I was missing out on.

I was absolutely thrilled when my Auntie Connie and Uncle Gary (Dad's brother) sent me a Christmas present in the mail. I didn't know why out of all the years, she picked that year, but it made my Christmas. It was Love's Baby Soft lotion that all the girls at school smelled like.

Thou Shall Not Bear False Witness Unless Your Name is Summer

Speaking of Christmas, this one won the prize for worst ever. It was the annual Stoner's Christmas party. Each year it was hosted by the older parents of two of the popular softball players. They were like the team's grandparents. I was around twelve or thirteen.

Jimmy's girlfriend, Emma often showed kindness to us four girls and taught us how to do facials and apply makeup. Before the party, she boiled a pot of water and showed us how to put a towel over our heads to steam our pores open, clean our faces, and apply her creams and makeup. Emma helped us put on blush, eyeshadow, black eyeliner, mascara, and lipstick. For the first time we all felt pampered and pretty.

Leah and Summer were arch enemies, just like Misty and me. Summer was gifted at manipulating Mom and used the house dynamics to her benefit. Anyone could tell Misty was Eddy's favorite and Summer wasn't by smack count alone. Because of that, Mom lavished Summer with extra love and attention as recompense. It was equally obvious Leah was not Mom's favorite because she reminded Mom of Dad. Mom often said to Leah, "You're just like your father!" with palpable disdain. Clever Summer often cried out to Mom, "Paaaaaaaat! Leah did (some horrible thing)!" to which Mom would immediately discipline Leah without finding out what really happened. Leah was an easy scapegoat and Summer seemed to delight in getting her in trouble. When boys were nearby, the conflict between Leah and Summer was magnified.

The adults were inside the three-bedroom house, drinking and laughing near a flocked Christmas tree and blazing fireplace while the kids hung out in a variety of huddles on the front lawn. There was a punchbowl of eggnog on the kitchen counter. I helped myself to a frothy cup and a candy cane and headed outside.

Summer decided to provoke Leah by shitchatting to other kids about Leah like, "Did you see Leah's eyeshadow? Don't you think she looks like a clown?" News traveled fast and it got back to Leah that Summer was talking about her.

Ballsy Leah got fed up and approached Summer, "If you have something to say, you better say it to my face," and confidently walked away.

Summer didn't follow Leah's instructions and soon Leah caught her in the gossiping act and confronted her, "If you don't stop, you're going to get hit."

Summer had the confidence an audience brings and answered, "Oh yeah, what are you going to do about it?!"

All the kids peeled away from their separate huddles and surrounded Leah and Summer. There were about twenty of us.

Leah didn't respond to Summer's question. Instead, she stepped forward and punched Summer in the nose.

Summer didn't fight back. She calmly walked away, stepped inside the house, and then began to cry, "Paaaaaaaaat!!!" Like she had it all planned.

Mom stormed out of the house with fire in her eyes and caught Leah off guard. She started punching, kicking, and wailing on Leah. It all happened so fast. She took Leah's arm, spun her around and slammed her to the ground. Mom got on top of her, straddled her and continued to uncontrollably hit Leah. A couple adults had to pull Mom off Leah. I stood there helpless, paralyzed, and scared for Leah.

I couldn't believe Mom just beat the crap out of Leah—and in front of everyone. Mom seemed demon-possessed when she was drunk. The slightest things triggered her rage. She hurt and humiliated poor Leah in an attempt to show the drunken crowd her badass-ness. Or maybe it was her way of working out all her anger towards Dad on a nearby focal point that happened to be her daughter. It was a horrible chaotic scene of yelling, crying, and hitting. It was worse than all the beatings any of us kids ever got, combined in that single moment.

I was sad and embarrassed for Leah and ashamed of my mom. I wished I could be like the Invisible Man and disappear. I wondered why Mom always took Summer and Misty's side and treated her own girls worse. That evening, Summer seemed pleased and Misty unfazed.

Leah disappeared to the backyard. She told me she was done and was going to walk to Dad's house to live with him. Eddy came outside and found my sister quietly sniffling by the fence, her pretty makeup ruined and face swollen. Eddy, for the first and only time consoled my sister. He put his arm around her and apologized for Mom, saying, "I can't believe what your mom just did." Eddy was visibly distraught over what Mom had done. Neither Mom nor Summer apologized to Leah for that night.

Dad later shared with me that around this time, Uncle Bruce, who hated Dad immensely, showed up at his studio, and announced, "You've got to take those kids away from Pat," while Dad was in the middle of a photography shoot.

When Dad told this story, I asked, "So why didn't you take us kids away?"

"I was busy with work," he said.

When I asked Uncle Bruce about it, he remembered it differently and said, "That's not true, I would NEVER go to your dad. He's an asshole!"

Leah tells me that was the night any remnant of self-esteem finally left her for good. We now both agree Leah was Mom's punching bag for all the things our dad represented. Mom loved Leah, but I'm certain she didn't like her. Mom might have even been jealous. Dad favored Leah and I'm sure that hurt Mom on some level since Dad rejected and left Mom.

My sister's makeup got thicker over the years, continually trying to hide her true self, likely because the world was not a safe place and required cosmetic armor.

I don't recall the kids receiving presents at the softball Christmas parties. The adults exchanged gifts as we watched from the sidelines. At that party, I watched a couple guests carry out the homeowner's ceramic lion statue. Stealing from people's houses was normal for the people we hung around. Misty's Aunt Marquis was close to our age and likely a kleptomaniac. I had many things come up missing when she visited. Misty bragged about her older Aunt Sapphire's husband who got stuff for free. She said he'd buy a large ice chest at a store. Which was no problem, but he'd stow away many valuable items in the ice chest, and not pay for those. The cashier never looked inside. I remember shopping with my mom and one of the softball players. He had this large decorative picture in his hands as he stood just beyond the checkout lane Mom was in. Nobody thought to ask him if he paid for it. He acted casual and walked out of the store with it in plain sight.

Honor Your Father and Leave Your Mother

Leah was teased at school for not having a bra. Mom didn't buy things like that. And I'm sure she didn't notice when Leah started to get boobs. The mean girls, who never missed an opportunity, teased, "Look—Leah can't even afford a bra!" When Leah started her period, I watched her at the kitchen table make homemade pads out of toilet paper and scotch tape. She was too scared to ask Mom for help. We all were. Leah got tired of being treated like crap, living at our scummy house, and left to go live with Dad. Mom, a master at guilt and blame, put on an extra thick guilt trip, crying on the drive over, her way of begging Leah to stay.

Leah tells me she left when she was in the 8th grade. Chance and I stayed put. I'm not sure why, but probably because we didn't want to further upset Mom. And we wanted to show our allegiance to her and hoped that we would win her affection and maybe sobriety. We knew she loved us and was strict. Even in her drunkenness she still made us go to school. And she taught us how to fend for ourselves. I would have given anything to see a Pepsi can in Mom's hand once again, with her mowing the lawn like she did before Dad split.

I didn't get mad at Leah for leaving. I was surprised she didn't do it sooner. Leah was always Dad's favorite, his princess. Leah knew how to direct Dad's divided attention to her by cracking a disgusting joke. I'd just watch and listen; there was no point in competing, nor could I get a word in edgewise.

At twelve and approaching the seventh grade, one of Dad's employees took me school shopping. Dad was busy working. She insisted I have a dress, but I was really hoping for everyday outfits and cool tennis shoes. She took me to the higher-end department store in town. She insisted I try on a Gunne Sax dress. It was a peasant style with miniature pink flowers. I wasn't going to argue, happy to go shopping. She also picked out a pair of pants, sweater, and dress sandals for my Gunne Sack dress. I had the first day of school outfit that was so critical in middle school. First impressions were key.

Dad remarried and I would soon have three more adorable siblings. I loved seeing Dad when I got the chance. He was affectionate and said he loved me. He'd spontaneously dance with me and sing.

Sometimes, I called my dad at his work, hoping to have a sliver of his time, and maybe ask him to come pick Chance and me up. He'd answer the phone slightly out of breath and distracted from something going on at his photography studio. Or his significant other would need to talk to him at exactly the same time that I called, consciously or unconsciously competing for his divided attention.

To this day, "The Cat's in the Cradle" song still makes my eyes tear up every time I hear it.

Thou Shall Not Steal Candy Bars

ONE MORNING, EDDY stormed in the house from the backyard and said, "Fucking Colonel's—sold me a bad heart." Eddy's red-tailed

Hawk, Baldy, died. We were all sad for the loss of such a beautiful creature.

Misty, Summer, and I joined Eddy in blaming the grocery store. We united in our anger and plotted our revenge on "Fucking Colonel's." We hopped on our bicycles and rode to the store, marched directly to the refrigerated meat aisle, and tore open packages with our dirty fingernails.

Our vandalism crime quickly escalated into stealing. We hit the candy aisle and dumped candy in our empty purses—Hershey's Kisses, Snickers, Whatchamacallits. I used a brown leather tooled purse that used to be Auntie Raven's. Misty used a Velcro clutch purse that was Leah's. Summer carried one of Mom's old, crocheted purses. I was scared the cashiers knew what we were up to. We quickly exited the store before someone noticed. After pedaling a hundred feet away, I was thrilled we didn't get caught and had a good stash of chocolate for our revenge work. It became addictive and we kept going back to steal more candy bars. One checker was on to us, I could tell by the way he kept looking at us, standing on his tippy toes while ringing up customers.

After several thefts, I decided to finally quit when I got scared straight. As usual, I stealthily slipped a Whatchamacallit for Leah and a Summit bar for me in my purse. Summit bars came out the same time Twix did, but I guess I was the only one who liked them, since they got discontinued. It was like a Twix and Kit Kat all in one.

I was in the checkout line buying something that Mom needed with Food Stamps, when suddenly there was a hand on my shoulder. The man said, "Hey kid, come with me." My heart fell to my stomach, I stopped breathing, and I began to sweat profusely. The guy seemed familiar. And then he started laughing. It was my Uncle Bruce's good friend, Tim, messing with me. I had never been so relieved in my life.

My career as a thief stopped right then and there. Except I relapsed later as an older teenager when I tried to act cool in front of my future best friend, and stole a bathing suit, thinking that would impress her. She wasn't impressed and I felt guilt every time I wore the floral one piece.

Thou Shall Not Use Thy Lord's Name in Vain – Or Burn Down Dad's House

I'D OFTEN WALK the few miles to Dad's brand-new home where he lived. Leah snooped and found Dad's porn videos and put them in the VCR. As I sat on Dad's brown leather couch, I was grossed out by what Debby did in Dallas and what was behind the Green Door. I preferred the '70s PG movies with a flute-heavy soundtrack on Dad's hijacked cable channel. I'd sift through the coffee table *Seventeen* magazines and see advertisements for United Colors of Benneton clothes with happy teenagers. Ads for Sea Breeze astringent, Love's Baby Soft lotion or Bonne Bell lip gloss littered the pages. I imagined being just like the happy people in the magazine.

I'd read the cover model's interview and they all claimed they kept in great shape by climbing the stairs to their high-rise apartments. They had great skin because they drank lots of water. I'm now calling bull crap on that; nobody has a perfect body from climbing stairs. And water alone doesn't give you great skin. Surely there was good genes, an eating disorder or addiction, plus some good photo editing.

Ambitious, positive-thinking Dad subscribed to *Success* magazine, but I never looked inside those, just his *Playboy* magazines for the inappropriate comics and centerfold interviews, curious to find out what their "Turn-Ons" and "Turn-Offs" were.

Dad consumed positive self-help books and believed in working hard. He'd tell me things like, "Winners do what they don't want to do, and losers don't" or "When life gives you chicken shit, make chicken salad."

Dad hardly had any food in the house, but I could always count on popcorn kernels and oil to make a batch of popcorn every visit. Dad was a health nut and once fed us mysterious, green-colored sausage for breakfast. Yet he drank an awful lot of Natural Light beer.

Dad lived in a new development that was once just a pile of river rocks. The houses were beautiful, much nicer than Mom's. His house smelled like fried eggs dusted with pepper, but that was just his persistent beer farts, with a top note of cat pee emanating from the litter box.

When I visited Leah at Dad's, I remember walking by this one house that was perfectly painted white and taupe; its basketball hoop backboard matched the house colors. The landscaping was lush with green grass and exotic-looking plants. Like ones you might find in Hawaii. I imagined myself living there. It was the prettiest house on the block.

One weekend, when Chance and I stayed the night at Dad's house, I attempted to clean out sausage grease in a pan by warming up the pan. After I turned on the burner, I went in the back room to hang out with my siblings and forgot about the pan.

I heard Dad yell, "GOD DAMMIT—FIRE!!!" We ran from the back room and saw dad frantically trying to beat the fire with a dishtowel and pour a box of salt everywhere. Nothing worked. I knew I had to do something. I ran to the next-door neighbor's house and banged on the door, screaming, "HELP!" Thankfully, Alfonso grabbed his fire extinguisher and ran to our house. He stopped the fire right before it spread to the attic. Dad's kitchen was severely burned. I felt horrible.

Dad later told me, "I had two weddings that day. Something inside me compelled me to come home in between weddings. You kids were playing in the back room when I walked in and saw smoke coming from the kitchen. I don't think you kids would have survived if I didn't come home that day."

Dad wouldn't fix the kitchen for months. I felt guilty for years. Thankfully Dad didn't hit kids, just doors and walls.

The year Leah left for Dad's, Mom got a part-time job. Maybe she was required to do it to continue welfare. It was at a liquor store with a deli, a couple miles down the road. It was a good thing she finally had a job since Eddy rarely worked now. That summer, my brother, Summer, Misty, and I often rode our bikes to the store where Mom worked. It was situated near a neighborhood with lots of apartments.

The bags of chips that didn't sell before the expiration date came home in a brown paper bag for us, and that was a tasty fringe benefit. I remembered seeing Mom behind the counter drinking out of a Pepsi can as she prepared deli sandwiches for customers while Ming, one of the neighborhood boys, conquered the store's Pac-Man game on one quarter. Ming's Pac-Man skills made me have a crush on him.

I got so excited to see the Pepsi can in my mom's hand. I wondered, "Does that mean she stopped drinking? Wait, do I have my mom back?" Looking closer, I saw the lip of the can had clear yellow bubbly liquid, and I knew it wasn't Ginger Ale. It was the beer the deli served on draft, another perk of the job.

Paradise is in California

SUMMER BREAKS MEANT traveling to Paradise to visit Grandma Lou, Grandpa, and Darlene for a few weeks. My grandparents moved there soon after Dad left. Paradise was widely advertised, and many retirees flocked to the area.

Grandma and Grandpa had an enormous double-wide trailer with three bedrooms and two bathrooms. Since Summer and

Misty's arrival, they also joined us for the visits. I didn't like sharing my bed, my clothes, or Mom, and now *my grandparents* with Summer and Misty. They even called them "Grandma and Grandpa," which annoyed the heck out of me.

Still, those summer vacations are by far my happiest memories. As soon as we rolled into town, I smelled Christmas trees and fresh air. I couldn't wait to have a glass of water from Grandma's tap; Paradise water was the freshest tasting I ever had. As we walked up the porch stairs, I saw swarms of hummingbirds zooming around Grandma's hummingbird feeder. Grandma filled it with sugar water every few days.

Grandma's garden was in full bloom with colorful snap dragons, irises, and a strawberry patch. Quail roamed her property and scattered through the manzanita bushes. Us kids saw the massive pile of four cords of wood waiting for us to stack neatly and help Grandma and Grandpa get ready for winter.

Inside, Grandma's pantry had plenty of food and snacks like cookies and chips. Her kitchen table had a ceramic fruit bowl containing all the bananas I could manage.

I took my paper bag of clothes to Aunt Darlene's room. She had the best room in the house. She had a king-sized bed with a floral bedspread. Her room was decorated with porcelain dolls and Avon perfume bottles. Underneath her bed was a never-ending supply of warm blackberry soda I could drink without asking. I'd sit on Darlene's bed, watching her favorite programs like, *Days of Our Lives, Lawrence Welk, Hee Haw,* and the *Barbara Mandrell and the Mandrell Sisters*. Darlene had the TV and radio going on at the same time and it was pure heaven hanging out with her. She called me "sweetheart" and repeatedly said, "It's so pretty outside" as she looked out her windows.

Sometimes the TV made Darlene cry and carry on unconsolably. It was always for the same reason. Something tragic happened on her favorite show, *The Days of Our Lives*. This went on for hours. Grandpa thought it was funny and continued to ask her questions about the show to keep her rant going.

During *Lawrence Welk*, Darlene held her bottle of Rosemilk during the commercial break advertising the lotion. I'd watch her pump a dollop on her hands and apply it to her rosy cheeks. She loved her perfume and had many bottles sitting on her vanity. Charlie was her favorite.

At Grandma's, I ate my fill without getting yelled at. Each morning, I woke up at 6 a.m. and tiptoed to the back porch and sat on the swing so I could be near my grandpa while he quietly read the newspaper. That way I had him all to myself. I cherished those mornings. Grandpa sometimes made SOS (shit on a shingle) for breakfast. He learned how to make that in the Army. It was ground beef and milk gravy served over toast. It was my favorite breakfast, and I ate gallons of it.

I had a good amount of downtime between stacking wood. I often stared at Grandma's VCR clock and did endless math equations using the blue numbers on the clock. If it was 2:34, I'd divide 34 by 2. I'd multiply 2 by 17. Then I'd figure out how many minutes it was until it was 8:00. That was fun for me. If any of the numbers had a six, I thought it was evil and I'd count until the clock changed.

Sometimes I'd sit quietly beside Grandma as she watched Bob Ross effortlessly paint a landscape. At night, Chance and I stayed up late to watch *David Letterman*, *Nightline* and *Saturday Night Live*. I had a huge crush on David Letterman and Ted Koppel. They seemed like strong and decent men. I dreamt of being on *Saturday Night Live*. They all looked happy.

One visit, I got a bloody nose that wouldn't quit no matter what I did. This went on for a couple weeks. Grandma supplied me with fresh washcloths for the blood and made me take her Geritol vitamin. She said it would help my blood.

One morning, I put on my metal-wheeled roller skates. Grandpa followed me in his little pickup truck and clocked me speeding down the steep hill at 20 miles an hour. He bought me a Dr. Pepper afterwards at the corner store and I felt special and loved as I sipped the cold can of soda.

All of us kids enjoyed playing card and board games like Yahtzee, Life, Rummy, and Spades. Sometimes we hung out with Grandma's friend Maxine. She took a liking to me and taught me how to play the organ and do some crafts. I learned to play Elvis' "Love Me Tender." She even gave me some clothes she made for her granddaughter. She said her granddaughter was ungrateful and didn't appreciate homemade clothes. I was thrilled to have the pink checkered knickers and matching top.

I loved it when we "went to town" which meant going to Kmart and the grocery store. When we rolled into the parking lot, I saw a gorgeous '65 pink Mustang convertible with a white top and tires. I fell in love with that car. We approached the lady putting her groceries in her trunk and asked about the car. She told us it used to be a Playboy Bunny car, and Hugh Heffner gave them to some of his Bunnies. Pink is my favorite color. Right then it became a dream of mine to have a pink car. I thought maybe I could be a Bunny and get one too.

At the grocery store, Grandma let me pick out extra snacks. I always chose banana chips and Albertson's brand cheese puffs. That brand had the perfect ratio of cheese to puff.

Our summer visits usually lasted three blissful weeks. We also visited during the holidays. On many Thanksgivings Grandma cooked for everyone. It was a scary drive when Eddy drove the Datsun. There were many spots on the road without guard rails to protect the car from crashing down what I thought was a ten-thousand-foot drop. I remained alert during those drives to make sure the car didn't careen down the cliff, as if I had any control from the backseat. Before the scary cliffs, we drove by miles of fruit trees planted neatly in rows. Depending on how I changed my perspective, I watched the moving geometric patterns play tricks on my eyes to pass the time.

Sometimes us kids would play the alphabet game trying to spot the letters A to Z by looking at the various license plates. During our early family visits to Paradise, Grandpa hid his liquor bottles in the snow and Leah found them as she made her snowballs to attack me. Grandpa finally sobered up a few years after they moved to Paradise.

On another summertime visit, Auntie Raven lived with Grandma and Grandpa after she had her first baby, Alice. Like any infant, Alice woke up in the night and started crying. Auntie Raven lost her temper and screamed at her baby to "SHUUUUTTT UP!" waking up everyone. Then minutes later she'd shapeshift into another person and sweetly say, "Momma loves you. Momma loves you," to Alice. Auntie Raven thought feeding her baby Jell-O water would help her stay full throughout the night. It didn't work out and wasn't good for her future teeth.

Grandma Lou was the kindest and most joyful person I ever met. I wanted to be just like her. She was a gifted poet, seamstress, cook and painter. She was also a great storyteller. One story she shared was about a man who suspiciously had each of his new brides die on their wedding night. She said that after a few wives, the father of the newest bride hid under the newlywed's bed to keep watch. On the marriage bed, the husband started to tickle his wife and didn't stop despite her protests. The father crawled out from under the bed and stopped the fatal tickling before it was too late, solving the mystery of how the former wives had died. The Tickler lived out his remaining years in prison.

Grandma never drank alcohol. She smoked for a few years, but really, it was more of an accessory. Her cigarettes went unattended in the ashtray with a long ash growing. Her imperfections were few: she loved food a bit too much and cursed like a sailor. It was hilarious to hear my sweet Grandma say a few bad words to give dramatic effect to her stories.

When I wasn't in Paradise, I wrote Grandma Lou using the stamped stationary she gave me to tell her how much I missed her saying, "I miss you sooooooooooooooooooooooooooooooooooooooooo much. I cannot wait to see you during the summer. Next time, can I please stay longer?" She would always write me back.

Surprise Dinner

ONE EVENING, SUMMER, Misty, Chance, and I were home alone. Mom and Eddy were out. The doorbell rang. We ran to the door to see who it was. It was Grandma Lou and Grandpa standing outside with wide grins on their faces. It was such a pleasant surprise, we yelled, "Grandma and Grandpa are here!!!"

Grandma asked, "You kids want to go out to dinner?" Of course we did! We ran around the house, excited, trying to find shoes so we could hurry up and go. Grandma and Grandpa drove us to Smorga Rob's. It was an all-you-can-eat restaurant with salty meat, unlimited mac and cheese, and an assortment of desserts and beverages. My favorite part was the chocolate and regular milk on tap. I loved mixing chocolate with a little bit of regular milk to get it exactly right—not too chocolatey and not too milky. I drank until my belly couldn't stand anymore, at least a quart. We refilled our plates and stuffed ourselves. Grandma and Grandpa dropped us back at home and returned to Paradise.

We soon learned Grandpa and Grandma were in town because Grandpa had to visit the local veteran hospital. He had colon cancer.

And it was spreading fast. We enjoyed the dinner out, clueless that Grandpa didn't have much time left.

During the next several weeks, we saw Grandma and Grandpa a lot more. They made regular visits to the local hospital for treatments. I visited Grandpa at the hospital and watched him spray his blackened tongue and sore throat with Chloraseptic to alleviate his pain.

On another visit, Grandma, Grandpa, and Darlene had to stay at our house for a few days. A hospital bed showed up, and Grandpa rested in the middle of the smoke-filled living room. Auntie Raven also drove from Reno to visit, since Grandpa's time was short. Our tiny home was bursting at the seams with overnight guests. It was already a full house. It made me think of a story Grandma once shared about a study[1] where mice were allowed to populate in a confined space and the results were examined. The mice fought, ate each other, and hurt their babies. It wasn't good. The moral of the story Grandma said was, "People fight when they don't have space to breathe." This experiment played out every day at the house I lived in.

That day, the fight was between Mom and Auntie Raven. At first, I didn't pay attention to the noise in the kitchen. My family members have naturally loud, booming voices, so it seemed perfectly normal. What wasn't normal was when Auntie Raven began wildly shrieking as she threw animalistic slaps and punches towards my mom. Grandma yelled at them to stop, and nobody had a more commanding voice than Grandma. But Mom and Auntie Raven were too far gone. There was no stopping them as they regressed back to their childhood ways. Mom backed up just a smidge and charged at Auntie Raven, sending her and Raven in a tangled

---

1 Calhoun, John B. (1973). "Death Squared: The Explosive Grown and Demise of a Mouse Population" Davis, Louise (1971). *"The Garden of Eden or Doomsday?"*. *Tennessean Magazine.*

mess from the kitchen, down the hall, into Mom's bedroom, onto her bed, and then down to the floor where Mom finally had her pinned. Raven screamed at Mom, "Stop pinching my nipple!" That was the TKO moment. Mom won the fight. Auntie Raven tapped out and Mom retained her alpha position in the pecking order. I'm sure Grandma and Grandpa questioned their decision to stay at our house and had other parental regrets. We were no better than the rodents in the study.

Auntie Raven always brought excitement. One time she took Leah and me to a house to collect empty soda bottles. We turned them in at the Circle K and got ten cents each. We had enough money to buy Lemonheads, Cheetos, and soda. It was awesome! We learned the bottles were not hers to return. Auntie Raven would end up getting fired from most of her jobs for allegedly stealing. The police were called when money came up missing at the local sandwich shop where she worked. She was fired again.

Auntie Raven's quest for fun was contagious. It made you want to join the party and avoid chores and obligations. The morning after the nipple-pinching fight, when it was time to walk to school, Mom and Auntie Raven were at the kitchen table, smoking, laughing, and living it up. I wanted to stay home and live it up too. "Mom, please, can I stay home from school, just this once?!" It was not a discussion. Mom said I had to go.

Summer at Auntie Raven's

It was the summer before eighth grade. We were unable to go visit Grandma and Grandpa because Grandpa was dying. Another worry of mine was about the next school year and my prospects for school clothes. There was zero chance I'd be taken to Kmart, Goodwill, or a dumpster to get school clothes for my next grade. Dad's business was in a slump and Mom had other priorities.

I had recurring dreams of finding new clothes in my closet.

Clothes that resembled the frilly dresses I wore at age seven but didn't fit anymore. In my dreams, I was so happy to have a wardrobe as I slept, knowing Mom and Dad were still together. It felt real. It was just like my dreams about finding a bag of money.

When I woke up, I realized it was just a dream. There was nothing to wear and Mom and Dad were divorced. I stayed in bed, trying to get back to that same dream so life could be good again. Sleep was always better than real life.

Mom and Eddy were in a downward Coors and Kessler spiral and wanted to be free of us kids for the summer. Leah was at Dad's. Summer and Misty were heading to their mom's. Summer planned to live with her mom permanently and drop out of school that year. Chance was the only one who got to go to Paradise.

Before Summer left for her mom's, she kept playing Ozzy Osbourne's "Crazy Train" song as she curled her hair and I sat on the bed. She bragged about how dropouts get to do whatever they wanted. I thought dropping out of school was a dumb plan but kept it to myself.

I was sent to Auntie Raven's house in Reno for the summer. The sales pitch was that I would babysit my adorable toddler cousin, Alice, in return for school clothes money. That sounded like a good deal, and at least I wouldn't see Eddy for a while. Plus, I would have some school clothes by the end of summer.

Auntie Raven worked at a casino and the local 7-11. Her husband, Uncle Matt worked as a plumber. My adorable cousin had Uncle Matt's blonde hair and Auntie Raven's round face.

I slept on the couch in the small living room of the duplex. The first week went well. Calm and obedient Alice listened to me. She was easily entertained with blocks and books. I had good fun watching cartoons in the morning and later MTV music videos for the better part of the day. Pat Benatar and Tina Turner kept us entertained for hours. The ultimate highlight of our days was walking to 7-11 to get a free Slurpee. Cola was my favorite flavor and I tried to make it last. I was practicing real mindfulness with my daily Slurpee.

After a week, I made it to my first payday and Uncle Matt handed me a ten-dollar bill with a warning, "Don't tell Raven I gave that to you, or she'll end up taking it." I didn't believe Auntie would do that, plus I was not good at keeping secrets, so I told her. Sure enough, she asked to "borrow" it and I didn't get it back.

My ultimate school clothes goal was securing a pair of Levi's 501 button fly denim jeans. Those were the ones you had to wash three times before they shrunk enough to be worn. That pair of jeans would secure my status as a semi-worthy human being in school, and hopefully help me blend in. And maybe, just maybe, a boy with a cool mullet and braces would look my way. As the weeks rolled on, I didn't get any more ten-dollar paydays. I figured they would pay me at the end of the summer.

Auntie Raven and Uncle Matt had an ugly black van that any respectable hobo would be embarrassed to ride in. It pushed out clouds of smoke from its tailpipe when we drove it to the grocery store, choking out anyone who was unfortunate enough to be behind us. I already felt less than human at the time, even more so while in that jalopy. Looking out the window, I noticed much happier Reno people staring at us from their clean, non-polluting, reliable cars and quickly turning away in disgust. It made me feel more worthless. Raven used a quart-sized Mason jar as her wallet and carried it as we went shopping. For some reason, the jar further mortified me. Life was already embarrassing and being nearly 14 made me even more aware of opportunities to feel ashamed.

Next to sipping the Slurpee, another favorite routine was laundromat day. Every Sunday we got McDonalds and hung out waiting for the laundry to finish. I called it "family day" because it felt like what normal families might do together, or maybe what church was like. I had never been, except to that one wedding and my baptism.

A few weeks into the summer, Auntie Raven took me and Alice to her friend's house. Lola was maybe 17, a runaway, and lived with an older man I never actually saw. Lola had olive skin, secretive eyes, and talked fast. Her mysterious roommate sold an assortment of drugs.

Lola and Raven took me into Lola's back room. We sat on the spare bed and Lola took out a small tin can and unscrewed the lid. They said it was for record players but got you high. She handed it to me and told me to smell it. I took one whiff and blacked out for a second, then my forehead pounded to the beat of my heart. They told me, "Do it again!" Eager to please, I obeyed. They giggled as they watched me unknowingly kill my brain cells.

That summer was much different than my summer visits to Paradise. Auntie Raven and I hung out a lot with Lola. They next taught me how to snort cocaine. It wasn't hard. They used a razorblade to chop the powder into a fine dust on one of those framed mirrors you could win at a carnival game. This mirror had Van Halen's logo on it. Lola rolled up a twenty-dollar bill and stuck it up her right nostril while plugging her left and sniffed up one of the three lines. She handed me the makeshift straw. I sniffed my line real hard to impress them and dabbed my finger on the remaining crumbs and rubbed it on my gums, just like Lola. Like a potato chip, you can't have just one. We kept doing it. They sipped Kahlua and cream on ice out of casino glasses. I preferred to eat scoops of Lola's chocolate ice milk out of a plastic bowl.

Another night, Lola brought out a baggy of something that looked like dirt and flaky wood chips. She took some of the dirt out of the bag, put it in my hand and told me to eat it. "What is it?" I asked as I swallowed the remnants of the dirt and wood chips.

"Mushrooms."

I had heard about those and got scared for a second, but then turned my attention to Led Zeppelin playing in the background. I found myself staring at Lola's *Stairway to Heaven* album cover for far too long, pondering what the hooded guy with the lantern was doing. Lola interrupted me and demanded, "Come to the bathroom, right now!"

Auntie Raven, Lola and I stood side by side in front of the wide bathroom mirror. "Ok, look at yourself in the mirror and try not to blink," Lola instructed.

I looked at my reflection. The sight of my face puzzled me. It all seemed so strange. Life was strange. I started giggling. Auntie and Lola did too. The sight of my face made me laugh so hard my stomach hurt. I couldn't stop laughing and moaned and groaned with my laughter to make it stop hurting. I never laughed that hard in my life. I decided drugs weren't such a bad thing. After all, drinking and drugs is what made all the people in my life happy. I told myself I could get used to this. That's when we heard several loud knocks on the front door.

Whatever mushroom-induced joy I felt immediately went to terror. Lola's three brothers were outside pounding on the front door. They were trying to get her to come back home, but at the time I thought they were going to kill us.

Lola made me hide in the back room that had a front-facing window. I peeked outside and thought I saw one of the brothers holding a lighted torch, maybe a pitchfork. It was probably just a flashlight. After what seemed like hours, they eventually left without rescuing their sister.

Lola and Raven wanted to do more mushrooms and lines. I told them I wanted to go lay down. Disappointed in me being a party-pooper, they let me crash on the cold floor in the spare bedroom. When the next morning came, we walked to the local corner store and bought more chocolate ice milk and ate it for breakfast.

While I babysat and did drugs in Reno, Mom continued to hang out with her new best friend, Donna. Boisterous Donna rocked her brunette beehive hairdo and penciled in tadpole eyebrows. Warren, her "old man," had wild eyes, and an Eddy Rabbit beard. He was a doppelganger of Charles Manson minus the forehead tattoo. When Donna and Warren came into my mom's life after meeting at a bar, Mom constantly roared with laughter. Donna was funny and enjoyed the same hobbies as my mom: drinking and smoking. Donna had a few front teeth missing thanks to Warren's fists. Both Mom and Donna often went on grocery store beer runs. No matter where they were, everyone in the store could hear their laughter, as if they were in the front row of a George Carlin concert. It was good to see Mom happy and have a friend. Donna's favorite phrase to say when she went on a rant about some injustice, "I'll tell you what it is. It's dirty, rotten, stinkin'!"

When Warren wasn't taking his anger out on Donna's face, he spontaneously busted out some dance moves. It was a cross between James Brown moves and clogging. Warren washed his beloved yellow Gremlin out front while Mom and Donna drank and smoked inside.

The best part of Donna was she had three handsome sons who visited our house to see their mom. I could tell they were horrified by their mom's situation as much as we were by ours. They too had a dad who lived in a nice home with a new family while their mom was on the brink of homelessness. The boys were our ages and brought along a gorgeous friend named, Romeo. He lived up to his name, with rock and roll hair and exotic features. Romeo and Donna's oldest boy drove crotch rocket motorcycles and must have been attracted to my older sister and Summer because they used to visit a lot under the guise of seeing Donna. Summer and Leah were always the primary targets of male attention and Summer would try to steal any attention away from Leah. Nobody was interested in me.

One of the girls soon gave in to the oldest boy's carnal desires and we hardly saw them after that. Summer was pretty and a favorite with the boys. I'm pretty sure it was her.

With no children at home, Mom and Eddy allowed Donna and Warren to crash in the bed Misty and I shared. One night the house awoke to lots of smoke. Donna or Warren hadn't extinguished a cigarette and caught the bed on fire. The house wasn't burnt to the ground, but news of the situation traveled to Reno.

Back at Reno, Uncle Matt had a friend from high school who was visiting. His name was Jack. Nightly, they went out to the casinos and Jack wore his same black muscle shirt with Japanese letters that spelled some unknown word. It could have said, "I'm a ding-dong" for all I knew. Jack knew about my home situation and the recent house fire. He looked at me one night and said, "I feel so sorry for you."

I usually have a comeback, but this time I was silent. I couldn't quite process his comment. It felt like a compliment of some sort, and I drank it in. I thought, "Someone actually took a moment to think about me." It felt foreign, like his muscle shirt. I thought he was kind of cute after that.

In my silence, Jack offered me a line of sympathy cocaine. I accepted his charity. Uncle Matt was in the background sitting at the living room desk, measuring mounds of white powder on a scale, and carefully placing it into miniature baggies. I'm not sure who the head supplier was; maybe it was Lola's roommate.

When Uncle Matt was in weights and measures mode, he was focused and professional, as if he were on a secret mission. Jack bragged that he knew the dealer who sold to the rock bands who performed at the casinos.

My Reno summer gig was nearing an end. I didn't have any 501s, school clothes, cash, or hair, but my addiction switch was set to the "on" position. Raven concocted a plan to save face and send me back with some clothes. She took me over to Lola's house and bought some of her dirty laundry. One pair of ill-fitting jeans and a couple of shirts would serve as my school clothes and babysitting paycheck. Lola charged Raven twenty dollars for those lame clothes. I pretended to be grateful, but I was crushed. I couldn't wait to get a real job where people paid their workers.

Auntie Raven's friend Colleen wanted to cut my long strawberry hair before I left to give me a fresh look. Colleen gave off a masculine vibe with her large biceps, wifebeater shirt, and permed mullet. Raven and Colleen gave me an Ogilvie home permanent in the kitchen. After the perm was done, they began to cut my hair. And cut. Once finished, I had the exact same hairdo as Colleen.

When I got back home, everyone was shocked with my new look. Not in a good way. I could tell by their wide-open mouths. I was awkward and insecure before, but without my crowning glory, my ugliness was more pronounced. Eddy said, "You look like a fucking dyke!" Leah said I looked like Opie from *Andy Griffith*. And to think there was a time when people thought I was cute and gave me stuffed animals just for showing up to elementary school. I couldn't wait for my hair to grow back.

Grandpa Joe

AFTER I CAME home from Raven's, Grandpa Joe died.

I wanted to look respectable for the funeral, so I hunted for a skirt and boots from the yard sale pile. I chose a floral knee-length skirt with black boots and tried them on. I was satisfied with my look.

At the same Catholic cemetery Uncle John and Larry were buried, I saw some especially handsome distant relatives my age, secretly hoping they liked my outfit and thought I was cute. They looked like they had nice normal lives, good clothes, a beautiful clean home, and a steady supply of toiletries and groceries. I overheard their mom say, "David uses egg whites to style his mohawk. It works better than hair gel. Oh, did you hear, Mickey is in the academy training to be a police officer." I thought, blah, blah, braggity, blah, blah.

These relatives were on a whole different level. They had hair gel, career goals, and parents who were proud of them. I was jealous, but kind of proud that my family tree had a few normal branches.

After the graveside funeral, Grandpa's casket was lowered into the ground. My silent tears turned to uncontrolled sobbing at the finality of it all. He was so kind to me, and now I was losing another important man in my life. First Uncle John, then Dad, and now Grandpa. I may as well have been lowered down with him.

After Grandma and Darlene drove back to Paradise, I wrote Grandma begging her to <u>PLEASE</u> let me live with her. I just couldn't stand my life, home, and situation anymore. I told her how I loved that I could have a banana whenever I wanted, and that I wasn't ever hungry when I visited her house. I wrote that I would help her with housework, go on walks with Darlene, and not be much trouble.

I didn't tell Mom or Dad about the letter. I pictured myself going to school in Paradise, having a normal life. A bed that wasn't scorched, school clothes, and groceries.

Shortly after I wrote the letter, Mom quit drinking—cold turkey. I think Grandma finally told my mom to get her shit together, or else.

Dad recalls a different version of Mom's sobriety. Mom hadn't made a single $125 monthly house payment since he left several years prior. It all caught up with her, and unbeknownst to me, we were all going to be locked out of the house. This was Mom's rock bottom. She approached Dad one day asking for help, "Why are your hands shaking?" Dad asked.

"I quit drinking because my liver started to hurt," Mom said.

She told him she needed money to pay the back mortgage so we wouldn't be kicked out. Dad agreed to make the back payments and let her live rent free for three more years. She just had to sign the house back over to him. Mom gladly accepted the offer.

It was all so anticlimactic when Mom got sober. She didn't go to rehab and muscled through delirium tremens. It took me some time before I noticed she wasn't drinking. Her gray face began to brighten every week and her eyes looked less angry.

Eddy kept drinking. Mom must have felt sorry for him and didn't kick him out as she evolved into a kinder, sober version of herself. By then I don't think they had any "relations" for quite some time. Eddy's equipment probably shut down due to his excessive drinking. But somehow, he had an active crush on a softball player's wife, Brandy. She sang well, especially to Crystal Gayle's "Don't It Make my Brown Eyes Blue." Eddy gave her more attention. Mom was mad about that and pouted whenever Brandy showed up.

Brandy's husband, Ace left occasional lines of cocaine for me in my room. I thought it was truly generous of him. Brandy gave us her pet lovebird, Pepe. We let him out of his cage, and Pepe would fly right towards me and freak me out. I had already watched Alfred Hitchcock's *The Birds* and knew what they were capable of.

Just Kill Me Already

WHEN MIDDLE SCHOOL cheerleading tryouts came, I knew I would be good at it, but it was not an option. I watched longingly as the girls performed their routines at the pep rallies, happy for them and wishing I were up there too. Some of the cheerleaders asked me why I didn't try out. It made me feel good that they thought I could be a part of the team. I lied and told them it was because my grandpa died. I was too embarrassed to tell them I couldn't afford the uniform. Annual school clothes were a thing of the past, with my Gunne Sax school shopping trip my last. School supplies were not purchased unless I bought them myself. My toupee-wearing English teacher marked my horrible grade down even more for not having a three-ringed binder. I tried to play it off like I didn't care, but I did.

This is around the time where Mom let herself out of a moving car after a fight with Eddy. With Mom and Eddy not working, and Mom in a full leg cast, I had the more frequent embarrassing task of taking Food Stamps to buy groceries. Each trip was so stressful knowing someone from school could see that I was on welfare and make fun of me. That was when Food Stamps were these brightly colored large bills announcing to the world that you were a piece of shit and living off other people's money. The cashiers loudly stamped these bills so anyone within a 100-foot radius knew what was going on in checkout lane number three. The welfare we had was called "Aid to Families with Dependent Children." It should have been called, "Aid to Depressed Mothers So She and Her Loser Boyfriend Can Buy What They Want and Neglect the Kids."

I parked my ten-speed bicycle out front and started walking towards the entrance with a list written on the back of an envelope and Food Stamps in my pocket. Also in tow was a note from my mom requesting the cashier to allow me to purchase Marlboro Reds. I had to use cash for cigarettes. Hyper alert, I prayed I wouldn't see anybody from school. As I approached the front door, I looked up and saw Jeff from my middle school art class walking towards me. He was a handsome kid with a prominent set of brown eyebrows. We recognized one another but didn't say anything because that's what you do at that age. I felt something drop to the ground as I got closer to him. My heart dropped. I was hoping it was the cash or the envelope.

I looked down and saw a wad of colorful Food Stamps on the ground a few feet in front of Jeff. With the speed of a red-faced ninja, I picked them up and kept walking. I knew he must've seen, and I felt a horrible sense of doom, shame, depression, and terror. I wanted to quit life.

I walked in the store to obediently complete my chore. I purchased the items, heading into what looked like the quickest line to avoid more shame, thinking, "Why didn't I drop the real money in front of Jeff!!?" I rode my bike back home, right hand struggling to hold the gallon of milk and handlebar simultaneously and the rest of the stuff in a bag cradled by my left arm. I could easily ride with no hands, but the gallon of milk was a bit much to negotiate. As I crossed a busy street, a car almost hit me. My survival instincts kicked in along with my guardian angel's help. I swerved and miraculously avoided getting hit.

Later that school night, I lay in bed frantically praying, "God, please just kill me in my sleep. I can't face tomorrow." I knew the whole school would find out and everyone would laugh at me. Life was hard enough, and I couldn't take anymore. I wished my chemistry set were still around.

Part III – Things Are Looking Up

The key is to keep company only with people who uplift you, whose presence calls forth your best. – Epictetus

Girlfriends

I WOKE UP the next day and walked to school. Jeff didn't say anything, and nobody pointed or laughed at me. Good thing God doesn't answer all our prayers.

Things started looking up in the friendship and life department. Shelly lived down the street and liked me no matter what my house looked like. We knew each other from elementary school and reconnected during first period. She was loved by the boys because of her bubbly personality, painted on jeans, and high heels. Little Chance even had a crush on her. After school, Shelly and I climbed the same fruitless mulberry tree I used to climb with my sister to play *Star Trek*.

Today we didn't play *Star Trek*. Instead, Shelly listened to me plot my escape from Alcatraz as I told her I could begin my career as a high paid escort or Playboy Bunny. It seemed like a good plan to my messed-up brain. The Bunnies had cute clothes, and they looked happy and pretty. Plus, they got paid in pink Mustangs. I didn't think about the other stuff. I was still a virgin by some heavenly miracle. I remembered Misty telling stories of her mom's escort job, making a ton of money. I heard about one of the dates where one escort was so rich, they ended up rubbing cocaine and money all over their bodies. It seemed like fun and a lucrative career choice. Afterall, Misty's mom was always smiling and laughing when she visited. This further burned into my brain that anyone who is happy must be on drugs. There was no other way to achieve happiness.

Shelly must've known Denise somehow and we all became thick as thieves. Denise had a natural blonde afro she tamed with mousse making it look like uncooked ramen noodles. She was the first clarinet chair in band and always wore perfect outfits and precise eye liner. I was most impressed with Denise when I watched her get a glass of water from her kitchen sink and it suddenly splashed all over her face and clothes. She didn't freak out like I would. She calmly looked up at me and smiled like it was no big deal. Denise lived with her mom and two younger sisters in the nearby apartments.

Monica came shortly after. She lived next door to Denise with her mom and brother. She gave off a tough girl vibe with her resting-gangster face. Monica fought anyone who talked shit and scared the hell out of everybody, including me. I learned she was as soft as an angora sweater, and never wanted to harm anyone—unless she had to. Monica taught us how to make homemade tortillas and fed us burritos. Misty was part of the friend group since she lived at my house.

Denise's mom was a fun, happy hippy with minimal rules, so we often slept over at her house and roamed the streets at night. Monica didn't have many rules either, but my now sober mom had even more rules. My friends and I were all scared of her.

When we walked to school together, we must have been quite a sight according to the whistles and honking noises coming from the cars. Denise and Monica were tall, with great hair and ginormous boobs. Shelly had the booty, and well, I just had hair (thankfully my mullet had started to grow out.) It was the '80s and big hair was a thing.

I felt safe with my nonjudgmental squad, sans Misty. I was the loud goofball cracking jokes. I tried to be pretty as well, although I didn't really know how to do my hair or makeup like they did. They seemed to like me too. I felt I brought the entertainment and dance skills to the table. Using the moves I learned watching *American Bandstand*, *Soul Train*, and *Solid Gold*, I choreographed a dance with us girls in Denise's living room. It was to Van Halen's "Jump" song.

We walked to school together daily and sang Scorpions, Ratt, and Motley Crue songs obnoxiously loud. I'm certain we woke up the neighborhood every morning doing our best to disturb the peace. Attention is what we were after, and we earned it. Denise, Monica, Misty, and Shelly wore high heels as we walked to school. I couldn't do that if I tried.

To fit in, I placed a black leather jacket from Wilson's Leather on layaway and couldn't wait to wear it. Next, I was going to buy those large silver monsterish rings to adorn my fingers to show the world I was a tough rocker chick. With the Scorpion's shirt I won at the fair and too much black eyeliner I melted with a lighter before I put on, I looked the part. Truth be told, I preferred R&B, Rap, and Hip-Hop music, but that's not the look we were going for.

Staying true to myself, I plastered my walls with Michael Jackson and Prince posters which caused Eddy to call me in his disgusted tone, "n****r digger," telling me that having a crush on a black person was not acceptable. I heard that word often come out of Eddy's mouth, along with other unkind slurs.

I kept loving Michael and Prince. And if by some miracle, they asked me out on a date, I would go, no matter what Eddy thought.

I sat in my room for hours listening to Prince's *Controversy* cassette over and over, and later did the same with *Purple Rain*. I imagined Prince was my boyfriend and he was singing to me. In our purple world, Prince and I understood each other. I was perfect for him. I dreamt that someday we'd bump into each other, and he'd instantly see something special in me and whisk me away on the back of his motorcycle to live happily ever after. He was my escape hatch, therapy, and long-term boyfriend.

Michael Jackson was my imaginary side piece. He came to a local ranch when I was younger, and all the kids were talking about it at school. He was always doing something nice for kids. There would be no way in heck that my mom would drive me there. Not asking for help or anything was now hard coded in my DNA.

Jimmy, my favorite softball player, worked as a sound man at concerts. He brought me a Michael Jackson concert shirt, knowing I loved Michael. I proudly wore it to school and had all the kids thinking I went to the concert. I was hoping they would notice. When asked, "Did you go to the concert!?" I sometimes answered honestly. But if I felt a little sassy, I avoided the question and played it off like, "Don't bother me with a stupid question, of course I did." Man, what I'd give to have that T-shirt again.

There was a commercial for a carbohydrate laden cereal at the time that said if you could pinch an inch, you needed to lose weight and eat their cereal. Who couldn't pinch an inch or seven!? My girls and I sat on my dirty couch watching this commercial and squeezed our perfect thighs so that the cottage cheese would emerge and say, "Look how fat I am!" We were all clueless to the fact that we had the best figures of our lives. The whole planet was still clueless to the evils of simple carbohydrates and sodas.

Trying to get skinnier, I was bulimic for a day after getting too full from a Snickers bar, and broccoli smothered in melted Government Cheese. After forcing myself to vomit, I felt guilt wash over me. I never did that again. I'd find my way into other addictions.

Thou Shall Have No Other Gods Before Me, Even Boys

You might guess by now I have daddy and mommy issues. I was a product of parenting by people who were dealing with their own junk and happened to have kids. What's a girl to do but seek male attention to prove she has some worth in this world? The only worth I thought I had was offering my body as a sacrifice. Boys became my false idols to worship. I was oblivious of the unhealthy thought patterns and habits I established as I searched for love in all the wrong places. I no longer knew healthy parental love, and certainly didn't know how to love myself.

I got my first kiss from Steven. He looked feminine with his long, blonde hair and the fact that puberty hadn't hit. Same as me. Misty and I walked home from middle school one day with a cluster of boys and got invited over to their house. We walked them well out of our way just to be in their orbit.

It all happened so fast, but I remember Steven and I were standing in one of the bedrooms that had a perfectly made bed. I guessed it was a mother's bedroom by the looks of it. His face was near mine and he quickly dove in and rammed his tongue down my throat. It lasted two seconds. I thought, "Ooooh, that must be a French kiss." I was thrilled somebody kissed me even if I didn't know how to kiss yet. I thought, "Yay, he likes me! Somebody likes me! I hope I did it right!"

Soon after my first kiss, Misty and I left their house and I thought I had a boyfriend. Once home, I quickly wrote "I Love Steven" on all my schoolbooks and on my hand. Steven ignored me within 24 hours. The ink on my hand hadn't even faded, I was devastated, and it only confirmed what I thought. I was faulty equipment and not worthy of love.

I allowed myself to imagine a different version of myself though. Instead of walking to school in the cheapest tennis shoes and uncool, unclean, cigarette smelling outfits, with pimply skin, I dreamt of walking to school wearing shiny hot pink spandex pants, cute '80s big hair, matching jewelry, thigh high leather boots, and a matching leather jacket. Kind of like how Olivia Newton John looked at the end of the movie *Grease*. All the boys would wonder who I was and finally I'd be discovered as someone worth something.

And then what? I didn't know. Maybe then everyone would like me, and I would be okay. I equated a clean home, attentive parents, groceries, toiletries, a wardrobe, and good looks as things that would make me an acceptable human.

I now know it's never a good thing to peak in elementary, junior, or high school. That doesn't seem to end well for most people. We all need a little humility, and thankfully I got plenty.

When I turned 14, things improved in the boy department. That's when I met my first long-term boyfriend, Axel. He looked the part of the bad boy with his facial acne and pockmarks, plus he had already been to juvenile hall. He had a wavy, red mullet and walked with a bowlegged swagger as only a confident convict could.

Axel attended the continuation school down the street. I met him one night when I snuck out of my bedroom window to hang out with Denise, Shelly, and Monica at the local school. Axel was there too. The first time we met, after a little small talk, he cut to the point and asked, "Do you give head?"

I wasn't taught that I had any ownership of my body or mind, nor how to pronounce the word, "No" so I didn't tell Axel, "Gross!" and leave his side. I didn't have that elusive stand-up-for-yourself muscle.

Mom barely gave me the birds and bees talk in the sixth grade. It was quick. She said, "A girl has three holes. A poop hole, a pee hole, and the middle hole. That's your baby hole. Guys only want one thing: to wet their willies in the middle hole." The end. Great talk, Mom. I should be grateful. Many girls didn't even get that. I knew girls who thought they only had two holes for the longest time. I wished Mom would have walked me through some scenarios or even role play so I could be prepared to say no or taught me that being promiscuous doesn't improve one's self-esteem. Better yet, I wished my mom and dad filled up my soul with stable parental love, so I wouldn't feel so incomplete.

Not wanting to mess up an encounter with a potential boyfriend and hopefully fill some of my emptiness, I tried to calmly react to his crude question and said, "I never have." It didn't occur to me that it was an option to say no and not do something I didn't want to do. I had to be a good sport and sacrifice my body and dignity to get a boyfriend, which I equated with love.

I thoughtlessly gave away a priceless gift and lost my virginity that night when Axel took me back to his mom and stepdad's house. They were home asleep when he smuggled me inside. It lasted maybe two minutes and hurt like heck. I'm sure his bedsheets were wrecked. His stepdad must've heard noises, and he announced himself in the dark hallway near Axel's door. I was frightened. Axel quickly got me out of there and partially walked me home so I could climb back through my bedroom window.

Having my virginity gone made me feel loved and important and somewhat superior to girls who hadn't yet had that "honor." The next day at school, I even bragged about it to anyone who'd listen, including boys in my P.E. class. I'm certain now they must have thought I was a slut or crazy, and here I thought I was proving to them that I was cool. As if to say, "See everyone, I'm worth something! Someone wants me! I'm not so awful after all!" Sick, I know.

I felt so free and happy walking the streets at night. Unfortunately, one evening Misty joined me and was too loud as she climbed out the window causing mom to check in and catch us in the act. The next day she asked Uncle Bruce to caulk the bedroom window shut. Uncle Bruce laughed the whole time about us getting busted as he applied the caulk. My freedom and safe escape from a house fire was now gone.

After a whole three weeks, Axel and I were finished. The only time I could see him was when I snuck out of my bedroom window. And Mom wouldn't let me go outside when he showed up at my house. I learned that to keep a boyfriend you had to keep your body available. Misty and Mom always ruined everything.

Night Terrors

I OFTEN HAD night terrors. I didn't know that's what they were at the time. Nobody did. I usually got them when I had fevers. I later learned night terrors can be caused by stress, sleep deprivation, or fever. I had a horrible fever after the end-of-middle-school party at the lake. Sunscreen wasn't a thing back then. Covering our bodies with baby oil and lying on a towel that looked like aluminum foil was.

I came home with my fair skin burnt to a crisp, bright red, and blistering in spots. I didn't receive a Noxzema treatment from the loving hands of a parent, like I saw on TV. That night I had a 103 fever.

The next day I missed my 9th grade graduation. While I slept in Chance's bed, Misty helped herself to my special Gunne Sax dress and shoes. Mom and Eddy took Misty to graduation. Jimmy was hanging out at the house.

In the grips of another night terror, I bolted out of bed and ran towards the front door screaming gibberish. Jimmy didn't know what to do. I felt the whole world was ending and the universe was collapsing into itself. Like the opposite of the Big Bang. A sense of doom suffocated me and there was wailing and gnashing of teeth. I had to escape. Jimmy somehow stopped me at the front door, and despite my cries and flailing arms, he got me to sit down in the living room.

Out of the periphery of my semi-conscious mind, I noticed Jimmy clumsily pick up the phone, trying to call for help. I had thousands of thoughts racing in my head and I couldn't keep up with everything. I remember one of the random questions that flew out of my mouth. I asked Jimmy, "Am I going to graduate?!"

Relieved I was making sense, Jimmy laughed and said, "Yes, Bernstein." That was his nickname for me because I was extremely frugal with money. He nicknamed most people. It was a compliment, not intended as anti-Semitism. Jimmy doesn't have a mean bone in his body.

The real world came into blurry focus, and I was so happy to learn it wasn't ending. After my fever subsided several days later, I grew clusters of cold sores that covered my top and bottom lips. Each night the top and bottom fused together, and by morning I had to carefully pry my mouth open without causing too much bleeding. The sores lasted the better part of the summer.

When Shelly and I hung out at the local community pool, schoolmates asked, "What happened to you!?" We told them I got in a fight since it made for a better story. Perhaps I should have stayed away from the community pool with those monstrosities on my face. Oopsie.

On weekdays, Mom and Jimmy watched *General Hospital* together when Luke and Laura were a hot item. Jimmy still had his girlfriend Emma who'd come over too. She loved hamburgers, cocaine, and Motley Crue. I watched her eat juicy burgers from the local parking lot burger shack, "Moe's." Mayo-laden special sauce dripped from her pretty fingernails as she devoured her burger. Emma taught me that chicken tasted best when dipped in mayonnaise. How right she was! Jimmy would take a bullet for her and asked her to marry him.

Misty and I were invited to their wedding and Chance was the adorable ring bearer, wearing a white tux with tails. Emma bought fancy dresses for Misty and me. As I sat in the folded chair during the backyard ceremony, the preacher waved his arms like Vanna White, showcasing the newly installed decking and landscaping saying, "All of this means nothing if the marital vows are not taken seriously." It was like he knew what we were all thinking; this union wouldn't last as long as the redwood decking.

Misty and I were Emma's faithful buddies. We loved it when she took us places in her silver Trans-Am. Misty would always call shotgun before I could think of it, so I sat in the back. We felt special riding in that car. So special that Misty yelled out the window to people innocently walking down the street calling them, "BIIIITCH!" and other derogatory terms like that.

I loved staying the night at Emma's house because she had plenty of Agree shampoo and conditioner. It smelled like heaven. My hair got super clean and smelled perfumy, just like the popular girls in school. On those days, I'd even take the time to carefully put Emma's makeup on before school. The girls at school asked me, "Who do you like?" thinking I was on the hunt with my fancy face, which I was.

On weekends, Emma took Misty and me to the local adult dance club, Ponderosa Saloon. We were too young to enter, so she went in to buy her cocaine while we waited in the car. One night she came running out of the club and quickly got in the car and sped away. Another car started chasing us.

Emma drove us out of the parking lot like a sprint-car driver. We didn't ask questions, but it became clear she didn't pay for the cocaine. A car full of angry men were chasing us. Somehow, we lost them and continued to drive around town and listen to Motley Crue songs. Later that night, Emma drove us back to the Ponderosa

Saloon. I didn't feel good about that decision. Guess who was in the parking lot, waiting for us?

"Oh shit," Emma said as she spotted them. Their oncoming car sped toward us, trying to hit us head on. Emma jerked her car to the right. The driver's side of the Trans Am crunched and the whole car shook. It felt like bumper cars, only scarier. Thanks to Emma's driving skills, we got away again.

Happily, we made it home safe and agreed on our story about the wrecked car. We'd say it was a hit and run. Misty and I were happy to back up Emma's alibi. She took good care of us and gave us trinkets, access to her toiletries, and drove us around in her cool car. That was an exciting summer.

Planned Promiscuity

MY HIGH SCHOOL's smoking area had cement picnic benches and ashtrays so kids could smoke before class and during lunch. It was a busy place. Before school, there were several packs of friends crowding the area, and a tired-looking girl sitting on her boyfriend's lap to mark her property. Anyone could easily sneak a few tokes off a joint if we held it like a cigarette.

Denise, Monica, Shelly, Misty, and I smoked cigarettes before school every morning. I got surprisingly good at blowing smoke rings with minimal practice but didn't stick with it. First, I'm too cheap, and second, I really didn't get the point. It didn't even give me a buzz, and it cost too much. I tried to exhale all the smoke to not pollute my lungs with each drag.

Cinnamon, a rocker chick with permed black hair and a potty mouth, walked up to us and bummed a smoke. She was chatty and asked us if we were on the pill yet. None of us were. She described in detail how we could score some birth control pills.

"Go to the fucking Planned Parenthood and tell 'em you don't have any insurance when they ask. Let 'em know you're sexually active. They'll give you a bag full of birth control pills—for free! No shit! You don't even have to give 'em any information. It's all confidential."

My girlfriends and I hung onto her every word. We thought it was a smart plan since we were boy crazy and didn't want to be moms yet. I couldn't talk to my mom about much, let alone birth control. I concocted a plan to get Jimmy to drive me to Planned Parenthood. It was across the river, about ten miles away. There was no way we could walk or ride our bikes.

Frugal and a lover of free stuff, I often tried to win radio station contests. All I had to do was be the lucky caller. I won many times, thanks to the redial button and fast fingers. When I heard ringing instead of the busy signal, my heart skipped a beat. I knew I won. I scored concert tickets, a Police album, and water park tickets.

To get to Planned Parenthood, I told Jimmy I needed to pick up another prize from a radio station down the street. I asked if he wouldn't mind driving Shelly and me. He unwittingly drove us to Planned Parenthood. We had him park in their parking lot and wait for us. It worked just like Cinnamon said. We left with a brown paper bag full of birth control pills. Jimmy didn't ask any questions when he drove us home.

I felt like a grown up placing the pill container in my pleather purse, comingling with my pack of gum and lip gloss.

Cinnamon, a seemingly great friend, decided to make a move on Denise's boyfriend within a couple of weeks. She was now a villain and we ostracized her, rightfully so. And Denise's cheating boyfriend was kicked to the curb.

I felt bad about lying to Jimmy, and I gave him a whale I made in ceramic class as an apology. He still has "Humphrey" and proudly displays it as any proxy dad would.

Working Girl

SINCE I WAS as broke as a church mouse, I got my work permit as soon as possible. I needed some moola to buy clothes, school supplies, toiletries, candy bars, and other essentials like alcohol and drugs. I landed a job working at my school's front office answering the phones for the office manager, Mrs. Chan. It must have been because I was a fast typist. My keyboarding teacher recommended me for the job and local typing contest. I didn't win the contest because I caved under pressure, but at least I landed a job.

Mrs. Chan was strict and scary, but I felt important working in an office and made a little less than $3 an hour because the school's payroll department hadn't caught up to the new minimum wage of $3.35.

I answered the phones, "Valley High School, may I help you?" My coworker, Duncan, our class president told me, "You should answer the phone. "Valley *Senior* High School." He thought adding the word "senior" made it sound more professional. I thought it was cool that someone important enough to be elected as class president talked to little ol' me.

I didn't get my job back when I left for Grandma's house for three weeks during the summer. I could have been a better communicator about my summer vacation. In fact, I didn't tell Mrs. Chan I'd be gone. I was too scared of her. But I would have rather lost my job than miss out on visiting Grandma and Darlene.

Not long after my return, still fourteen, I saw a "Help Wanted, Inquire Within" sign on the door of the local thrift store. It was next door to the Colonel's grocery store, and Food Stamp pickup place, a quick walk from my house. Since I had experience selling used items from my front lawn, I knew I was a good job fit. I walked home and changed into my interview outfit. I chose a collared shirt and my fake Guess jeans that had the upside-down triangle on the right rear pocket. My triangle said, "Palmetto's" instead of Guess. I walked through the door and inquired with the manager, Carmen. She had short copper hair and wore large Sally Jessy Raphael eyeglasses trimmed in gold to match her jewelry. She looked me up and down and I felt glad to be wearing a collared shirt. She asked, "When can you start?"

"Right away!" I replied. I started the next morning.

On my first day, I walked inside the store and my nostrils were instantly assaulted by a potent smell of urine and other dreadful aromas. It was a hot day, and this full-figured lady was too close to the swamp cooler. Her funky-town situation permeated the whole place. Nobody seemed to notice, but my keen sense of smell picked up everything. I tried to breathe through my mouth. I asked my coworker, Lydia, a mother of three, "Does it always smell like this?"

"I no sure." She answered in her best English.

Finally, one of my coworkers found the offending cup of piss in the aisle that sold sheets, blankets, stuffed animals, and curtains. A customer must have decided the cup made a good porta-potty. It didn't smell so horrible after the lady left and the cup of pee was removed.

Still, the job was not fun, and the bosses were scary. The owner sat in his office perched way above the store so he could watch his employees like a hawk. I felt like I was doing something wrong even if I wasn't, like when Eddy was around.

I worked there for a couple of years and was grateful to work the cash register rather than clean up the floor mess that customers made. It was fun to shop for forty-cent shirts and eighty-cent pants while I worked. I was pleasantly surprised to get an occasional twenty-five cent bump in my hourly pay. I guess Hawk Eye was OK with me and the fact that I never called in sick, and my register always balanced. One of my coworkers got a job at the grocery store next door and the whole store was so happy she made it to the big leagues. When she walked out after working her last day, it felt like the end of *An Officer and a Gentleman* where Debra Winger gets whisked away from her factory job by uniformed Richard Gere.

During the summers, I worked full time and it was miserable, but I needed the cash. Once school started, I worked daily from 5 p.m. to 9 p.m., scrubbing dirty old shoes in the back room.

On my days off, I'd walk by the store on my way to Denise's house and daydream about it catching on fire so that I wouldn't have to go back. It never did. I wished Drew Barrymore from the *Firestarter* movie would do me a favor.

When I worked a full day, I splurged and bought a large soda and a frozen microwaveable meal from Colonel's for lunch. Sometimes I bought chocolate Kisses and they kept me company, sitting in my apron pocket as I worked.

On weekends, when the boss wasn't there, I suggested to my coworkers that we all pitch in and get some Spanada and 7 up to make wine coolers, like some of my mom's friends. They thought it was a great idea. I was so happy my college-aged coworkers could buy our booze. We sipped our cocktails out of red Solo cups all day and didn't get caught. I now feel bad about that, but we did take care of our work responsibilities while enjoying our beverages. Plus, it boosted our morale.

Dudley

NOT TOO LONG after Axel, while I was still fourteen but looked no more than twelve, my best friends found my next boyfriend. My girls were walking in the neighborhood when a car full of older boys drove by and asked, "You wanna party?" Soon we all met up at their two-bedroom apartment.

The boys drove us to the nearby liquor store to buy some beer. Dudley had abnormally large eyes and a devilish smile. Robert was the handsomest and my first pick, because he looked exactly like a black-haired Rod Stewart with a strong pointy nose. Sheamus had personality and charisma, but he was in no way good looking to me. Just an ordinary faceless rocker guy. He was the oldest and had the nicest car, a Chevelle.

Monica, Shelly, and I waited in the car. As we watched them walk in the store, we quickly divided the boys. I asked, "Who do you like?"

"Robert's cute." Monica said.

I was bummed because I wanted Robert. Shelly already claimed Sheamus. "Ok Monica, you can have Robert, I'll go for Dudley." It was settled.

They all came from West Virginia hoping for more excitement in California. Once here, they put in applications everywhere to land a job. They were quickly hired at a local tool and die shop.

Dudley and Robert shared a room. They crammed two twin beds in there and hung a poster of their favorite guitarist, Randy Rhoads. Dudley told me Randy was the best guitar player that ever lived. He played with Ozzy Osbourne and Quiet Riot before he died in a plane crash. Sheamus had the master bedroom. Their fridge always had beer and a block of Government Cheese, just like my house.

A couple days into our relationship, as Dudley and I cuddled on his couch, he said, "You shouldn't tell your parents we're dating. We need to keep it a secret."

"Why?" I asked.

"The last girl I was with told her parents. They turned me in, and I got charged for statutory rape. I don't want to go to jail this time."

I was fourteen and he was nineteen. "What's her name?"

"Becky."

I knew who she was and became jealous since she got to him first and she's one grade below me. I disliked her instantly.

I was so happy to have another male figure pay attention to me after Axel broke my heart. I didn't care about the age difference, or criminal record. Even Sheamus called us "jailbait" when we visited. My boyfriend was a convicted pedophile. At the time, I thought it was love. I was malnourished in that department.

Later, Dudley took me on a date to the local parking lot carnival. I felt so proud to walk around with an older guy on my arm to show everyone I had a boyfriend. I walked taller and scanned the crowd hoping that someone from school would see me, especially Axel, Steven, or Fay. I won an extra-large stuffed animal by shooting a pyramid of clear plastic cups. I hoped carrying that big stuffed dog would increase my odds of getting noticed.

We lasted off and on for about two years and, after year one, I finally introduced him to my mom and Eddy. We lied about his age and made him a couple years younger.

Despite my worries, Mom and Eddy were fine with Dudley. He was charming and polite in social settings. They didn't get to see the angry version. Dudley felt comfortable out at my house and tinkered on his beat-up pickup in my front yard. He even helped himself to chunks of our Government Cheese without Eddy getting mad and yelling, "Don't let him eat our food!"

Dudley was very reactive. He often punched holes in doors and walls. His violent temper nearly killed us on many occasions. He'd get so mad at other drivers. He would angrily accelerate his pickup, nearly rear-ending or sideswiping them on the freeway as he yelled curse words, trying to pick fights and teach them a lesson. I begged him to stop, but that only made him angrier.

When Dudley drank tequila, his temper got worse. He'd get an evil look in his eyes like he was possessed. He got so mad and drunk one night about some perceived insult, he punched a glass window. He sliced himself up so badly he had to be taken to the emergency room. He was out of work for a while and got hit with a large medical expense he couldn't afford.

After he had his arm in a cast for several weeks, I drove with him to pay an installment on his medical bill. The professionally dressed lady sitting at the front desk impressed me. I watched her switch from speaking Spanish to English on the phone and help people waiting in line to pay their bills. I thought to myself, "Dang, she has a good job—and she's bilingual. Maybe I could have a good government job like that someday. Maybe I could learn Spanish."

When Dudley was able to work again, in between paychecks, he borrowed money from me to buy ham, swiss cheese, and a loaf of bread so he would have food. He'd always pay me back.

As the months rolled on, we started to visit his buddy, Dwight the dealer, to do coke. I saw one of the popular girls from school sitting on Dwight's couch and felt cool for a minute being in the same room with her, a cheerleader who was also voted "Best Hair." We didn't speak. Everyone sat awkwardly on Dwight's living room furniture hoping to be lucky enough to be called back to his room to do free lines. Dudley was good friends with Dwight and that helped prioritize our charity case. It's a pitiful situation, the whole protocol of getting free drugs. But then again, I love free stuff.

That night Dudley and I were invited to go to the drive-in theatres with Dwight and a bunch of friends. The last time I went to the drive-ins was with Mom, Dad, and Leah. I remembered hearing Paul McCartney's theme song to James Bond's *Live and Let Die* as I ate Mom's buttery popcorn out of a paper grocery bag. Those were the good days.

On this trip to the drive-ins, I had no idea what the movie was about because every few minutes we were fiending for the next line. Dwight's dealing business was booming, so he decided to rent a Camaro for the week. He didn't bother to turn it in, so it was essentially stolen after the rental period. I loved it when he picked me up from my thrift store job. I felt important, like a groupie.

On hot days, I hung out at the apartment pool with Dwight, his wife Lucy, and Dudley. There were kids splashing in the pool from the apartment complex, and one innocently asked me, "Are you a kid or a grown up?"

I didn't know what to say and I felt embarrassed by this kid's bold question. I stammered for a minute and finally said, "I'm.... somewhere in between." I had always looked younger than my age, and obvious to everyone, including that kid, I didn't fit in with this older crowd.

With Dudley, I had fleeting moments of clarity where I'd question, "What the hell am I doing with this person!?" I remember working at my high school's snack shack serving hot dogs and sodas. He stood off in the distance, sitting on his ten-speed bicycle wearing his Iron Maiden hat that no longer fit his watermelon head, and unflattering '70s sunglasses. I saw him with crystal clear clarity in that moment. He had a horrible temper, no goals, and he wasn't going anywhere in life. As for my goals, I imagined being a bilingual receptionist, working at a grocery store, or as a Kmart cashier. I suppressed these intelligent thoughts of leaving and stayed with Dudley.

Dudley must have felt me pulling away because he bought me a small promise ring. It kept me tethered longer. I didn't want to hurt his feelings or speak up, plus the diamond ring was the most expensive thing anyone ever bought me, even though he borrowed money from me to buy it.

I finally got the courage to break up with him after him breaking my heart, cheating on me, and giving me another STD with zero satisfaction. I had no idea what an "O" was but pretended like I did just to get his sweaty body off me. Yes, I can be slow. I was around 16 when I finally worked up the nerve. That meant he was 21.

To think, there was a time when I imagined myself living in his hometown in West Virginia, in a manufactured home, standing behind a dusty screen door just barely making ends meet with a crying dirty-faced baby on my hip. Thankfully, God sent me on a new path.

I got back on the hunt. I had my eyes on this cutie for a while. I was sixteen and starting my senior year of high school. He had rocker hair, great teeth, full lips, and a car.

I thought Finn was handsome, and that's all that counted. I overlooked how he often used big words incorrectly and tried to sound smart to people who didn't have a "vocabulation." He'd spontaneously blurt out impersonations of an extremely popular comedian, Sam Kinison. I tried to get his attention while I was the teacher's assistant in Auto Shop class.

I was doing well in school when Mr. C, the auto shop teacher, asked me to be his assistant. I hoped he would since I campaigned the year prior by acing all his tests and being the only girl in class. Auto Shop was full of guys. That's why I took the class in the first place.

I replayed the scene in my head of how Finn and I would fall in love. I'd walk around the corner from Mr. C's office with a clipboard in my arms, acting like I had an important mission. As I turned the corner, Finn would just so happen to be there, bump into me, look into my beady eyes, and it would be love at first sight. It didn't exactly go down that way.

I got impatient and told Finn, "Hey, we should go out to lunch." That did the trick. Finn and I went to the local McDonald's that day and each day after.

After a week, Finn finally kissed me while we hung out in his room. Partially proud yet embarrassed to be so experienced for my age, I learned I was Finn's first intimate experience, excluding one of his kissing cousins he told me about.

Finn and I had lots of fun together. He took me to his favorite Mexican restaurant. He invited me to his grandma's house. We watched movies and ate dinner with his family. I loved how his family was normal. His mom and dad both worked and were unaddicted.

I realized Finn would want to come over to see my house too. I couldn't put him off any longer. I just knew he'd break up with me once he saw my living situation. A few weeks into our relationship, the dreaded day came.

On the way over I got extra anxious. I blurted out rapid-fire distractions, "We have piranhas. My mom's boyfriend is an asshole. You want to get high later? What are we doing this weekend?"

He parked his brown Toyota Celica in front of my house. I felt sick to my stomach. We walked through the door and saw shirtless Eddy perched on the couch, hunched over and smoking. Mom was sitting at the kitchen table. I introduced Finn to Mom and Eddy and showed him the piranhas. I didn't dare let him see my room or use the bathroom.

After the brief visit, we got the heck out of there. During our car ride back to his place, Finn accurately assessed and named my house. He had a way with words, even when he made them up. "Your house is horrible, and what the hell is up with Eddy? It's like you live at...at...*The House of **Death***." I agreed and thought to myself, "Huh, I never thought to name my home, 'The House of Death', but it's totally accurate." He didn't break up with me. I felt like I dodged a bullet.

We hung out at his place most of the time. We smoked a lot of weed together, even during lunch. We'd head back to class after putting Visine in our eyes, trying to act normal and pretend to pay attention in class.

One weekend, we drove with my sister to score some cocaine. She dropped us off in front of some random liquor store so she could drive to her dealer's house around the corner for, "Just a few minutes." It was 35-degrees, and the wind blew right through my parachute pants and leopard shirt. The dealer, aka "The General," was paranoid and didn't trust many people, especially some strange boy. Plus, he had done time before. My sister preferred to freebase her cocaine, which took time. A "few minutes" turned into an hour and a half as Finn and I huddled close to keep warm. I hated being cold and I didn't own a proper jacket. I was mad and thought, "If I didn't have Finn with me, I'd be able to go in The General's house, just like the last time." During my prior visits, I'd watch my sister's excitement grow as she sanded down a glass cigar case she'd use to freebase.

Fina-friggen-ly, I saw the familiar headlights of Leah's 1978 Honda Accord. She rolled up without apologizing for the delay, eyes extra wide. She drove to a vacant parking spot so we could snort cocaine with our frostbitten noses.

The next morning, at my thrift store job, I noticed the prices of some of the nicer bedroom furniture. I realized with the money I spent on cocaine; I could buy the furniture with my money instead of snorting it. I decided it was too expensive to sustain a cocaine habit. I told myself I would only do it if it was free.

Near the end of our senior year, Finn and I went to Senior Prom, but didn't dance a single dance. Instead, we left and hung out in a hotel room and ordered his favorite Mexican food and snorted cocaine. I would have preferred to dance.

I can't thank Mr. C enough for landing me a boyfriend my age and telling me how important college was. I listened to Mr. C. He was kind and encouraged me, a great male figure in my life. He loved that I could type his lesson plans super-fast into his Commodore 64 computer. Sorry if there were tons of typos, Mr C!

Working for Dad

I FINALLY GOT a better job. I got to work for Dad since his photography business was doing so well and he had a vacancy.

By then, Dad fulfilled a lifelong dream of his—to have all the high school students coming to him for their senior portraits and dance pictures. My sister stopped working for Dad since she got a really good job, the mother of all jobs—a government job.

Mom told Leah about the job. By then, the welfare-to-work program helped Mom get a seasonal job, working for a government agency sorting mail. Now both my mom and sister were making good money. Mom, with the help from the state, was weaning herself off public assistance. We went from eating Government Cheese to earning government cheddar. It was even better than a grocery store job with amazing health benefits and a pension.

Like Leah, I was good at keeping up and taking care of the customers, but Dad's studio wasn't an organized shop. My dad was great at taking photos and schmoozing with his customers, but the office management details suffered.

Dad was a workaholic, with the work ethic of Elon Musk. At the studio, he'd entertain us by throwing daily tantrums, kicking and punching walls, and shouting expletives as he processed film in his dark room. It was laughable and embarrassing when customers were in earshot. I put as much order to the chaos as possible, including apologizing to customers for unmet promises.

My coworker Kendra and I were organized and consistent employees. Dad was charming and could disarm people and get them from pissed to laughing in seconds. Thanks to my upbringing, so could I. It was crisis management all day every day, and I was skilled at damage control. It was a great education in how to run a shop and deal with crazy personalities and crises—a great skill for any job.

That experience made me realize owning my own business could never be fun for me. I'd never want to take over Dad's business, even if it was extremely profitable. Plus, I thought Dad's second batch of kids would probably want it.

On two separate occasions, I remember looking out the front window of my dad's office and seeing Axel and Steven walking with their girlfriends and pushing a stroller. I wasn't sure if the babies were theirs. A part of me thought, "What's wrong with me? Why did they break up with me?" The sensible part of me was grateful to not have a child by either one of them.

The funny thing is that my schoolmates thought I was rich. Realizing the photographer for their senior and dance portraits had the same last name as me they asked, "Is *that* your dad?!" As if they were surprised that little old me had a dad who owned a business and drove a beamer.

I'd shrug and say, "Yeah," acting nonchalant, as if it were no big deal. But it *was* a big deal. I imagined with each question, that they thought I lived in a normal home, with a normal happy life—something much better than my reality. It was just like when my classmates asked about Leah, "*That's* your sister!?" surprised that I was related to someone so beautiful.

I lived a dual existence and hoped people wouldn't learn the truth. On one hand, Dad owned three houses: the nice one he and his new family and my sister lived in, the slum I slept in and tried to avoid, and the remodeled home that now served as his photography studio. It seemed like life was good when you looked at my dad or sister. On the other hand, Chance, Mom, and I lived in squalor thanks to the decade of my home serving as non-stop party central. I was grateful most of my classmates had no idea about the situation I lived in, and I wasn't about to tell them or invite them over for a Government Cheese sandwich.

Girl Time

As usual, I was always on the go. I couldn't stand being at home or around Eddy. During our free time, my best friends and I hung out at the clay banks of the local river, wearing our '80s high-cut fluorescent bikinis and cheap sunglasses. Our current boyfriends sometimes joined us. The river was a popular spot for stoners, drinkers, and hoodlums like us. Boys jumped their BMX bikes off the cliffs and into the water to impress girls.

In between sunbathing and imbibing, we walked upstream to jump off one of the clay banks and float on our backs to cool down. We were totally oblivious to the dangers of the river. On one jump, we thought it was wise to take the box of Franzia wine we borrowed from a parent's refrigerator. It seemed like a good idea. I staggered upstream with my girls and jumped into the river with the box. The shock of the cold water helped me realize how drunk I was. We found ourselves washed up on the rocky shore, laughing, with the box of wine within arm's reach. That summer a couple of us also dabbled in meth since it was cheaper than cocaine and easily accessible. Plus, we looked extra thin in our bikinis since meth curbed our appetites. We thought it was a good diet plan and didn't have as many inches to pinch.

The best part of our senior year was when Denise's mom bought a light blue Samurai Suzuki four-wheel drive. Our stock price in coolness soared when Denise drove. We felt like we were the shit and got lots of attention. I remember driving to a concert at the state fair with our hair blowing in the wind as the cassette player blasted, "Rock You Like a Hurricane" by the Scorpions.

My favorite part of my senior year was when Misty left to join Summer and live with her mom. I was thrilled to have my friends, clothes, and room all to myself without Misty's negativity. I was cautiously happy that Mom remained sober. I thought life couldn't get any better.

Sometimes we'd take the Suzuki to the local lake along with a twelve pack of beer. On one occasion, the police spotted us, and most of us dropped our beers quickly to hide the evidence. Monica wasn't quick enough in ditching hers. It still dangled from her beer cooler necklace as the officers approached. She got the only citation for drinking underage. She took the fall for all of us. Sorry, Monica!

We thought the most embarrassing part was when the cops made us pour out our precious remaining beers in the sand in front of all the other beachgoers. We dusted off our pride, acquired more beer and continued to party after the cops left.

White Trash

THE SUMMER AFTER my senior year, Leah, Chance, and I got to go on a road trip with Dad. Leah gave Dad a hard time and told him, "Your younger kids get all of your time, and you never take us anywhere!"

Dad's business was doing very well, so he took us to the amusement park near Los Angeles. We pretty much forced him at gunpoint using Leah's sharp-shooting guilt gun. Chance and I added to the guilt letting him know how messed up it was that his second family got most of his time; we wanted him all to ourselves for one friggin' weekend.

The trip was a blast. We got to ride in dad's gray 325 I BMW. Leah sat in front, with Chance and me in the back. We sang loudly to Whitesnake's, "Here I Go Again," when it came on the radio. Leah talked so dang much the whole drive, clearly cherishing the fact Dad was a captive audience, hitting him with disgusting shock jock type quips, causing him to belly laugh and snort and say, "Stop it! You're gross!" Chance was equally hilarious and got some good ones in too. I settled into my observer role. Chance and Leah craved Dad's attention even more than me and I wanted them to have it.

The next morning, we had breakfast at a local diner before we hit the park. Chance ordered a side of biscuits and gravy. All of a sudden, our health nut Dad started howling with uncontrollable laughter. We didn't get what was so funny and asked why he was laughing.

Dad explained, "Chance, biscuits and gravy are soooo white trash!" Chance's face turned red.

Leah quickly chimed in and said, "Dad, in case you didn't notice, we ARE white trash."

While Leah, Chance, and I ran from ride to ride, Dad was happy to take naps on any available park bench. He could fall asleep anywhere.

After the road trip with Dad, Eddy's daughters returned to visit. They brought along four extra visitors. They each had a long-haired-rock-concert-shirt-wearing boyfriend. And both carried in beautiful bright-eyed bundles of joy.

The baby girls were adorable, with chubby feet, cheeks, and black hair. They looked like twins. I didn't know Misty and Summer were pregnant. I noticed that Summer and Misty spoke differently. They now shared the same Latino accents of their boyfriends. I thought they didn't leave that long ago to pick up a new accent.

I really liked Misty's boyfriend. He was the nicest. He was normal, polite, and gentle. I noticed that Misty was different in a good way. She even said something nice to me during this visit. I told her I was thinking about going to college and she said, "I knew you would always do good." It was a huge compliment coming from her. I never knew she thought that highly of me. Maybe being a mom softened her up. Eddy was happy to see his daughters and their babies. His mood brightened.

Not much changed with their dad since they last saw him.

He was still perched on the same dirty couch, in the same dreary house, Kessler's bottle nearby, unemployed, looking more pitiful with each passing day. So pitiful, many of the Stoners stopped coming around.

The visit was short, just a weekend and they were on their way back to Southern California where they now lived. My sister and I went back to our hard-working and hard-partying lives. Eddy's prediction of Leah and I having babies at sixteen didn't come true. My sister and I had no intention of being moms yet. We were having too much fun running away from our demons.

I didn't ask, but I wondered why Mom didn't kick Eddy out once she got sober. I think she felt sorry for him. He had nowhere else to go and would probably end up homeless. Mom saw Grandma Lou tolerate Grandpa's excessive drinking, so it was a family tradition to stay together no matter what.

To earn a little cash, sometimes Eddy ran errands for my dad's business. Dad had a way of making everyone his personal secretary. Eddy used the Dart muscle car Dad bought for him. In between errands, Eddy asked me, "Can I borrow a few dollars?" I'd reluctantly hand it to him, knowing I'd never get it back. In between my "loans" and Dad's errands, Eddy began stealing whiskey from the grocery store.

After getting home from work or school, I noticed Eddy helped himself to microwave meals I bought for myself. And yes, without asking. I felt sorry for Eddy and didn't say anything.

Dad felt sorry for Eddy too and got him a job doing landscaping work for the local community park. That is what we referred to as, "a good job"—a steady one with benefits. On his first day, Eddy quit within two hours since he started shaking violently from alcohol withdrawals. I felt pity for him when he came home before lunchtime and tried to comfort him in my codependent way. I hugged him and told him something I'm not sure I believed, "It's okay, at least you tried!"

A miracle happened shortly after Eddy quit. I don't recall the fight between Mom and Eddy, but suddenly he started loading up his clothes and hats in the trunk of his car. He threw his faded paystubs at Mom as she stood in the kitchen to prove that he once worked. He made such a big spectacle about leaving; I think he expected Mom and Chance to scream, "No, please don't go! We need you!"

None of us said a word. We couldn't believe our luck. Was this really happening? As Eddy made the few trips from Mom's room to his car, Mom, Chance, and I told each other with our eyes, "If we all play it cool, this really might happen."

When Eddy sped away, I felt like one of the munchkins from *The Wizard of Oz* when the Wicked Witch had the house fall on her. Ding dong, Eddy's gone!

Eddy came back the next day. He walked through the front door as if he still lived there. I was home alone, getting ready to go to work and miraculously found the courage to tell him to leave. I said, "You don't live here anymore. I'm calling Mom." Mom was at work. I picked up the phone from the kitchen wall and started dialing. That made him leave for good.

I couldn't believe it was that easy. I thanked God and the Academy. My brother, Mom, and I were now rid of Eddy and all his mess. From then on, we kept the door locked in case he tried to return. His departure meant all my problems were solved, right?

Dad sent me to hypnotherapy. With Eddy gone, I must have begun to share some of my experiences with him. Dad had extra hypnotherapy sessions on trade, and he said it helped people. He loved all that positive thinking stuff.

I showed up to the tiny one room office. The nerdy bespectacled hypnotherapist welcomed me and asked me to sit on his plastic couch. "So, tell me, what's the problem?"

"I don't have any problems. My mom's boyfriend just left, and his daughters no longer live in my house." No problems here, mister, can I go now? My appointment lasted fifteen minutes. Deep in denial, I was out of there.

Even though Mom was sober and Eddy and Misty were out of my house, the effects of my childhood would bubble up in my life, like a volcano, triggered by the darndest things. At the time, I had no clue what was in store. With all the defense mechanisms I unconsciously built, triggers programmed deep inside, and the trauma I stuffed away, I had no idea it would need to be acknowledged and addressed. But for now, I was on auto pilot, happy to live my life without Eddy and his daughters.

I'm Fine, Really!

Wherever you go you will find your teacher, as long as you have the eyes to see and the ears to hear. – Shunryu Suzuki

I WATCHED OTHERS and copied what seemed normal. I bought preppy clothes from the thrift shop and dressed conservatively, trying to play the part of "average girl" who lived in an ordinary home and never received ass-whoopin's or government assistance. But deep down, in the recesses of my soul, it felt like I'd fallen flat on my face, got my front teeth knocked out, had blood gushing from my nose, gravel lodged in my forehead, yet quickly popped up and told everyone, "I'm fine. It doesn't even hurt. Nothing to see here!"

I dressed and acted a certain way so I could convince an audience of strangers that I was living a normal life and doing just fine. I didn't realize the imaginary audience I was performing for and trying to convince was me.

I believed all the years of negative programming and piled on my own. I felt worthless, as if I had nothing to offer and zero talents. Just female anatomy and maybe a joke or dance move. I worked hard to be whoever I thought people wanted me to be, seeking a constant drip of other people's approval. I certainly didn't approve of myself. I didn't know who I was anyway.

I hungered for the simple things. Maybe one day I could have a good job. Maybe one day, I could afford all the groceries I needed without stressing out as I faced the cashier with my armpits sweaty, face red, heart racing, calculating ten times to make sure I had enough money. Maybe one day, I wouldn't feel as if the cashiers were judging me as if I were paying with Food Stamps, even though I now paid in cash and coupons. Maybe one day, I would have an apartment or house that didn't embarrass me if someone came over. I certainly wouldn't have any stinky pets or clothes that smelled like an ashtray, and my bathroom would be sparkly clean and smell like pine trees. One day.

I didn't realize yet that I was a masterpiece created by God and that nothing I do can add to or subtract from that beautiful truth. I had no clue that we all receive God-given talents, and nobody gets left out on talent-distribution day. I had no clue that I didn't have to earn my right to exist. God already did that by making me. I wished someone had told me that. I had to learn these truths the hard way.

Pills, Thrills, and Guys Feeding Me Meals

RIGHT BEFORE HIGH school graduation, Finn broke up with me. He got so mad because I chose to stay with his parents in their living room and watch TV instead of joining him in his room for some hanky panky. He kept yelling for me from his bedroom, and I ignored him. When I finally walked in, I saw he had torn up his photograph of me. I thought it was an overreaction. After that evening, he stopped calling me. It didn't bother me too much. I felt like I was outgrowing him anyway.

In auto shop class, my teacher and surrogate father, Mr. C, asked me what I was going to do after graduation and suggested community college. I asked him to tell me more. He said it was a good idea, so I obediently filled out the forms he handed me, not sure what I was doing.

I told Dad my plans to go to community college. He said he'd help pay for my books and tuition. I even won a scholarship from the local rotary club just by writing an essay about my goals. Mom reviewed it and made sure I put in there, "My dad does not provide any child support." She'd often tell Chance and me what a terrible person Dad was. She wanted his friends at the rotary club to think it too. I also wrote, "I plan to get my degree and be a contributing, tax-paying member of society." I hoped they'd like that part.

I was so grateful to have the scholarship and Dad's help. Sure, I had to be as persistent as a bill collector to get him or his significant other to write me a check, but I didn't care. It took a couple hours for them to get around to it during my collection visits, but it was worth the wait.

A few months shy of my eighteenth birthday, the first day of college came. I made the 30-minute drive and picked up a girlfriend along the way. I noticed everybody wore their JanSport backpacks over one shoulder. I copied them with my plastic backpack from Kmart. I wanted to fit in.

I planned to sit on the left side of each class because I thought the right side of my face was less ugly. I can't stand my left eye. It's noticeably smaller than my right, and both eyes are beady.

During my 8 a.m. math class, I was so tired, I daydreamed about sleeping on an imaginary mattress that hovered above our desks, knowing I could easily fall asleep. I sat behind a girl who used to have a crush on my ex-boyfriend Finn and noticed how pretty she was in her fashionable clothes. She was wearing pristine white Keds, acid-washed designer jeans, and a collared preppy shirt. Behind me sat a clone of my ex-boyfriend, Dudley, both in looks and temper. He seemed familiar, so I ended up hanging out with him for a hot minute until I came to my senses.

On our first date, I brought a girlfriend for protection, and we visited a vacant apartment in a seedy part of town. Dudley #2 took me aside and whispered that he planned to score us some cocaine and his plans didn't allow for an additional set of nostrils. Instead, Dudley #2 handed my girlfriend and me a cross top pill. It was a cheaper alternative he didn't mind sharing. The whole situation felt dangerous, and my girlfriend and I left. We drove to a local club to dance off our cross tops.

The next week, Dudley #2 got thrown out of class when he talked back to the beatnik-looking teacher. As Dudley #2 stormed out of class, Mr. Beatnik pointed and said, "That's what we call a bad actor!" I never saw Dudley #2 again.

Mike, my next boyfriend, came on strong and scared me. He was handing out flyers for an afterparty while Denise, Monica, and I danced the night away at the Ponderosa Saloon. This was the same place that Jimmy's girlfriend Emma took Misty and me to purchase her cocaine. Mike was hot, with a clean, dark brown haircut and a face that looked like the lead singer of Depeche Mode. After Dudley and Finn, I preferred clean-cut guys or Prince.

Denise, Monica, and I had fake IDs by now. Mine said I was Christine Connor. As we drove to our over-21 destination, we'd recite our fake ID addresses in case we encountered a suspicious bouncer. I knew Christine's birthdate made her a Pisces and remembered that in case the bouncer asked my astrological sign.

We showed up to the afterparty. Mike spotted us. I felt cute with my '80s hair and borrowed clothes from Denise's closet. Mike dressed preppy and kept his hair high and tight like he was in the military.

Mike and I hit it off and he took me for a drive in his Volkswagen Rabbit. He told me how his dad was rich and drove me past his dad's mansion to prove it. He said he barely attended class and just showed up for quizzes. He was probably hoping to inherit dad's cash and just pretend to go to college. He must have thought I had money since I had borrowed my dad's BMW that night.

On our first date, Mike made me his favorite meal at his duplex. Beef gravy with rice and peas. As we ate, he called me, "sweetheart" and said all the things a girl wants to hear. I wasn't used to positive words of affirmation and drank them in like a tall glass of water after a long night of drinking. He insisted that I take a spare house key. I resisted him coming on so strong at first, maybe I had some kind of bullshit meter. It didn't take much effort for him to wear me down, daddy issues and all.

After dinner, we retreated to his bedroom. A few minutes later there was a loud knocking on his door. Whoever it was must have a key to his house. He left me in his room, and I heard the whispers of a female voice. I hoped she'd leave and wondered how many people had a key to his place. Once he returned, he apologized, "Sorry, it was my ex, she's having a hard time letting go." I didn't ask questions although I noticed female toiletries still on his bathroom counter.

The dreaded day came when Mike visited me at The House of Death. I think my living situation shocked him. He didn't even want to see the piranhas. I'm guessing he realized I didn't have anything to offer economically like my dad's BMW might have suggested. And he no longer had a challenge. I had already fallen— hook, line, and sinker. He stopped calling me.

Hoping to win him back, Denise and I went to the next party his friends were hosting after working at one of Dad's high school dances. I imagined Mike seeing me in a tight purple dress, realize his mistake and want me back.

I spotted him in the crowd and my heart fluttered. He noticed me. My stomach churned. I hoped for the best. I started walking towards him. He was standing by a brunette and another guy. After glancing at me, he turned his head to ram his tongue down the brunette's mouth. She was cute, with a short and sassy haircut.

I stopped and made Denise walk outside with me. I was crushed and pissed. I concluded she was the same girlfriend who banged on his bedroom door and still had her eye makeup removal bottle sitting on his bathroom counter.

I learned to be wary of guys who seem too perfect, talk about their rich dad, call you sweetheart, and tell you all that you want to hear. They're all talk and rarely come through.

I was back on the market and needed to hurry up and find my next host, I mean boyfriend, to latch onto and feed my insatiable validation appetite. Mary didn't like being hungry.

The next weekend, Denise, Monica, and I drank a few beers as we made our hair big and put on our faces for another one of Mike's parties downtown. Hey, they were great parties!

I borrowed another tight-fitting dress from Denise's closet and Dad's BMW. I looked the part of upper-middle-class college girl despite me living in The House of Death. Denise and Monica, with their height and beauty, looked like professional models.

After parking Dad's car in the parking lot, we strutted into the converted mansion downtown. We scanned the situation and made a beeline for the bar where the party drink was a Funky Cold Medina. It was a blue concoction served from a large vat with dry ice for effect. A couple Medina's down the hatch, we headed to the dance floor where my girls and I could bust a move.

Before I got to the dance floor, Brad approached and asked me to dance. He had a square jaw and perpetually tanned skin. He looked like a Ken doll but with more chest hair. I wondered how a guy as hot as him wanted to dance with me.

As we danced, I thought his moves were dorky, but his stunning beauty more than compensated. Yes, I was shallow. After a few songs, we took a break in a corner and made small talk.

"Do you have a girlfriend?" I asked.

"We broke up." I thought, *YES! He's a free man.*

"Why?" I asked.

"She says I'm a dick," he laughed nervously.

I laughed along, not sure how to respond to that. I should've known better to tangle with him with that comment, but my need for male attention coupled with his disarming looks overshadowed any common sense. We exchanged phone numbers at the end of the evening.

After three long days of waiting for him to call, I couldn't stand the suspense and called him. We made plans to go out to dinner. I suggested we meet at his place since I couldn't have him see my house after what happened with Mike.

When I arrived at his apartment entrance, he had to buzz me in. I stood nervously in the fancily furnished lobby. He walked down the stairs and greeted me with a kiss on the cheek. I thought, "Oh goody, he still likes me—and daaaaaang, he's way hotter than I remembered." I felt honored to be in his presence. I tried to be charming, perfect, and not desperate.

We went out for Thai, and I hoped he didn't expect me to pay half the bill. The food tasted incredible, like a fireworks explosion of flavors with every bite. I had no clue food could be so delicious and wondered what else I was missing out on. I hoped our date meant he was my fiancé. He paid the bill and we made plans for the next weekend, and the weekend after that.

Most of the time, I'd drive fifteen miles downtown to visit him. Every Saturday, we'd drive to pick up a small mushroom pizza and rent a Blockbuster video. I wanted to eat more than one slice of pizza but didn't want to annoy him. I ate my one self-allotted piece slowly, secretly wanting a second. To think, I used to eat a huge portion of a large Domino's pizza with Finn after we got stoned. Afterwards, we watched SNL. It bothered me how he'd laugh nervously at jokes he didn't understand. I wouldn't dare tell him that and risk losing him.

One weeknight, I cut class to visit him. I told him so, and thought he'd be happy to see me. He got mad and told me, "Don't ever do that again, you have to finish school!"

I'm thankful he didn't approve. I didn't approve either. On one hand, I knew I didn't want to end up like my mom, who had nothing after Dad left. I wanted to have options. Another part of me would've loved a sugar daddy, but I knew I couldn't depend on a man. They usually leave.

Brad showered me with gifts and expensive perfumes. He upgraded his sedan to a BMW and blasted the B52's as we drove. I soon grew tired of "Love Shack." I wanted to take charge of the music and play Hip Hop but didn't dare verbalize my desires or make any demands. I wanted him to stay with me forever and think of me as the perfect girlfriend. I saw him as my perfect boyfriend.

Thanksgiving was on the horizon and Brad asked, "What are we doing for Thanksgiving?" I stiffened. In a normal situation, I'd invite him over instead of freaking out. Mom always cooked a Thanksgiving meal. I knew If Brad came over, he would soon see that I wasn't worthy of his time and had nothing to offer. And if he had to use the restroom, that would be the tipping point of my anxiety, game over.

"My mom usually cooks, what are you doing?"

"My sister and brother-in-law are out of town, so I don't have plans this year."

Crap! Now I *have* to invite him. "Maybe you could come over for Thanksgiving?" I asked hoping he'd decline.

"Yeah, that sounds good. And I can meet your mom."

I prayed when people came over, that they would never need to use the bathroom, especially Brad.

Before Brad's Thanksgiving visit, I bought brown towels and a bathmat to spruce up the bathroom and make it more presentable, just in case he had to use it. I hated brown but thought it would blend in with Mom's color palate: dirty, ugly brown, yellow, and green.

I swept the front walkway and tried to remove the dust-caked cobwebs from the entryway. No amount of hosing down, scouring, or vacuuming could undo years of neglect or turn The House of Death into something presentable.

The dreadful day came. Brad walked in and shook my mom's hand. He did a good job pretending to not see the squalor.

After complimenting Mom on a delicious dinner, he stayed to play Pictionary with my mom and a few other softball friends. I was overjoyed he didn't leave abruptly and still deemed me to be an acceptable accessory in his life. I thought I hit the boyfriend jackpot and maybe he could be my meal ticket out of poverty and the overall suck of life. Maybe someday I could even live off his fortune. Working long hours and attending college full-time wasn't easy. All I had to do was give him the only thing of value I thought I had.

After the visit, Brad started calling me by a new name, Punky. After the freckly-faced scrappy orphan from the TV show *Punky Brewster*. Punky's dad walked out on her too, but I hoped he called me Punky because of my spunky attitude and freckles. I've got to hand it to Brad; he never said a word about my living situation.

Brad looked like he had a ton of money, but selling insurance wasn't profitable at the time. He later confessed he had a massive credit card debt, was broke, and could only pay his bills thanks to his older sister. I think he must have felt safe telling me that only after he visited my House of Death.

Brad must have met someone else because after nearly a year, he broke up with me. But he waited until after we spring cleaned his well-decorated apartment in the downtown area. We scoured his cream-colored apartment from top to bottom, including his matching leather couch. The timing of this deep cleaning project was suspicious.

He tried to console me, "Think of our relationship like, uh like—a flower being picked. You never know, it might grow back."

I sobbed uncontrollably. Snot and tears involuntary gushed forth from my orifices.

I'm embarrassed to tell you that I begged to please still "see" him from time to time. I desperately needed to keep some type of link to a man, any man, to fill the limitless void I had inside, especially one who looked like Brad. Being a piece of shit, he took me up on that offer.

After our breakup, he'd call me late at night and I'd score him some cocaine or just visit. I only stopped hanging around when I met the next toad who could fill my abyss on a more full-time basis.

It ticks me off how not having a full-time engaged father figure made me so needy in the male department back then. On a positive note, I am forever thankful Brad introduced me to Thai food and expensive perfume. Childhood trauma may have screwed me, but at least I smelled amazing and knew the joys of sticky rice and mango.

I Got an Office Job!

I GOT ANOTHER job offer that year. After a ton of complaining about the chaos at my dad's thriving business and my unreliable coworker, my best friend gave me the break I needed. Denise told me that her mom's office was hiring. Her mom was a secretary, and they needed a student helper. It was a government office. They were backfilling a student job, so I applied and got it. I was only going to be there until the former student, Renee, returned.

Thankfully, Renee never came back. So, while I went to college full-time, I worked there, first part-time, and then full-time. I was making government cheddar, like my mom and sister. I was nineteen when I started. I typed contracts, office correspondence, and made a whopping $9.11 an hour. I was rich!

At the office, there was an especially challenging engineer. Darla had rightfully earned the reputation for being mean and scary. You never knew what she was going to say, but it was usually unpleasant. As she returned a signed project invoice, she asked, "Why do you keep distracting me and changing the subject?"

I didn't realize I was doing that until she pointed it out. My coping mechanisms automatically kicked in when I caught a whiff of judgment or Eddy. I interrupted Darla with distracting jokes and random questions to try to get her to crack a smile and prevent an imminent attack. I was relieved when Darla left my desk and returned to her office without grilling me further.

My spastic distraction chatter wasn't such a bad thing I suppose. There were plenty of versions of Eddy in the world, and it made me a pleasing, agreeable, and hyper-productive employee. According to Strengths Finders,[2] "Woo" was one of my top five strengths, which means I like to win people over. As a child, I felt as if my survival depended on it. But as I started life in the workplace, it became my superpower. I got a lot of work done without pissing people off too much. Although I pissed off my coworker Gladys because she thought I cheated somehow when I finished up my

---

2   StrengthsFinder is a test that helps people learn what they're naturally good at.

contracts so fast. She preferred the typewriter while I used macros on WordPerfect.

I learned about office gossip quick. The whole office knew this one male architect was having an affair with an analyst. They were both married. Before I knew of the affair, the analyst brought her young child into work, and we all gushed over her cuteness. I sweetly asked, "How old are you?"

Her mom said to me indirectly, responding for her daughter in a singsong tone, "Say, I'm not a trained seal." My silent voice called her a bitch for that.

When I learned of the affair, I was thoroughly disgusted by both of them. And despite the fact that I was a good employee, I went out of my way to be unhelpful to the adulterer architect even though it was my job.

My anger towards my dad was transferred to both of them, misdirected from my unaddressed daddy issues. Philandering Phil asked me one day, "You don't like me, do you!?" I was both embarrassed by the direct question and satisfied that he noticed I didn't like him. It pissed me off that he was having an affair with the bitch lady at work. Didn't they care that they were married!? They weren't even trying to hide it and could be seen making out at lunch. I don't remember how I answered his question, but I hope it was good.

Addicted

WHILE WORKING AND going to school, I made rapid progress with my new love—meth. Monica was busy with her beautiful daughter, my adorable niece, Angelica. Shelly was always working. And Denise was in Florida, hanging out with her boyfriend. My sister was also busy with her boyfriend from high school, so I hung out more with my new friend, Violet. She had the body of a trained athlete and oozed confidence.

Violet could effortlessly replicate any dance move she saw and was a great teacher. She urged me to perform the moves she taught me in front of her friends. I'd happily entertain, always active with my disease to please. She said, "You dance good for a white girl." I felt six feet tall around Violet.

Violet could've been a famous comedienne or choreographer if meth hadn't sidetracked her; she was that good. She could entertain anyone with her stories and sense of humor for hours. I later learned she convinced our dealer friends that I had a crush on them, and that earned her free drugs. I typically had a boyfriend, and that prevented me from being available to our dealer friends. Plus, they scared me with their unpredictable employment and paranoid moods.

OK, I didn't plan on getting addicted. Does anybody? I socially snorted a little here and there. Yes, I drank a lot, smoked pot on a routine basis, and was addicted to numbing myself with various substances and boys. If we're being honest, yes, my addict gene was easily triggered during my Reno Summer vacation at Auntie Raven's. Drugs were my shortcut to those elusive happy feelings I lacked, thanks to my actual life and the fact that I screwed up my brain's reward system by using so much.

One Friday night, Mom relaxed on the couch after a long day of work, watching *Wheel of Fortune*. She had a stack of movies she had rented sitting on top of the console TV. She said, "Why don't you stay in tonight and watch movies with me?"

I contemplated it for a half a second. It sounded like good clean fun, and a smarter choice. I thought it was nice that Mom wanted me to hang out. She'd been sober for a while, but I wasn't.

My darker desire was too strong. "Sorry, Mom. me and Violet are going out dancing."

She gave me that knowing look. I walked out of the house with a pang of guilt I quickly squashed down. I hopped in my gold Fiesta

I bought for $1,000 and drove to Violet's. She was waiting for me out front of her apartment. Soon we were on our way to the dealer's house. I didn't have a radio, so we sang our favorite songs on the way, Guy's "Goodbye Love" and Karyn White's "Superwoman." Violet had the best dance moves, even while she was sitting in the passenger's seat. I tried to do them too while shifting gears, when suddenly my stomach began to churn with the excited anticipation of our first hit.

"Dang it, I have to poop," I said.

"Stop at Paco's Tacos, I can have a beer there," Violet said.

This having to poop thing always happened right before I did drugs. My mind and body knew what was going to happen and the nerves went straight to my bowels. We stopped and I ordered a chicken taco and rice. It was the least I could do since I was about ready to blow up their bathroom.

Violet and I fueled up on food. We knew we wouldn't have an appetite for the next few days. I'll have to remind myself to eat when I was home so Mom wouldn't suspect anything. All Mom had to do was take one look at my eyeballs and see my pupils dilated. Good thing I rarely made eye contact.

Shortly after we finished at Paco's, we made it to Marvin's apartment. He was our usual supplier. Marvin had a jheri-curl hairdo and a medium build. He was generous with his stash, and Violet said he had a crush on me. I was oblivious to his overtures.

Unlike cocaine, when I snorted meth, it burned my nasal cavity and drained an awful chemical taste down the back of my throat. I heard how some users burned holes in their sinuses when they snorted too much. I learned from Violet and Marvin that it was better to smoke it, and it was more powerful that way. I sprinkled the meth pebbles in the fold of my small sheet of aluminum foil just like Violet. I took my soda straw and placed it in my mouth and held the aluminum foil in one hand and lit the underside of the foil with the other. It took a couple seconds for the meth crumbs to bubble and turn to smoke. I inhaled the smoke through the straw to make sure I didn't waste any of it.

The meth vapor smelled like rotting oranges infused with gasoline and Campho Phenique. I was high within a couple of minutes and that numbed away most feelings of worthlessness. I felt euphoric and had plenty of energy to stay up all night or run a marathon. I thought all things were possible while on meth. Violet and I made grand plans to jog every morning, get a second job, and travel the world while high. I was far away from knowing the scripture from Matthew 19:26 "…with God, all things are possible."

Violet and I said our goodbyes and drove to the club to dance our asses off. While on the dance floor, it was just Violet and me, the music, and our high. Before we knew it, last call came at 4 a.m. We'd head home singing our favorite songs with even more zeal than at the beginning of the night. At home, I'd pretend to sleep but wouldn't be able to until Saturday evening.

Violet kept her party going. She'd do her usual several-day meth binge and smell like burnt hair and a just-lit match. After, she'd pass out at home for a few days of rest and was ready for another round of meth madness by the following weekend.

After getting it free for several months, I wore out my welcome and had to spend my money on it—money I should be spending on necessities. It should've been a warning sign when I began to smoke it and pay for it. Violet and I were transforming into Crankenstein and Spinderella.

I usually made it home by 5 a.m. and every white crumb on my bedroom floor tricked me into thinking it was the drug. Sometimes it *was* a crumb, and I continued my party. Most of the time, it was a mirage or just a fuzz ball.

During some of my binges, I chillaxed and feverishly plowed

through crossword puzzles at Violet's house or all by my lonesome. Sometimes we played "bones," aka dominos, at the dealer's house for hours, talking some serious shit while playing. I got pretty skilled at bones and puzzles, but not the shit-talking; that was Violet's specialty. It was amazing how much focus we gave these activities while on meth.

I took Saturday and Sunday off to detox and do homework so I could be ready for school and work the following Monday. I showed up to school and work no matter what and thought that meant I wasn't as addicted as Violet was. She did meth on weekdays. I incorrectly thought I was better than her because of it.

As I progressed with my addiction, Violet and I also hung out with a few other friends, I mean addicts. I became like the boiled frog. Put a frog in water. Incrementally heat the water. The frog won't notice she's being boiled and dies. Although some say this fable is untrue, it makes sense.

Jen had a cute short blonde haircut, the chiseled face of a model, and a New York attitude. Doing meth was our pre-club routine. I remember getting ready at Jen's house and wondering why we didn't hurry up and go dancing already. Jen and Violet preferred to primp and pregame with meth and booze more than being at the actual club dancing. I was the opposite. I was very much an impatient and efficient Type A personality. Their routine irritated the crap out of me—or was that the meth? Soon, I would irritate them, and they'd tell me to knock it off. Finally, we headed to the club around 10 p.m., pupils dilated. Booze and meth fueled our dancing.

That night, I was almost put into human trafficking—I'm pretty sure. This well-dressed guy approached and told me the prince of some country I couldn't pronounce wanted to dance with me. So, we did. Prince Charming smiled the whole time but didn't say a word. He had brown skin and an extra bushy unibrow. I'm not sure if he spoke English—he didn't respond to my small talk.

After we danced, his buddy translated for his friend and told me, "The Prince would like to have you as his girlfriend. He would like to take you to his mansion where all your needs will be taken care of."

If I agreed, the limo was waiting outside, and we could begin our new life. It sounded like a great answer to my misery and lack of funds. A life plan where I didn't have to worry about money?! I'm in! Where do I sign?!

I found Jen and told her that I met a prince, and we should go hang out with these guys. She wasn't having any of it and said, "Hell no, they're full of it."

I kept pressing, "Come on Jen, I'm serious! He's a prince and they have a limo!" She kept saying no and blocked my dream of being free. I thought she was jealous. By some miracle I obeyed Jen and didn't leave with those guys.

I don't know why I looked to Jen for permission, who knows what would have happened if she hadn't stepped in that night. I'd be a concubine, human trafficked, or maybe Princess Mary. How many untold horrors have I been saved from, making my poor guardian angel tired? Only God knows, but I'm certain that night was one of them.

The lights went on for last call and we went to Jen's house to continue getting high. But we dressed it up by calling it, "partying."

By the time I left Jen's house, the sun had begun to rise. I hated when I got home after the sun came up. It never felt right. It was a more painful last call because it's God's last call. His daily sunrise is his way of turning on the planet's club lights telling all of us addicts, "It's last call, go home! Repent and sin no more!"

I'm ashamed to admit that, on Thanksgiving that year at Grandma's house, I smoked meth inside her Paradise bathroom and blew it out her window. I chose meth over Grandma's turkey, and nobody noticed. I hadn't hit my rock bottom, but I stooped to a new low.

While I was busy filling my soul's swiss cheese holes with meth and boys, Mom found love. She met a nice man who didn't drink, had a government job, no kids, and owned a home in the foothills. They met through one of her girlfriends from work at a dance event for divorced people called "Parents Without Partners."

Lionel bore a slight resemblance to Eddy but was the total opposite in values and finances. And Lionel smiled. It was so great to see Mom laughing and in love. She had a pep in her step and was always on the go instead of stuck on the couch. She was either driving to see Lionel or headed to work. She was even moving up the ladder at her job. Mom was the happiest I'd ever seen, and the best version of several I'd ever met.

As Mom and Dad previously agreed, Mom lived rent-free in The House of Death for three years after she got sober. Three years turned into four. Of course, my brother and I were also living there and had stable shelter thanks to their arrangement. I'm sure my brother and I would have made Dad's house extra crowded, so it was a win-win.

By this time, the house value had appreciated tremendously. Dad told me that Mom, most likely pissed that he would make a ton of money on the house, told everyone that he had stolen the house, and they believed it.

Because Dad admitted to me that he gave Mom "the clap" while she was pregnant with Chance, I believed this story too. Mom didn't share the part about her not paying the mortgage while she was on her eight-year bender, so complete strangers approached Dad and told him how awful he was for "stealing Mom's house."

Now that Mom planned to move in with Lionel, Dad decided to fix up the house. It was thoroughly trashed by the abuse from the alcoholics, pot-smokers, chain-smokers, line-snorters, and transients that had passed through over the years. I wished he would've done that during my formative years, but I get it. I'm frugal too. Why pay to fix something up that wasn't going to be taken care of anyway?

The middle-aged contractor he hired happened to be engaged. Lester bartered with Dad to fix up the house in exchange for his wedding photos and other photography services. The soon-to-be married Lester came over to work while I was home alone. He had a curly head of brown hair reminiscent of Richard Simmons, but with a contractor's build and a belly brought to you by bad food and twelve packs. I was wearing my nightgown inside out, sitting on the couch watching TV before work.

Lester was chatty and I was doing my polite people-pleasing routine. The next thing I knew, in between our small talk, he moved swiftly to the couch and climbed on top of me. I was shocked and paralyzed, processing what was happening. I had no words, but either he realized his mistake or maybe I pushed him away because he suddenly got up before anything worse happened. Knowing how I react in stressful situations; I don't think I put up a fight.

After Lester left, I called my dad's office, and his spouse picked up. I blurted out what happened and thankfully, she said she would handle it. She was gifted at confrontations. Dad still used Lester as the contractor. I tried to avoid him.

It didn't occur to me how messed up it was that Dad still used Lester as his contractor after that incident. Dad preferred to save money using trade versus punching the guy and calling the police. It also never occurred to me that I could've called the police.

I wonder if Lester's still married. I doubt he turned out to be the faithful kind.

Kurt

It didn't take long after Brad dumped me to secure my next boyfriend. Kurt was a nephew and coworker of Ned, the neighbor across the street. Ned was a divorced guy who shared custody of his three daughters. I had noticed Kurt a while back always showing up to carpool with Ned at 7:30 a.m. He looked like a brunette Hercules. Tall, tan, and beefy and a couple years older than me. I knew Kurt first as Ned's husky nephew who helped clean wild game after their hunting trips. I remembered him as a giggly and easy-going boy. All grown up, he was a stunning, upgraded version of Brad.

I peeked out the window and noticed Kurt was in Ned's driveway waiting for his uncle, right on time. I grabbed my keys and backpack and sashayed to my car. I tried to look especially cute with my curly ponytail secured on top of my head with a large scrunchie. I braided my dampened hair the night before to make it extra curly.

I saw Kurt turn his head to look my way. I hoped that meant he would ask me out. That night Ned called and invited me over for a weekend barbeque to re-introduce me to Kurt. My plan worked! Ned shared that Kurt's last girlfriend had broken up with him out of the blue, even though he took her on a picnic with chocolate covered strawberries and champagne. Ned couldn't understand why Kurt couldn't find a good girlfriend. I couldn't either.

It took nearly the whole barbeque for me to summon the courage to wade in the backyard pool. That was the icebreaker we needed to awkwardly begin talking.

Kurt joined me in the pool. Dang, his muscles were big. We made small talk and planned to go to a popular BBQ joint in town. We soon became a couple.

A few times a week, I drove to Kurt's house and watched

him lift weights in his backyard along with his peeping Tammy neighbor. I acted like I was having fun watching him, oohing and aahing on how strong he was, but soon became thoroughly bored by his peacocking. Yes, I was that desperate to keep a boy in my life.

The older version of Kurt looked amazing on the outside, but inside, he was still the chubby insecure kid. Here we were, two insecure people trying to be normal young adults, yet still carrying our childhood luggage. I was pleased to have handsome male arm candy that might impress strangers. He seemed happy to have a girlfriend after the last one broke his heart.

I was still addicted to meth, and I remember going out to dinner with him and some of his friends and getting sideways glances because I ordered a side of green beans for dinner. They probably thought I had an eating disorder instead of a meth addiction. I didn't look like a poster child for meth or anorexia yet but was on my way. Kurt didn't seem to catch on to my consistent weekend habit.

One weekend, we went on a double date with his best friend and his girlfriend, Cheyenne, to an amusement park. Cheyenne was a cheerful cutie patootie with clear skin. Since adolescence, I always had a flock of angry zits on my chin that wouldn't go away. I wished I had skin like Cheyenne's. In between rollercoaster rides, I tried to perform surgery on my massive cystic chin zit in the poorly lit bathroom. My botched procedure only made my chin more inflamed and noticeable.

On the long drive back home from our date, I pretended to sleep. I listened to Kurt and his friend make fun of my zits and giggle about it. "Did you see that cyclops on her chin?" Kurt whispered to his friend. My fragile feelings were massively wounded, and then I got pissed.

A few weeks later, Kurt forgot my birthday. It hurt enough that my parents didn't remember birthdays, and now Kurt opened fresh stab wounds. First, he talked crap about my zits, and then he forgot my birthday—I don't freaking think so! His two strikes injured me enough to hunt for my next boyfriend so there wouldn't be an air gap in between boys. After Brad, I learned to make sure I had one on deck so I wouldn't risk being alone.

I met my next prospect at a college party. Mickey became my next fix. I wasn't wholly human yet. I was still auditioning for the role and needed the constant crutch of a boyfriend to prop me up. Mickey attended the same college as I did and was taking difficult chemistry classes. He was smart, had chicken legs, and could easily fit in my khaki shorts. He was soft-spoken and kind with a receding hairline and sideburns. He looked like Luke Perry from *Beverly Hills 90210*. He and I struck up a conversation while standing around the keg and soon snuggled on the couch while The Cure played in the background. Near the end of the night, he gave me a tentative peck on the cheek. I liked that he didn't try to get to third base. I was hooked. I broke it off with Kurt that night, but I didn't tell him. Mickey and I made plans to hang out again.

Kurt saw Mickey's red Fiat parked out front of The House of Death and realized he had competition. He left several tearful voicemails trying to win me back saying, "This is Kurt, I'm sorry I blew it. I'll make it up to you. Call me. Please." I'm usually overly empathetic, but in this case, I felt zero sympathy for his untimely tears and thought less of him because he wanted me back. I moved on. Had he paid me this kind of attention before and not forgotten my birthday, I would have gladly stayed forever.

Mom packed up 13-year-old Chance to move in with her new husband. I was so glad that my mom went from borrowing my Ford Fiesta to driving a reliable, respectable-looking, Oldsmobile and living with a decent man. She was moving on up in the world, to the East side, to a deluxe manufactured home in the hills. Miracles were possible!

I had The House of Death to myself for a whole month before I had to scramble and find a place to rent, since Dad wanted to rent it out and get some of his money back. I don't remember Dad asking me to come live with him. Leah had already moved in with her boyfriend from high school.

I either had to rent a place or move thirty miles away from my college with Chance and Mom. I knew I would never finish my degree if I moved in with Mom and Lionel, because it was so far away from school. Denise just got back from Florida and offered to rent me a room at her house for $400 a month, which was a steal at the time. My best friends always came through.

I was still partying hard, getting high on weed and alcohol during the week, and meth and alcohol on weekends. One weekday I was passed out in my bed, and barely woke up in time to roll over just enough to puke in an empty pizza box on the floor. I fell back asleep with my stick of berry-flavored gum stuck to my teeth. The next day, I washed up and went to school and work with chemicals trying to escape through my pores. My supervisor noticed. "Wow, your cheeks are flushed, are you ok?"

His question made my cheeks even redder. Did he know my secrets? I lied. "Yeah, I'm fine. Just had a rough night studying for a test."

What I hated most about meth was that I couldn't sleep at night once the partying was over. The meth and my racing heart wouldn't allow it. I snuck off to the bathroom to hide my habit from sweet Mickey and then felt guilty about it. One weekend, he stayed the night at the nearly vacant House of Death. I pretended to sleep but was still high. He asked me why my heart was beating so fast. I told him it was because I was nervous. That was partially true. I decided I really needed to quit meth. I would have to start paying $400 a month in rent and I wouldn't have extra money for it anyway.

When it finally came time for me to leave The House of Death, Uncle Bruce and Mom helped me move a dresser and a twin bed to Denise's house. I loved my new little room and being so close to Denise and her mom. And Mickey lived a convenient three miles away.

A few months later, I learned Kurt accidentally killed himself during a camping trip. I prayed it was an accident as it was told to me and not because I broke up with him. A neighbor shared he was cleaning his handgun at a picnic table and said, "Oh shit" as the gun fired.

I felt sad for his sweet parents and the life Kurt could have lived. May his soul rest in peace.

Broken Promise

IT TOOK CHANCE almost dying to make me quit meth.

Chance started pooping out blood and losing a ton of weight. He didn't think to mention it until Mom found blood in the toilet and questioned him. He fessed up that he'd been pooping blood for months. Mom took one good look at him, suddenly realized how pale and skinny he was, and drove him straight to the emergency room. The hospital admitted him. After further tests, he was diagnosed with ulcerative colitis at the age of thirteen. He needed immediate surgery, medicine, and prayers.

The doctors took years to realize he had an autoimmune disease known as Crohn's. Leah was experiencing her own auto-immune symptoms. As for me, my issues exist in between my ears. I believe all the crap Chance and Leah endured ended up activating their diseases.[3] I bet it didn't help how often Eddy punched Chance in the stomach, thinking it made him tough.

---

3 I've since learned that Adverse Childhood Experiences, known as ACES, made us more susceptible to auto-immune diseases, mental illnesses and drug abuse. ACES include experiencing divorced parents, physical and

I visited Chance every day in between work and school. I cried out to God as I stood beside Chance unconscious in his ICU bed and begged, "I promise to quit if you please save my brother. Please!"

A few days later Chance improved. God took me up on the offer, even though I only talked to him when I needed something. My brother finally left the hospital. I broke my promise six months later.

The not-so-funny thing was it happened after watching a news report on the impacts of addiction. The images of the lines of cocaine on a mirror and realistic crackpipes triggered me to think it was a good idea to call my old dealer, Marvin. I'm certain the journalist wasn't hoping to cause an addict to relapse when she put together that news report.

I knew better than to call Violet, knowing I would fall too deep. She and I had tons of fun together, but we weren't bringing out the best in each other. I stopped hanging out with her after I moved in with Denise. First, I didn't like that I began to require the same amount of meth Violet used. I had thought she was the addict, not me. I was wrong. Second, Violet had already worn out her welcome with several of our meth friends by owing us money. And third, I was treading water at poverty level.

Marvin was happy to hear from me. I asked him for $10 worth so I could "study" for a final exam. When I showed up to his new shabbier place, we were alone; he no longer had roommates or much furniture. I sat on his unvacuumed carpet while he sat in a recliner. We smoked a little bit of his stash before I handed over my $10 in exchange for a small baggie.

---

mental abuse, addiction, and neglect from caregivers. All these count towards an overall "ACES" score. Chance, Leah, Summer, Misty, and I have pretty decent scores from our extended stay at The House of Death. Our lives are testimonies to the well-documented research.

We sat there in silence, waiting for the high to kick in when suddenly I heard a vibrating sound coming from behind. He had a handheld massager and moved it towards my thigh, asking "You wanna massage?"

It freaked me out, so I bolted up and said, "Sorry Marvin, I've got to get back to studying. Call you later?!" I got the heck out of there. I guess Violet was right. He did have a crush on me.

That night I couldn't fall asleep. I regretted calling Marvin but didn't stop using until I finished my supply. I couldn't stand wasting things, even toxic drugs.

I told myself I wasn't ever going to do it again. My relapse and broken God promise made me feel ashamed. And exhausted. I loved and needed sleep way too much to keep on doing it and I didn't want to make Chance get sick again. I hoped God would forgive me for breaking our deal and keep Chance alive.

A few days later my life was threatened over a piece of pizza.

I had leftovers in the fridge that I looked forward to after a long day of school and work. I may not have had a warm winter jacket, but made sure I had food. I couldn't find my foil-wrapped pizza leftovers in the fridge. I asked Denise if she knew what happened. She didn't know. I asked Antichrist Andy, Denise's mom's biker boyfriend, "Did you eat my pizza?" I was so proud of my hungry and timid self for confronting him.

He glared at me and walked away. Moments later I heard loud banging noises in the back of the house and wondered what it was.

I soon learned it was Andy throwing a big-boy tantrum in the back bedroom, punching holes in the walls. While I stood in the kitchen wondering what to eat, the angry 6'4" gigantic Leprechaun-looking Andy rushed towards me yelling and pointing, "You better fucking leave or I'm going to kill you!" I have no memory of what happened immediately after.

I don't know who called 911, but thankfully the cops showed up before I was injured. The cops didn't even cuff him. Andy calmly showed the cops a stack of his mail addressed to Denise's house. That mail gave him the right to live there too. This leftover thief knew the game. The cops said one of us had to leave and Andy wasn't budging.

I packed up my clothes and toothbrush and drove to Mickey's house. The next day Mickey paid first and last month's rent on an apartment and packed up his childhood bedroom to save his damsel in distress. We loaded up Mickey's mattress and moved in a small apartment complex near our college. We budgeted $35 a week for ramen noodles and frozen burritos, and Mickey brought home leftovers from his job at Red Lobster. My meth days were officially over.

It was time for Mickey to meet my mom and her new husband, Lionel. They invited us to a BBQ at the local park with some of their new foothill friends, Chester and Peggy. Their friends seemed nice. As we all stood around the sizzling BBQ, Chester decided to tell us a joke. I don't recall it, but the punchline involved his hands squeezing my boobs and saying, "Honk, honk!"

I stood there stunned for a second until my people pleasing kicked in and I laughed along like it was funny. Mom and Lionel joined in the laughter.

Mickey and I left after eating our hamburgers and Mom's homemade potato salad. Once in the car, he yelled, "I can't believe your parents let that guy touch your boobs!"

I was surprised by his reaction though it was more appropriate than mine. I wished I had a better sense of what was right and wrong and how to vocalize boundaries. I learned slowly, seeing through the lenses of properly parented people like Mickey.

Things were great with Mickey. His parents loved me, and I loved them. They were non-drinking vegetarians who said prayers before dinner and gave out hugs. Mickey was the second oldest of six children. The rest were girls, all beauties. Mickey treated me to an expensive NordicTrack skiing machine and Rollerblades for Christmas. I was grateful for his generous gifts since my ramen noodles and no meth had caught up to my hips.

With no need to escape a horrible living situation, I became domesticated and wanted to stay home during my downtime to do homework or watch TV. Not quite 21, I had already partied enough for a couple of lifetimes and didn't feel like doing it anymore. I was tired from long days of work and school, I wanted Mickey to stay home with me, but he preferred to go out.

I woke up one morning for school and saw Mickey passed out on the couch with fresh stamps on his hands from the local club when he was supposed to be at the library with his study group. I left him a note saying, "I know you lied! Get the fuck out!"

He didn't come home for a few days. I didn't want to believe he was cheating but my intuition told me otherwise.

Near the end of our 18-month relationship, Mickey was arrested. He was charged with kicking a girl in the head and fracturing her eye socket while he was at a party.

The morning after, he looked pale when he told me he drank too much the night before and that the sheriffs were coming to arrest him. He said, "I accidentally kicked a girl with my boot. I was only trying to step over her while she was passed out on the floor." It didn't add up, like the time he told me the girl hugging him at school was his gay friend.

He asked me to have his mom pull out all his savings and use it to bail him out as soon as possible. His mom and I withdrew his money and posted bail. On the way home, he said he found God and read the Bible. I was hoping that was true. I liked the God-loving Mickey; his eyes looked happier and more awakened. By the next weekend, he misplaced God and continued his excessive drinking.

A few weeks later, while I was at work, I answered the phone, "Office of Engineering Services, this is Mary, how can I help you?"

I noticed the familiar pause from the caller and my heart raced. "Um, oh hi, this is Brad." He wanted to see me again and catch up. This was code for, "I'm in between girlfriends and I need someone to fill my bed."

I tried to not act too excited, knowing it was time to leave Mickey, and I needed another life preserver, I mean boyfriend to cling to. I agreed to meet Brad.

Using a page from Mickey's playbook, I told him I had "group study." I met Brad at our favorite Thai restaurant where you could look out the windows and watch rats climb the outdoor bushes. As we sat in the booth, he said "I'm so sorry about what happened. It wasn't right. I've changed. If you'll have me, I'd like to give us another try." It was weird to be the one who was in semi-control for a moment. I wished I'd had the patience and self-restraint to stay quiet and make him work harder for it. Part of me believed that he had changed and that we were meant to be together, but way down deep somewhere, a smarter part of me knew better.

Before we were done with sticky rice and mango, trying to disguise my desperation, I gave him back control and said, "I missed you too. Ok, let's see how this goes."

I didn't feel good about blurring the lines between relationships. It felt wrong even though I told myself Mickey and I were done.

I broke it off with alcoholic-cheating Mickey. Leah had just left her alcoholic boyfriend too, and we decided to join forces and become roommates. I asked Dad if I could please crash at his house for a couple weeks until Leah and I could find an apartment. He was happy to have me. My sweet younger sibling let me sleep in her bed.

Mickey didn't beg me to stay. He too was done, though he had the nerve to ask for "goodbye luvins." I declined. I packed up my Rollerblades and Nordic Track and left our thinly walled apartment, the roaches, and the next-door neighbor who blasted Neil Diamond on heavy rotation at all hours. Mickey changed his major, learned how to play the drums, and joined a band. I don't know what happened with his assault charges nor cared to find out.

Trying to look the part, I now wore sneakers with my skirts like most girls. I felt so proud of myself, already landing a permanent government job before graduation, making government cheddar like my mom and sister. I could afford more groceries and clothes and started saving for a better car.

Brad didn't change like he'd said. I spent a total of three years off and on with him and the dude couldn't say, "I love you." I was just a play toy for a man who was never going to commit to anyone. I wasn't brave enough to ask him if he loved me. I was afraid of the answer.

I had to kiss a few toads to get my prince. I desperately needed male attention and approval and did not know how to pick a decent boyfriend. I thought they had to pick me. I wasn't a healthy choice for any of them either. Each lesson led me to the next guy so I could finally graduate to a guy worthy of marriage. Hopefully, a man for all seasons, including my crazy-town emotions as my past bubbled up and forced me to heal or have a mental breakdown. Or both.

Part IV – Can I Get Some Dessert with These Crap Sandwiches?

We know that all things work together for good for those who love God, for those who are called according to His purpose.
– Romans 8:28

Marriage Material

ON ROUND TWO of dating the fiscally irresponsible yet handsome Brad, I found my future husband. I was still in the "stickers on the back of my car phase." You know, where you basically put any sticker that you think makes you look cool on the back of your car.

My sister and I shared our adorable two-bedroom apartment at the time. She helped decorate my room using my favorite color, pink. Her bedroom was purple. Every Saturday morning, we'd blast Motley Crue or Metallica as we scoured our apartment for hours making sure there was no resemblance to The House of Death. I would rather have blasted Prince, but it was her stereo. I bought a lovely '80s patterned sectional sofa from Big Daddy's Furniture for $299. I got my second promotion at the Office of Engineering Services while finishing up school. I bought a reliable car with a radio. I selected a used, blue, four-door Pontiac Grand Am. I thought it made me look respectable and classy, especially with my stickers.

I had my normal routine of going to school, then work, then school, then home. Not a moment was wasted. I studied for tests while riding the commuter train and made flashcards on my breaks.

My happiest times were when I could read on the train for pleasure while on spring or Christmas break. The joy of only going to work and not having school responsibilities was a simple one and gave me a glimpse into a nice quiet life that I could get used to.

I'd come home on a Friday night, lock myself in my pink room, and read another romance novel without any regard to what the clock said. This was a stark contrast to my meth-induced all-nighters. I relished it. Consuming mass quantities of romance novels during breaks was one of the happiest, simplest times of my life. I understood why Grandma consumed grocery bags full of romance novels after Grampa died. It was her escape from her sad thoughts and loss of two sons and two husbands.

Around this time, my Grandma Lou moved from Paradise to a trailer park close to Mom. She didn't want to die alone with her and Darlene being so isolated. She had already seen too many widows die alone in her retirement community. On moving day, the whole clan swarmed her mobile home, loaded up all the belongings in a U-Haul and moved them into their new place.

Even though Grandpa had served in the Army most of his life and through the Korean War, somehow Grandma didn't receive much as a widow and was essentially broke after purchasing her new place. I went to the VA with her to fill out the paperwork to get her and Darlene some benefits. The paperwork didn't go anywhere despite me following up several times. The guy at the local VA office was nice, but by the looks of the piles of his disorganized papers, I realized he did nothing to help move the paperwork along.

After months of no progress, I finally looked up the name of the Secretary of Veteran's Affairs and wrote him a letter detailing the facts. I questioned their mission statement that claimed they took care of their vets and families. I documented how my Grandma Lou lost her first husband in Pearl Harbor and my grandpa, also a veteran, to cancer.

My letter did the trick. Grandma soon received a response and called me at home. She shared the good news that because both husbands were gone, the benefits she'd receive would be from her first husband who died in Pearl Harbor. That letter got Grandma out of poverty and she and Darlene had enough to pay the bills and have fun shopping at the local Kmart. I felt true and real unmedicated joy for doing a good deed. I was learning that I didn't need drugs, boys, and booze to feel good. After I got off the phone, I danced in my living room, and looked up and sang out to the Lord, "Thank you, oh my God, thank you!"

It was pitiful how much I obsessed about when Brad would finally profess his love for me. It never happened. Stewing about it while at work, I got so mad that I shoved the framed photo of us underneath a stack of papers to teach him a lesson, since I was too chicken to just ask him if he loved me. The next morning, I came in and the photo was moved from underneath the papers and prominently placed on the middle of my desk. I thought it was odd and wondered if somebody was messing with me. I put the photo back under the papers. The next day, the picture showed up again, in the same prominent place. Now I *knew* someone was messing with me.

At the time there was a swing-shift crew of network installers working. One of them was Frank, who was tan, had strong eyebrows, full lips, and a toothy smile. I didn't know it, but he was an addict too. Only his addictions were not destructive. He loved rebuilding classic cars and buying single-purpose kitchen appliances. I think he noticed me too. Something in my heart skipped a beat and a voice in my head whispered, "That's marriage material" as he walked by. I now know that it was the Holy Spirit. He never whispered those words with the other guys I dated.

These network guys happened to take their break at 6 p.m. each night, the time when my workday ended, and my studying continued. We'd make uncomfortable small talk as I waited for the elevator. Unknown to me at the time, Frank and his coworker Rodney talked about me. Rodney said he was going to ask me out. Frank told Rodney he'd give him three weeks to do it, otherwise Frank would ask me out. Frank didn't wait the three weeks. Good thing, I would've politely declined Rodney's request, since I didn't like dating fair-skinned boys or blondes. They looked too much like family.

One afternoon when I was filling in for the front office receptionist while she took a break, Frank walked up to me and said, "Do you want to go out to dinner or something?"

I stammered and said, "Uh…let me think about it." I knew I still had Brad. I was hot in the face and sweaty, and the green turtleneck sweater I wore didn't help. I told Frank I'd get back to him.

When I walked to the train station after work, I had a spring in my step and smiled the whole way, replaying the interaction with Frank.

Finally, I got home to my apartment. Brad was waiting so I could make him dinner like usual. He was up to his perfect jawline in debt again, never saving his commissions. We were eighteen months into our second try. As we were eating Tater Tots and fish sticks, I finally found the nerve to say, "Is this going anywhere?"

He put down his Tot and said, "Well, I, I'm not in a position to commit….."

I cut him off, "We shouldn't be together if this isn't going any further."

He indignantly replied, with food in his mouth, "Well you could've waited until we finished *dinner!*"

The way he pronounced "dinner" made it seem as if we were dining on lobster and caviar. No wonder my friends called him, "Biff." He was such a snob. Brad was officially dismissed from his position and my apartment. And it was me doing the dismissing! I finally found the courage to ask the million-dollar question after wasting a total three years with this polished turd. Honestly, I wouldn't have had the strength to do it without Frank waiting in the wings.

Now a free woman, I couldn't wait to see Frank at work. I felt proud of myself for not blurring the lines between relationships. I told Frank the next day, "Hey, I thought about it, and yes, let's go out." We scribbled our phone numbers on scraps of paper. I noticed his had the same prefix as mine. "Where do you live?" I asked.

"It's called 'The Preserve' in midtown."

"I live there too!" He asked me which apartment, and he realized that he had seen me before. He and his friend had noticed my sister and me from a distance, hanging out on our balcony.

We planned our first date. It wasn't dinner, it was the "or something." We decided to have a picnic. I offered to make lunch. I was nervous that morning and hoped he wouldn't realize I used semi-stale bread. We drove to the river, and I noticed him checking out my legs as they bounced to the music playing on his truck radio.

We sat on a blanket near the river, several miles upstream from where my friends and I smoked joints and drank too much a few years ago. Frank told me about his last girlfriend and how he looked forward to finding the "fire" again. He didn't tell me the part about her cheating on him with one of his good friends. That came later.

I thought, "What the hell am I!? Chopped liver? Is he not feeling my extra hot fire?" Mom and Lionel lived close to our picnic spot, so I asked Frank if he wanted to stop by and say hi. He did. It was a nice change to not worry about my former House of Death concerns. Mom and Lionel kept a clean, well-maintained home.

Mom and Lionel were sitting on their redwood deck as we drove up the long gravel driveway. Mom seemed pleased to see someone other than Brad. I could tell Lionel and Mom immediately approved of Frank. I think it helped that Frank was easy to talk to and wore work boots and jeans. Lionel and Frank talked about fishing and working on cars.

For our next date, we planned to meet at a local dance club. I brought my best friend Monica, and he brought his friend Tommy. A great song was playing, so I asked, "You wanna dance?"

"No. Not to this song," he said. So Monica and I danced.

The next thing I knew is he appeared next to us dancing with some other girl. I was red-hot pissed! I told Monica, "Let's go!" and quickly walked towards the door.

Frank followed us and grabbed my hand and said, "Hold on, hold on! Wait a minute!"

"Why'd you ask me out only to dance with someone else!?"

"I wanted to know if you really liked me." Against my better judgment and his game-playing, Monica and I stayed.

At our next date, we went fishing with my mom and Lionel at the river. Frank focused on fishing while I sat alone near the shore. Needy, insecure me felt ignored and grew more and more livid. I realized he must not like me after all. On the drive back I was quiet and sad. Almost home, I blurted, "I don't think you're enthusiastic enough about this relationship, we shouldn't see each other anymore!"

He took a couple breaths and said, "If that's what you think."

After he dropped me off at my door without a hug, I flung myself on my hot pink comforter, curled up and cried like a baby. I didn't have a man waiting in the wings as I let this one go. It was agonizing and I didn't feel right about not giving Frank a real shot.

Two days later Frank called. I was thrilled to hear his voice. He asked, "What are you up to?"

"Getting ready to wash my hair," I answered honestly.

"I think we should try this again."

"I'll be over after my shower."

With my spiral perm still wet, I walked to his apartment, and we talked about what happened during our fishing date. We concluded it was a misunderstanding and agreed to communicate better.

There was a knock at his door. Frank's friend, Tommy walked in and asked, "Hey, you wanna go out?"

Without consulting me, Frank stood up and replied, "Sure!"

I was red-hot pissed again. We just made up and he left me on his couch to go hang out with trouble-making Tommy. We obviously hadn't improved our communication.

Later Frank took me out to a lobster dinner to make amends for this infraction. So many times, we were on the verge of stopping before we even got started.

Our misfires settled down and we moved into another apartment in the same complex together. My sister reunited with her ex-boyfriend, Tony. He was funny and nice, but she could never be herself around Tony, and even used a strange voice I didn't recognize as hers. I used to do that with my boyfriends too, but not with Frank. Leah hadn't kissed as many frogs as I, so she hadn't learned as many lessons. With all my frogs, I learned what I didn't want by process of elimination.

I think back to all the scheming, manipulating, and begging just to make sure I kept a guy in my life. I was too busy being an anxious chameleon, trying to be whatever the situation called for and changing into what I thought they wanted, suppressing who God made me to be, whoever that was. I hadn't met her yet. I wished I knew back then that it was best to have God pick my boyfriends.

Life seemed to be such hard work that I thought everything should be hard. I had a bad habit of trying to do everything myself, trying to pull myself up from my thrift-store bootstraps. I came from a place of fear and scarcity, when really, I had God all along; all I needed to do was invite him in.

With all my struggles, it NEVER occurred to me to ask for God's help on one of the biggest decisions in life, one that could set my life's trajectory towards better or worse. Meeting Frank was effortless, being with him felt easy despite our rough start. The Holy Spirit even whispered a clue when he walked by. I'm a slow learner and, had I dated Frank before all the other frogs, I wouldn't have known how great of a guy he was without the unsavory comparisons.

Brad, Take #3?

A YEAR AND a half later, right on schedule in between girlfriends who figured out his game and wanted more of a commitment, Brad called my dad's business looking for me. I took him back once, but of course he was the same old Brad, not wanting more than a steady, warm body. In exchange, he'd provide perfume, dinners, and his handsome face. My dad's spouse made me proud and relayed the story to me. Speaking to him on the phone, she strung him along and told him, "Oh, Mary? She's not here. Yes, she's doing well. She graduated from college."

"Great!"

"Oh, and she bought a house."

"Wow!"

Building on his excitement, "Oh, and Mary got another promotion at work. Oh yeah… (pause)… and she got engaged."

"Oh," Brad said quietly. His enthusiastic mood changed. I'm thankful for her great work.

Writing this book, I looked him up on social media and noticed he had a girl in his profile picture who looked similar to me, and the one before me, and I'm sure like the ones before and after that.

By the looks of their left hands, he is still not ready to make a commitment.

I occasionally have nightmares about us getting back together and it frightens me more than a night terror. Our relationship was purely superficial and had no depth. It was like dating a handsome robot. I hadn't yet begun to inhabit my body and soul, nor did I know that I hadn't. I was just happy to be on the arm of a male specimen who looked as beautiful as him, to show perfect strangers, "Hey look at me! Someone handsome is dating me. See, I have value!" I used to love seeing the looks on people's faces as their eyes darted from him to me, and back and forth. In hindsight, those looks might have been them thinking, "What the hell is that young girl doing with that older man?" I had always looked younger than I was. I was seeking approval from extrinsic sources. Although I had found my match made in heaven, I hadn't quite yet learned that all extrinsic sources of happiness are futile pursuits.

The Happiest Year Ever!

I WAS ALMOST 24. My meth, pot, and heavy drinking days were in the not-so-distant past. Much to my surprise, I graduated from college. The first one in my family. I had been promoted a few times in my government employment, earning more cheddar. My sister gave birth to my beautiful nephew, Kyle. Frank and I bought a house. I thought all my problems were behind me. My mom was sober and with a kind man. Chance was living a normal teenage life with access to plenty of food and un-embarrassing school clothes. My adorable younger siblings lived around the corner from me and often visited. On graduation day, Frank and I hosted a barbeque for my family to celebrate. Everybody was there. Grandma Lou, Darlene, Mom, Lionel, Chance, Leah and her family, my younger siblings, Uncle Bruce and his lovely wife, Auntie Eleanor. Sipping lime Kool-Aid, eating hotdogs and baked beans, we looked like a normal family without any baggage.

Frank and I enjoyed the simple things in life like going to the park to play tennis with Phillip, our friend from the apartments. After work, I'd put my Rollerblades on and dance-skated around the neighborhood listening to Prince's *Controversy* album on a portable CD player. I loved not having homework anymore. I had occasional nightmares that I hadn't graduated, forgot to study for an exam, or worse, that I was still stuck with Brad or Dudley.

I was in the garage sweeping one Saturday when I noticed an old basketball backboard left by the previous owners. It triggered a memory from my teens. It was the same custom backboard of the house I admired when I walked to meet my sister when she lived with Dad. Frank and I had bought the same house I had dreamt of living in. It now makes me think of the scripture, "…He will give you the desires of your heart." (Psalm 37:4). Is God great or what? He wanted to give me heavenly presents. I just had to knock off the stupid stuff to make room for them.

Three months after we moved into our home, I happened to have a Monday off from work. As I was pouring Cheerios into a bowl, I overheard Frank on the phone. "I'm not coming in today. I need the day off. I'm getting married." That's how Frank proposed.

In past conversations, Frank told me his dad warned him to never get married. I wasn't going to wait three years like I did with Brad and told him so. I hated wasting time, and I had wasted enough with Brad and his predecessors. Frank caught the hint and handed me a ring from our local Mervyn's jewelry counter. I picked up a simple white dress (yes, white—don't judge!) and made a bouquet of silk flowers and stuffed it in my closet, so I could be ready. After purchasing our house together, we knew we were in it for the long haul.

That Monday, we drove up to Nevada with Leah's boyfriend,

Tony, so he could be our witness. Tony preferred drinking to working, so he was available. At the chapel, I alternated between hysterical crying and laughter as the preacher asked us to repeat our vows. My eyeliner and mascara became a hot mess.

As we drove back home in Frank's '65 Mustang, we got a speeding ticket. The officer had zero sympathy for newlyweds. We stopped by Grandma's house to share our happy news and call Mom at work. Grandma and Darlene joined us at a local restaurant and arcade to celebrate. After lunch, Grandma took the only photo from that day, a small Polaroid I framed. Afterwards, we headed to the Department of Motor Vehicles to change my name.

We went to work the next day.

As the months followed, I was in the honeymoon phase of a normal existence. The one I'd always dreamed of. It was so unusual and good. I began to worry Frank would die any day because life was usually not this good. And when it was, something bad was about to happen.

Working It

WHEN I FIRST started my government career, I sensed judging eyes, just like Eddy's. I looked like a 14-year-old for some time, despite my hard-partying years. That didn't help matters.

When I got another promotion, I hoped it wouldn't be long for me to get to the next level, since my new college degree gave me more options.

I wasn't at my new job long when I heard chatter in the bathroom about the upcoming promotional test. The girls in the bathroom spoke as if they were experts in all matters. I washed my hands slowly so I could eavesdrop, and my scrappy competitiveness kicked in. I resolved to get a higher score so I could "show them." I was hungry to be seen, and not dismissed as some invisible girl in the bathroom. And I wanted to climb the ladder to get further away from my impoverished past.

I asked my trainers tons of questions to help prepare. I studied. I crafted and memorized an opening spiel that answered the typical question, "How do you qualify for this position?" I became obsessed with the interview on the horizon. I wanted to walk into the interview room showing the confidence I wished I had, which was the biggest battle for me. I treated it like a role in a play.

The day of the interview finally arrived. I dressed in my best skirt and collared shirt, put on fake pearls, and tied my hair in a low business-like ponytail. I walked into the interview room smiling and shook hands with the three panel members, forcing myself to make eye contact with each one. I confidently answered all the questions and remembered what I wanted to say. The panel wrote a lot on their notepads, which I took as a good sign. After the interview they said it would take four weeks to get my results.

A month later, I picked up my mail and saw a white envelope with the Department of Progress as the return address. My heart raced. I tore it open and saw 95%. I made it into Rank One! I got the highest score possible without being a military veteran.

This was before scores were hidden to protect privacy, and everyone could see everyone else's scores. The devious and prideful part of me couldn't wait for others to see my high score and realize that they shouldn't underestimate me. I was still that little girl trying to prove herself to a world that couldn't care less.

I showed up to work and there was a buzz in the office. My girl buddies that I started with were happy for me. They did well too. One other person, Sebastian, also got 95%. He had been in that unit for a while, and I overheard the higher-level manager congratulate him and tell him his score was well-deserved.

She didn't stop by my desk to say anything, and I disliked her immediately because of it. Sebastian had been there for a few years; I had only been there two months and was one of the top producers. I guess she didn't think *my* score was well-deserved.

One of my office buddies told me a guy in the adjacent office heard about my score and said, "*THAT* little girl got 95%?!" Ty had black permed hair cut into a mullet. Business in the front, party in the back. He wore a farmer's cap and was a magician on the side. I found my courage and confronted him, "By the way, I'm not a little girl, I'm an educated woman!" I shocked Ty, myself, and those around us. I felt like Anne Shirley from *Anne of Green Gables* when she put mean people in their place.

Ty and I became pizza buffet lunch buddies after he apologized.

Thanks to my high score, I promoted to my next job quickly. I still didn't have much of a wardrobe and it was time for the Christmas luncheon that I really didn't want to participate in because Frank and I were on a tight budget. I splurged and paid the overpriced lunch fee, trying to be a team player. I decided to dress extra fancy since all the executive leadership would be there, thinking that would be a good move.

I wore an old party dress that I paid good money for at Weinstocks. I never got it dry cleaned like I should have, and the buttonholes were stretched out from my clubbing days. The dress was made of rayon, with black and white leopard print and tiny buttons cinching it up the middle. Some of the buttons around my belly wouldn't stay closed and kept popping open, three at a time if I moved or breathed too much. I was super self-conscious, and worried about my buttons, so I wore my jacket the whole time, just in case. I felt guilty, like everyone knew I was hiding something. I hoped someday I might be able to afford a suit from Lerner's, Casual Corner, or Petite Sophisticate. That would make me fit in.

There was a lady at the luncheon who worked in the area near me and had a resting-bitch face (RBF). Whenever I saw her in the halls, I immediately thought her scowl was because of something

I did. Just like I did with anyone who rolled their eyes or looked mad. I took on the responsibility of everyone's frowns as if it was my fault. I didn't realize RBF was her default-face setting, and that it had nothing to do with me. I wasn't a strong enough person back then. I thought about it entirely too much, and after the luncheon, I wrote a tagline on my email signature that said, "If you're happy and you know it, inform your face." I couldn't think of a better outlet to express my discomfort.

Are You There Mary? It's Me, God

I WAS AN analyst writing studies about process improvements. My team didn't seem to have enough work for the number of people it employed, and a couple of my coworkers played solitaire for an alarming amount of time. I asked my coworker from New Jersey, "What's up with this place?"

He said, in his thick accent, "Look kid, you gonna be busy—tryin' to look busy."

I made work for myself so I could stay productive. I took public-speaking classes and volunteered for any and every assignment. I couldn't *not* earn my paycheck. I was too insecure for that nonsense. I was so happy when we got a surge of phone calls. Finally, we were busy! Wanting to do a good job, and then quickly move onto the next call, I sometimes guessed at the answers, hoping I was right and that I sounded smart to both my nearby coworkers and to the callers. One of my coworkers told on me for giving out incorrect information and I got a stern talking to. I deserved the feedback even though I didn't like it.

My boss Martha was a short-statured gravelly voiced turd whose personality was better suited for solitary work. Not having much money for work clothes, I shopped in the cheaper junior's section. I wore a ruffled baby doll dress to work one day, feeling extra cute.

She looked me up and down, with her crinkled pug nose and

said, "You're dressed like a little girl!" I felt my face redden and flashed back to when Eddy and Misty picked on me.

Martha was not meant to lead people. And I'd really like to know who the heck decided otherwise. She referred to her team as "my staff," saying the word "staff" with a hint of a British accent and disdain as if we were inferior.

My coworkers were interesting. Libby didn't do much work and I'm guessing she was not well. She would be happy and kind one day and horrible the next. People called her Sybil behind her back. On a horrible day, I cracked a joke during our unit meeting.

"You fucking bitch!" She said straight to my face. For once, Martha was speechless. The conference room full of people fell silent, shocked by Libby's outburst. You could hear office crickets off in the distance. Libby went home for the rest of the day.

One afternoon, happy Libby invited me to her church's Christmas play. Unable to say no, I said I'd go.

The night of the play, Frank and I showed up to a full church and squeezed in a back pew to watch the performance. I saw all these happy teenagers dancing in the aisles before the play. I wondered why everyone was so happy. Like, what kind of drugs were they on? I wondered if Libby invited me to a cult meeting. After an opening prayer, the play began, and I immediately started to sob uncontrollably for no apparent reason. The play wasn't sad, neither was I. Or so I thought.

Thinking back, I know it was my soul hungry for the Lord and being in one of His houses hit something deep inside of me, cracking my wall of denial that kept an ocean of pain at bay. I blubbered and held back my snot with my sleeve so nobody would notice. I once heard someone say, "First we conceal, then we reveal, then we deal, so we can heal." I was still in the conceal phase.

After the play, I didn't think too deeply about my cry fest. I didn't catch the Holy Spirit's hint about how much I needed Him to heal me.

Work was my new addiction, and it distracted me from myself. Putting in another late night, a senior leader caught me crying at my desk and asked me what was wrong.

"I just found out I didn't get the training job. They said I was their second choice."

"Why do you want to leave?"

I had lied before, telling everyone I wanted to be a trainer. Truth was, I despised public speaking and wanted to be far away from Martha and my multiple-personality mentor. It had been a year of heck with these she-devils. "I just can't work for Martha anymore. She's horrible!"

"I know. Let me see what I can do."

The next week, he moved me to a new assignment and Martha was no longer my boss. Hallelujah!

My new boss, Cherise, was a radiant beauty who wore tailored work suits. I marveled at her perfect makeup and arched eyebrows. She spoke so eloquently and confidently. She was the whole package. I was her go-to girl, knowing what needed to be done before being asked. She showed sincere appreciation and told me that I did great work. I ate her positive reinforcement up like a bowl of homemade cookie dough. She asked my opinion on work matters, trying to coach and mentor me. I really didn't have an opinion on anything. I didn't know what to say and my face got hot whenever she asked.

I wanted to make Cherise, and everybody else happy. I was discovering who I was. I'd try on other people's personalities to see what fit. I decided I should be Cherise. I bought clothes she might wear. I cut my hair short like hers. I worked hard in my speaking class to help my stage fright and stop my face from turning red every time I spoke.

No matter how hard I tried, Cherise's personality didn't fit. Neither did her hair. I was being a phony baloney and not meant to be her. She was already taken. The real Mary was trying to hatch like a baby chick, but she couldn't quite break free from her stubborn shell. I still hadn't inhabited my body or put my feet on the ground, but I was trying. When I got frustrated at work, I couldn't help but get emotional, slip a few F-bombs, and blurt out my thoughts without filtering. Cherise never did that.

Frank and I settled into a routine. On Saturday nights, I sat in my pink polka-dotted bean bag near our fireplace while Frank and I watched the Spanish TV channel. I might have a glass of boxed wine. I might not. This was the same flavor I floated down the river with, only this time I bought it rather than take it from someone's refrigerator. The same box sat in the fridge for weeks and I didn't feel the familiar need to numb myself. Yet.

One evening, I remember listening to an inspirational tape while doing dishes. A coworker had given it to me. I loved positive books and inspirational speakers, just like my dad. It helped me. Frank came in the kitchen and turned off my cassette player. Why did he care what I listened to?

I got so mad I freaked out at his attempt to control me and screamed, "HOW DARE YOU DICTATE WHAT I CAN OR CAN'T LISTEN TO!! DON'T YOU EVER DO THAT AGAIN!!" He hadn't seen that side of me yet but was getting glimpses. I was living up to another nickname Leah gave me a long time ago, "Psycho Mary." Frank's attempt to control me triggered the beast. I did not want anyone to control me. I had enough of that in my life. Frank apologized.

I took Grandma Lou's advice to be married for at least two years before having children. She said it was important to build a relationship and enjoy one another before the kids came.

Always punctual, we got pregnant in October of 1996. Just like

Grandma suggested. I threw out the stale box of wine and tried to not have any bursts of anger to keep a hospitable environment for my little baby. I didn't want any part of my ugly self to seep through to her. I hoped she wasn't like me.

Somewhere-else-itis Relapse

If men had all they wished, they would be often ruined.
— Aesop's Fable, The Tortoise, and the Eagle

I HAD A recurring condition. Its symptoms were discontentedness, a longing to be somewhere else, acne, and explosive diarrhea. I'll call it somewhere-else-itis. Growing up, I was always on the run, trying to be elsewhere. I wanted different circumstances. A different set of parents. A different life. A different face. Another home. A better boyfriend.

I was in remission when somewhere-else-itis resurfaced. I had a picture-perfect life and it felt wrong. Whenever things became uncomfortably comfortable, I unconsciously manufactured drama because I wasn't used to normal. Frank hadn't dropped dead, as I previously feared he would, so I found other things to focus my obsessive thoughts. Worry was my new meth.

While I was pregnant with Grace, I obsessed about how I could be a stay-at-home mom and still pay the mortgage. Living in California, it wasn't easy to live off two paychecks, let alone one. No matter how many spreadsheets I created, the math didn't work. Being pregnant and hormonal, I grew increasingly irritated that the feminist movement fought so hard for us women to work. It was nearly impossible to be a stay-at-home mom and pay the bills. Nobody asked me if I wanted to work full-time while being a mom. We've come a long way, baby? I didn't think so.

Also weighing on my mind was an exit strategy in case Frank left. My parents' divorce showed me marriage vows were easily broken. I knew I'd better have an income or else I'd live in poverty when Frank grew tired of me. I had a good government job. I couldn't give up that security blanket and risk losing everything if Frank didn't stay.

Thanks to Dad's departure and Mom's destructive liquid pain management, I had an irrational fear of abandonment when we argued like normal couples do. After each squabble, I just knew Frank despised me and was going to pack his bags. To mitigate the risk, my long to-do list included the requisite two to three marital embraces a week, no matter how exhausted I felt. Otherwise, I thought he'd absolutely leave me. So yeah, I was officially a nervous wreck, just like normal. In a twisted way, it was soothing.

One day at work, I was chatting with my coworker about my dream to be a stay-at-home mom. As I rambled on, Johnny said, "I got this guy who owns his own business, he might be able to help you out."

"Really?" I was intrigued.

"Yeah, I heard him say he was looking for people who wanted to work from home."

Falling for what was dubbed the "curiosity approach," I said, "That'd be great if you could talk to him for me!"

"I'll let you know."

"Cool!"

After work, I told Frank that we had some people coming over to the house to talk to us about a business opportunity that might allow me to stay at home. Frank was immediately suspicious and asked, "Is it Amway?"

"I don't think so."

"If it is, I don't want anything to do with it." Frank told me about his good friend from his military days who tried to get him to sell Amway, and Frank knew better. He was not happy with my bright idea nor our soon-to-be arriving houseguests.

I learned Amway was a network-marketing company. You basically buy your groceries, toiletries, vitamins, etc. through the company, and sign up other people to do the same. If you signed up six people, and those six signed up four, and the four signed up two, you would be a "Diamond" and RICH! And if you only signed up three people who signed up four who signed up two, you would be an "Emerald" and sitting pretty. If you signed up one who signed up four who signed up two, you would be a "Direct" and you could quit your job. Not too shabby.

A team of four, including Johnny and his wife, descended upon our house. Frank blunted their eager smiles and asked, "Is this Amway?"

Johnny's friend, Patrick, deflected and handed me a business card, "It's called Royal Enterprises. Have you ever heard of it?" Patrick was clean cut and looked just like one of the handsome Mormon sons of my former neighbor. He brought his equally clean-cut wife who wore a lace-collared floral dress.

Sitting at our kitchen table, they asked me about my hopes and dreams. I told them that I'd love to be a stay-at-home mom and maybe travel and buy a pink car. They took down my answers in a shiny brochure as if they were chronicling mission-critical secrets. After the interview, pretending to calculate some algorithm in his head, Patrick assured me, "Well, I'm happy to tell you, YES, YOU CAN realize all your dreams with this opportunity!" I breathed a sigh of relief, hoping they would tell me good news.

Patrick said I could easily be a Diamond and showered me with compliments. I look back and think I was being "love bombed." I was all in!

From his briefcase, Patrick took out something that resembled a yearbook and handed it to me. He pointed out successful Amway business owners who were making tons of money.

"That guy right there, Chuck, he's a Diamond. He started out showing the plan on his bicycle. He didn't even have a car."

As I perused the pages, I noticed the women all wore bedazzled red, white, and blue blouses with their perfect makeup and extra-large, unmovable, bouffant hairdos.

I signed the forms and wrote a check for my starter kit. I was the proud owner of my own Amway business.

The next thing I knew, the love bombing lessened and Johnny's wife, Gina aggressively bossed me around on the dos and don'ts of Amway with her daily calls. She must've been 4'8' and weighed ninety pounds, but she had balls the size of Gibraltar. I hadn't yet grown a pair of my own.

As Gina demanded, I hosted an Amway makeup party. I invited my best girlfriends so I could make some sales and generate interest. Before the party got started, Gina inspected my set up and was horrified about my washcloths.

She ushered me to a corner. "Mary, we need to talk."

I thought, "Oh crap, now what."

"I needed you to get *white* washcloths—I thought I told you white will better show the dirt from the facials. You need to go fix this right away! Is there a store close by?"

She was so dang rude about it and scolded me like I was a child. Gina was another version of Eddy and Misty, and I still didn't know how to stand up to those types of people. My old pattern of submitting and not fighting back kicked in. I obediently drove to Kmart down the street and picked up the white washcloths. I kept my irritation towards Gina hidden.

The day after my unsuccessful makeup party, my phone rang and I hurried to pick it up, smacking my baby toe on the coffee table in the process. I hadn't kicked the lifelong habit of running for the phone in case it was a boy. It was Gina, speaking to me in her condescending voice, giving me action items, telling me what to do next time.

I wanted to scream because of my broken toe, but calmly had a conversation and pretended to take notes saying, "Uh huh. Yes. Ok. Right," as if my toe wasn't throbbing and a teardrop wasn't streaming down my cheek. What the heck was wrong with me!?

Gina did have a generous side. She was kind enough to loan me some of her maternity clothes.

A few months later, I dragged poor Frank to the Georgia Amway conference because Gina said it was mandatory and a "game changer" for my business.

When we arrived at the concert-like venue, I thought everyone seemed so fake happy, like Stepford people. On stage, ladies with big hair and glittery gowns sang uplifting songs in between Amway superstars delivering their tearful testimonies telling us how Amway has changed their lives. Everyone seemed so into it, like those speakers had all the answers to life's questions. I thought they were high or insane. I just didn't get it. Neither did Frank. But still, I purchased the monthly motivational cassette tapes from the superstars so I could stay "plugged in" or as Gina and Patrick put it, "using the tools." I later heard, selling these tools was how Amway superstars made a lot of their fortunes.

Frank dutifully accompanied me to the monthly meetings thirty miles away where we were supposed to be motivated by other folks in the business. I was pregnant and exhausted, but I didn't want to piss off Gina. Plus, I thought maybe I could stay at home with this little girl growing inside of me.

During the meetings, we were led by a couple who were already "Directs" in the business. In the rented hotel conference room, a tall lady with a large Texas hairdo and her cornfed husband led us in singing "God Bless America" before each meeting. I imagined they were probably homecoming king and queen in high school.

After the meeting, everyone was expected to report how much they "showed the plan" to prove they were working on growing their business. One couple consistently and suspiciously stood up and said they showed the plan twenty times a month. I didn't buy their bull crap for one minute.

After Grace was born, Frank and I still had to drive twenty miles to do "product pickup" to collect our toilet paper, cookies, and microwave popcorn from the homes of people higher up in the Amway food chain. We showed the plan here and there. We signed up Frank's dad and our next-door neighbor, and a coworker of mine. To this day I feel horrible about it when I see him in the hallway.

My high hopes of being able to quit my day job fizzled out. I was sleep deprived and done with Gina's bitchiness. I had my precious Grace, and I didn't want to spend any moment away from her. Amway wasn't what I thought it was and I wanted out. I think that must be what leaving a cult felt like.

Like most of my breakups with boyfriends, I just ghosted Gina and the team rather than tell them exactly what was on my mind. I was scared Gina would come knocking on my door at any moment. If she did, I planned to hide and pretend to not be home.

I thought their products were expensive, and we were instructed not to compare them because our "Directs" had already run the comparisons, and yes, the "prices were comparable." Comparable to what I didn't know. Maybe if I bought my groceries at a gas station or airport shop.

After we escaped the cult, I mean Amway, I think they made a good move by making things easier so that you could order stuff and get it auto shipped. No more inefficient product pickup! Amway was onto something brilliant, and Amazon hadn't quite branched out. If they hadn't given off such a cult vibe and price their stuff so out of reach, we might not know Jeff Bezos' name.

During my Amway detour, I didn't make any money. I donated it to Amway, their Directs, Emeralds, and Diamonds. This experience made me hyper aware of when some stranger at the grocery store makes small talk with me, feigning an interest, only to ask me if I'm interested in making extra money selling plastic containers, candles, or jewelry. I'm immediately triggered, and I powerfully and firmly say, "<u>NO,</u> thank you!" and run away. For that reason, I'm grateful for Amway.

Family Time

Any book that inspires us to lead a better life is a good book.
– Bishop Fulton J. Sheen

GRACE WAS THE most beautiful baby I had ever met. She had bright blue eyes, Grandma Lou's perfectly arched eyebrows, a mess of blond hair, and chubby porcelain skin. My pregnancy was easy, except for getting shingles on the right side of my head and neck, likely triggered by me overworking. I remembered staring at Grace as we lay in the hospital, concerned that she inherited my small left eye. I prayed fervently in the hospital room that she wouldn't.

Grace was the easiest baby from pregnancy to birth and afterwards. Except for the part when I pushed for three hours because her watermelon head got stuck, and she had to be vacuumed out. She had an alien-shaped head for a few days, but it's all good now. Grace even slept through the night after only seven weeks. Grandma Lou said that Grace was the best baby she had ever known, and Grandma should know since she raised six of her own.

When Grace was a few months old, we flew to Kentucky to have her meet Frank's family. Frank's Grandma saw Grace sucking her thumb and declared in her country accent, "Finger suckers make good babies!" Grace's best friend was her thumb. She'd go to town as she quietly watched everything like an owl, taking it all in.

During a blissful four-month maternity leave, Grace and I had simple days. I focused on feeding, loving, and caring for her. She loved Dr. Seuss books, especially, *One Fish, Two Fish, Red Fish, Blue Fish*. A feeling of sadness and melancholy began to envelope me. I was quicker to anger and closer to tears. It was a familiar feeling that I used to numb with drugs. I hadn't felt this way since meeting Frank.

I always enjoyed reading and, by the grace of God, I picked up a book from a yard sale called *The Road Less Traveled*, by M. Scott Peck. His book taught me that life was supposed to be difficult. That was so profound to me. I had never heard that before. I had thought life was supposed to be happy all the time and I got left out. I devoured every word he wrote. In his pages, I understood myself a little better. His book miraculously snapped me out of my melancholic postpartum. I didn't lean on drugs to make me feel better. At the time I also read *Man's Search for Meaning*, by Viktor Frankl. Books chased away my blues.

Since *The Road Less Traveled*, I've consumed hundreds of self-help books, biographies, and memoirs, trying to make some sense of my life and feelings by looking through the lens of other people's experiences. It's like getting access to the most skilled and wise therapists, only cheaper, and I love a bargain. Books were my therapy and anti-depressant, my prose-zac. Words became my whisky without the side-effects. I'd also listen to Dr. Laura's radio show during the day. I enjoyed her simple logical answers and hearing how other people had problems too. It was like mental algebra, rewiring my messed-up thinking.

It was time to return to work and leave Grace. The night before felt a million times worse than the last day of a summer break. I could've stayed home forever with my baby girl, and I wanted that more than anything, but we had a mortgage and bills. We had Frank work part-time so we could maximize our incomes and parental time with Grace. I worked an alternative schedule which allowed me to work four ten-hour days and have three full days with Grace. On Sundays we'd drive up to get Grandma Lou and Darlene to have them stay with us so they could watch Grace on Monday and Tuesday. It was perfect. We didn't have to put Grace's care in the hands of strangers, and I got to hang out more with my favorite ladies, Grandma Lou, and Darlene.

Mom and Lionel, who by now we called Grampa, were also an active and positive part of our lives. Mom, settling into her marriage and working life was a much kinder person without Eddy and alcohol. Grampa was a gifted mechanic and helped my husband work on cars. Mom and I always hugged each other when we visited and said "I love you" multiple times. It was a great and newish routine. Mom hosted larger family get-togethers during the holidays with my siblings and their children, Uncle Bruce, Auntie Eleanor, Grandma, and Darlene. It was like we were making up for lost time, doing what normal families do, without booze, drugs, and assholes.

As the months rolled by, during our frequent holiday and family events, Leah, Chance, and I shared stories about our not-so-distant past, like, "Remember our fried egg and Government Cheese sandwiches? Those were the best!" or "Remember when Uncle Bruce rewired our gas when the utility company turned it off?" "Did you hear Summer had her fourth child and all were taken…she's still using." It was our way of processing our past and doing our own version of group therapy. We tried to start these conversations when Mom was close by, our not-so-subtle attempt to get her to engage and introduce her to the elephant in the room. She never took the bait and disappeared to the next room. We were hoping Mom would join in and shed some light on what she was thinking, and maybe apologize. With concealing, revealing, dealing, and healing, Leah, Chance and I were crossing into the revealing and dealing territory. Mom preferred the conceal phase. And she never liked elephants.

Chance had graduated from high school and started taking college classes. Before long, he met his wife, and soon had three lovely sons. Around this time, Leah finally left her baby daddy for good. The final straw was when she came home from work and found their son crying unattended while the baby daddy was passed out.

After a year of being free from her ex, Leah soon met a nice man named Lance and they married. Lance was a former wrestler turned entrepreneur. He promised Leah he would love Kyle as his own.

My nephew, too young to remember his dad, thought Lance was his dad. My sister insisted she would tell him the truth when Kyle was ready. We were all unwillingly complicit in this family secret. My beautiful niece arrived a year after they married. Thanks to Lance's successful business, Leah was able to quit her government job. When she told me she quit, I thought she had made the biggest mistake of her life and begged her to reconsider. I explained, "What if the marriage doesn't work out or business slows down? You gotta have a backup plan and not be dependent on a man. You don't want to be like Mom!" She told me I didn't understand.

Lance and Leah made money hand over fist, earning and burning millions. The whole situation made me nervous.

Disease to Please

DEEP DOWN I still felt unworthy to occupy space on this planet. Like I had to earn my keep and prove my worth. When I was younger, I offered my body. Once I started my career, I sacrificed myself at the altar of other people's approval through work. I gravitated towards hard jobs and had an unhealthy workaholic ethic. I worked long hours and obsessed about being perfect so

I might earn more approval and another promotion. I didn't rest or have good self-care. I later learned that it was normal for adult children of alcoholics to have issues like these, but we sure make great employees.

Another issue that children of alcoholics have is the need for control. I felt so out of control as a child, that I tried to control my present world. I obsessively cleaned. I took on other people's jobs. If something didn't go as I intended, I freaked out. After a good run of sobriety and semi-normalcy, our sweet son, Joey was born. That was when I reached my tipping point.

My second pregnancy was more difficult. During one of my appointments, the doctor told me that my son likely had Down Syndrome. He suggested an amniocentesis.

"What's the worst that can happen if I agree?"

"About 20% of the time there could be complications or even miscarriage after the amniocentesis."

I didn't like those odds and I didn't want to put my baby at risk. I also thought about what the heck I would do even if my son had it? I knew I wouldn't abort my baby, so I declined the test and hoped and prayed for his health. After all, Aunt Darlene was a gift to our family, and Grandma did a great job raising a special needs child. Maybe I could too.

The thought of raising a special needs child probably impacted me somewhat, along with my fast-paced job and me not taking time to rest. I worked right up to the minute of delivery, just like I did with Grace.

The night I went into labor, I was sleeping on my left side, sawing logs. If I slept in any other position, baby Joey did non-stop gymnastics. I was snoring extra loud, so Frank woke me up and told me to roll over. As soon as I did, I felt a gush of water in between my legs. It was nearly four weeks before my due date. I wasn't too surprised since it felt like Joey would fall out of my baby hole every time I waddled. There was a lot of pressure in my nether regions thanks to me gaining sixty pounds by enjoying a steady diet of tacos and Thai food.

My Thai food addiction slowed down when Frank found a snake head in my chicken and broccoli dish. That helped curb my appetite. Seated in our booth, I called the waiter over and asked, "Is this supposed to be a part of the dish?" I knew the answer. The waiter's eyes got big, and he took my plate back to the kitchen. The owner came over to our table to apologize. I interrupted, "I want the check now."

The owner hurried to get our check and didn't offer a refund. Like a good girl, I paid the bill and we drove home without our leftovers. Once home, I went from shock to anger. "How could they let me pay the bill and not profusely apologize and send me home with complimentary sticky rice and mango?! I can't believe I friggin' paid!"

I called the restaurant. "Yeah, this is Mary, the one who found a snake head in her broccoli? Yeah, so I'm pretty upset that you *actually took* my money and let me pay the bill. And I'm really mad at myself for paying it. I'd like a refund, and you really shouldn't have let me pay the bill."

"Oh. Um yes, we can give you a refund. Come back any time and we'll take care of it."

So, I went back a few days later and got my refund. I also called the health department and told everybody I knew about my experience. Too bad we weren't using cell phones back then; I'd have pictures. Thankfully, Frank's eagle eyes never missed a detail. He spotted the head before I put the fork in my mouth.

At the hospital, my labor was not progressing, so the nurses increased my Pitocin to speed things along. About twelve hours later, it was time for an epidural. The inexperienced anesthesiologist gave me a spinal tap instead, and my heart rate climbed as if I were on meth. An extra handsome male OBGYN rushed in and injected me with more drugs to calm my heart down. I loved the attention.

Family and friends came in and out of my room during the lengthy labor. Not wanting to be rude, I had an open-door policy for the births of my babies. My best friends, all my siblings, Mom, Dad, Grandma, the postman, and UPS driver were all invited. I wanted people to feel welcome and not left out. As usual, my performance switch was on. I felt like I had to entertain and take care of my guests. "Can I get you anything? Would you like some of my ice chips? I'm sorry labor is so slow; I'll try to hurry."

For a moment, everyone left to get food and it got quiet. Once all my resources weren't aimed at pleasing people, I could finally feel things happening down there since I didn't have to be "ON" anymore. In the silence, my mind and body knew what to do. I should have learned from this. In the silence is where we give birth to ideas, peace, and humans.

Gratefully, Grace's large melon paved the way for Joey. But pushing was always hard. I couldn't isolate the muscles it took to push a baby from the ones it took to relieve myself. Joey was almost out when they wheeled me into another room. I was exhausted and didn't want to push anymore. The doctor said, "Reach down and feel his head!"

"I can't!" I didn't have the energy to move my arms. She grabbed my hand and made me touch his beautiful wet hairy head. That gave me all the motivation to push him out. She knew what she was doing.

Once he was out, I asked, "Does he have Down's?"

He didn't. Joey weighed in at 7 pounds 14 ounces, a few ounces less than his big sister. After the doctors tended to his premature lungs, he cried constantly. Nothing comforted him. Even Grandma Lou couldn't console him and said, "I've never seen a baby cry so much!" Joey wasn't thrilled about nursing like his big sister was. Nothing satisfied my little guy.

My stressful pregnancy, my job, Joey's incessant crying, and my inability to relax or ask for help made me especially fragile. I should have known I was a mess of hormones when I developed a crush on the male OBGYN and got jealous when he tended to the other mom in our hospital room. He only loved me during my spinal tap crisis.

When Joey was about eight weeks old, I told Frank, "We need to get Joey baptized, and we should start attending church." Mom made sure all her kids were baptized and I knew I had to make sure to check that box. The purpose of baptism was never explained to me, nor did I bother to study it. It was more of a to do list item than freeing my baby's soul from Adam and Eve's original sin. I don't know why I felt we needed to attend church. I didn't think too deeply about it, but something inside made me place church on my family's schedule.

"How about that one huge church in town?" I asked. Frank is easy going and never puts his foot down, even when I get crazy ideas like painting our bedroom hot pink.

He calmly and firmly said, "No. We're Catholic."

That was the end of our discussion.

Frank didn't want to disappoint his now deceased Grandma Celeste. Ten-year old Frank and his lovely younger sister had been sent to live with Grandma Celeste while their parents divorced. Frank's mom and dad stayed behind in Italy while his dad finished his military assignment. Grandma Celeste had made it her mission to get Frank and his sister baptized and confirmed in the Catholic church.

Frank loved his grandma and didn't dare deviate from what she set in motion. I called our local Catholic church and told them I'd like to get my son baptized and get closer to God. Both true statements. The lady on the phone explained that we would need to attend baptism classes on Sundays after mass. And that the Godparents would have to be practicing Catholics.

When we had Grace baptized in Frank's hometown church, we didn't have to take baptismal classes or promise we'd go to church. In Kentucky things were easier.

While sitting in the requisite baptism classes with twenty smiling moms and dads, I really didn't understand what we were doing. My religious background consisted of a baptism, and a few Catholic catechism classes until Mom and Dad divorced. I knew God existed, and prayed here and there, but that was about it. The volunteer teacher asked us to go around the circle and share our family traditions. I immediately panicked. I didn't know what she meant by that question. Family traditions? What the heck are those?

The instructor started and shared, "When my family does our annual Easter egg hunt, and someone finds an egg, they yell, 'Christ is risen!'" I looked around and wondered what the hell was going on. By the looks of their unchanged faces, the rest of the group didn't think her words were strange.

I looked over at this one mom who had a permanent and genuine opened-mouth smile on her face. I wished I felt like she did. I wondered, "Why is everyone so happy?" Like everyone had life figured out but me. I imagined they had a normal upbringing that gave them a great childhood and zero addictions. I guessed that their husbands had high-paying jobs that allowed them to stay at home and care for the kids. As I sat there and listened to their traditions, I felt so unhappy and empty inside. Baptism classes were sucking the remaining life force out of me.

I discovered that I had a huge theological knowledge gap. The only tradition I could think of to say was, "I bake homemade cookies every weekend."

The teacher asked, "Share with the group why you chose the name you did for your child."

I didn't have a biblical answer like the rest of the class, so I said, "I chose Joey for obvious reasons." My face flushed like it did when I got called on in class. What were the obvious reasons? I had no clue. I hoped they didn't ask.

I racked my brain and thought about Adam and Eve. Wait, wasn't there a Joseph? I just knew my classmates would find out that I was an imposter.

On weeknights, I attended my own confirmation classes while working full time and trying to be a good mom. I showed up every week despite how awful and depleted I felt. I needed one more obligation like I needed a hole in my head, but I didn't see it back then. The classes took a whole year and I'm no quitter even when I should be. Joey was baptized at three months, and he didn't cry as much after that. I should have splashed him with holy water a long time ago! We started attending church as a family.

Joey stopped nursing before he hit twelve months, I wondered if he had an undiagnosed allergy that caused all his earlier crying. Or maybe he was mirroring what his mom felt. Years later we learned he was allergic to most plant life.

After he stopped nursing, I made a sudden decision to get a tubal ligation at 29. I was overwhelmed and couldn't imagine one more chore, let alone one more child. The doctor made me take a series of classes to ensure I knew what I was doing. Nobody could talk me out of it.

Much later I'd come to regret that irreversible decision. It saddens me that I had no way to see beyond my current reality and that I made that hasty decision. I wished my doctor had refused to do a permanent procedure on a younger mom like I hear they do today. I tell all the young mothers I know to NOT make an irreversible, rash decision just because you cannot see beyond the current situation. This too shall pass, and you'll wish you hadn't acted so hastily.

Ritz Made me Too Big for my Britches

Pride goes before destruction, and an arrogant spirit before a fall.
– Proverbs 16:18

My sister and her husband continued to rake in millions with their business. Leah showered Chance, me, and our families with expensive gifts on birthdays and Christmas. I loved the pink leather outfits, jewelry, and shoes. I would never have bought that stuff for myself.

Annually, Leah took Mom and me on a girls' weekend to the nearest Ritz Carlton. On one trip, we got picked up by a limousine and my sister handed us an envelope of cash to use as shopping money. I was happy to get away from my weekend chores and looked forward to my shopping spree.

Once we arrived, the bellman insisted on carrying my yard sale luggage to our room. That meant I had to tip him. I fretted over the proper amount as he lingered way too long and showed us the bathroom and beds, as if we couldn't figure it out. I cringed in pain as I handed him $5.

After settling in, we walked to the elevator in our matching velour sweatsuits. I couldn't wait to head to the club level so we could drink the free booze and eat the gourmet appetizers. I guzzled at least three flutes of champagne and snacked on hummus, stuffed dates, cheese, and minimal crackers to conserve my carb intake for booze. I was back to leaning on alcohol to get through life, and I couldn't stop after one drink.

Our plan was always the same. Binge at the club level. Order room service popcorn with extra butter and watch a movie. The next day we'd hit Leah's favorites. First, Christian Dior, then Juicy

Couture. My favorites were much cheaper. My frugal gene insisted I save money and shop at the bargain stores.

Leah was not a morning person, and Mom and I didn't like to waste the day, so we woke up early and let Leah sleep. Mom and I shared a bed. Her restless COPD breathing kept me up and I was a jerk and mentioned it. She had developed a horrible case of Crohn's disease and worse case of COPD that made it hard for her to breathe and walk the city streets. It was the last trip she went on due to her declining health.

Each morning, I got my workout clothes on quietly, and Mom and I proceeded to the club level for breakfast. I had coffee, raspberries, and cantaloupe as my pre-workout treat.

I took the elevator down to the gym and scanned the room for an available cardio-type machine. I found one vacant elliptical and saw a tall brunette man working out in flip flops. I got on the machine, looked up at him and we greeted each other with, "Good morning." It took a second to register, but OMGosh. It was friggin' Al Gore. The former vice president before he ran for president. I was freaking out inside but acted nonchalant.

Our elliptical machines had TVs and he had his on some random program. I turned mine on and scanned the stations for something to impress Al Gore, since impressing others was still my crooked priority. I landed on *Meet the Press*. Tim Russert was speaking; God rest his soul. Al Gore changed his machine's TV to *Meet the Press* too.

After my workout, I walked into the elevator with endorphin-fueled confidence, feeling a little taller, as if to say to the non-working-out elevator passengers, "I worked out with Al Gore."

I arrived back at the club level to get more breakfast and find Mom. I proceeded to the tea service, looked up at a gentleman who was making his tea. I couldn't quite place where I knew him and only said, "Good morning, you sure look familiar," and then I realized it was Michael York.

"God, I hope so." We continued our small talk and he asked, "How long are you in town for?"

"Just the weekend. I'm here with my mom and sister on a girls' getaway."

I grabbed my green tea and joined Mom, sitting in one of the fancy chairs. I tried to be discreet and tell her all about Al Gore and Michael York. Mom saw Mr. York too. She didn't miss much. Then the elevator opened and there was Ozzy Osbourne with a young man walking to get their club-level breakfasts. Ozzy shuffled around and I decided to get more food just to be near him.

He commented to his friend, "Sharon would love some strawberries." I decided I wanted strawberries too. Mom was thrilled to see Ozzy since she watched his reality show.

I thought, "Whenever I play two truths and a lie, I can use, 'I shared strawberries with Ozzy Osbourne', or, 'I worked out with Al Gore.'"

Leah finally emerged from her slumber around 10:30 a.m. to get ready for the day at her usual sloth's pace. Our polar-opposite paces of life were a constant source of friction for us. It frustrated me so profoundly that it took her ten times longer than an average person to do a task. She's a detail-oriented perfectionist. I'm an efficient control freak. We don't mix well.

Around noon at the club level, Mom and I waited impatiently for Leah so we could finally go shopping. Once Leah was ready, Mom and I had fun watching her spend tons of money and have the sales associates treat her like royalty.

When we returned home after our trip, it was hard for me to come back to my small, non-luxurious home, with its simple furnishings, and my exhausting life. The fancy hotel and celebrities seduced me into thinking life should be like a weekend stay at the

Ritz. I felt a little too big for my britches and my non-celebrity normal husband, and I'm not proud of it. I realized how reality stars must feel after their fifteen minutes of fame only to head back to real life.

I grew more jealous of my sister's wealth and wished I had married someone rich so I could be a stay-at-home mom too. I remember talking crap to the pedicure salon technicians as my sister treated me to a pedicure and a spray-on tan. While Leah used the salon restroom, I'm ashamed to say I told the nail salon ladies, "She doesn't even have to work!!!" as if not working were a crime.

I'll tell you what I thought the crime was. It was that I had to work, and Leah didn't. She was living my dream. I second-guessed my choice in marriage partners, but not enough to covet Leah's husband, just his wallet.

Leah filled her days with shopping. So much that you couldn't even see what was in her large walk-in closet. I'd often get a ton of hand-me-downs when she hired a friend to help organize the chaos.

I'm grateful for my sister's help and generosity. She even watched my kids during summer breaks. Grace and Joey loved visiting and having sleepovers with their cousins. My kids played with their huge Rottweiler and swam in the pool alongside the pooch. It was like an amusement park in my sister's backyard. My niece's birthday parties were large productions with clowns, ponies, and magic shows.

A few years later, Leah's money dried up for reasons that could fill another book. This set off a downward spiral towards unfathomable circumstances.

Mama's Helper

Sometimes the only way the good Lord can get into some hearts is to break them. – Bishop Fulton J. Sheen

AFTER I COMPLETED my first communion and confirmation, the devil came after me hard to screw up my progress. He knew my weaknesses and I became his chew toy.

I popped by my dad's studio one day after work to visit. I must have told him and his friend about how stressed out I was. Dad slipped me some more Vicodin or Codeine pills, as he sometimes did, trying to be a supportive parent. I already used the stash of expired Vicodin I was prescribed when I had shingles. These pills helped me calm down and quieted my growing feelings of sadness. I always had an extra one tucked away in a pocket for moral support in case I needed it. As I exhausted my pill supply, they started to have the reverse effect, and made my heart race, like meth.

Dad's friend told me about his Reiki classes and asked to lay hands on me. I let him. I swear, in retrospect, I wonder if I got a curse right then and there as he explained how he used his sexuality to navigate work and life. His words made sense to my twisted mind back then. I felt peace for a moment as the Vicodin kicked in. It was false peace. I was looking for the peace and comfort only God can supply.

My blues soon turned to despair. I remember seeing people wearing shirts that said, "Life is good." I thought, "How dare they wear that! Life *is not* good! Why is everyone else happy except me?"

I sunk further into my depression and took up smoking weed and other drugs to destructively self-medicate. I had already screwed up my brain's reward system with my early drug use, and my volatile hormones did not help matters.

My pot addiction reignited when a friend of ours came for a

visit and happened to light up a joint. After taking a few discreet hits, I sat by our pool.

As the THC took effect, my tortured mind quieted. I heard birds singing. I noticed our beautiful redwood trees reaching to the sky. I felt the wind on my face. I inhabited my body and became present. I don't remember ever being this present and connected to nature or myself. I thought, "This is it! Pot is the answer to all my problems. Why didn't I try this sooner?"

What a freaking "Lie straight from the pit of hell," as my minister friend Ray would say. While it felt great for about a week, pot soon governed my life. I went from intermittently abusing pills and alcohol to a full-blown pot addict. For those of you who think it's not addictive, I'm here to tell you, *it absolutely is*, for many of us.[4] It held me tightly in its grip. Pot exponentially magnified my depression and postponed any hope for healing.

I was so tired of suffering and took destructive shortcuts to escape. Why hadn't I learned booze, drugs, or any other escapes do not eliminate pain? Why didn't I realize they only exacerbated all my problems, and added self-loathing to the mix? I hadn't learned to feel the pain when it comes, breathe through it, and lean on the Lord. Like Romans 5:3-5 explains, pain should make us happy. It produces perseverance and character. Pain is just part of the package of life. I should've re-read M. Scott Peck's book.

Many of us have our own version of mama's or papa's little helper. It ain't much help though. It just turned me into an empty shell. I was simply going through the motions that resembled a life to observers but made me feel like the walking dead. It quickly gets out of hand for those of us with the addict gene. It can be

---

[4] I realize there are many people who might be helped by using marijuana and/or have a much different experience. However, the people and addicts in my circle, including myself, did not realize any long-term benefits from using marijuana.

wine, vodka, pills, gambling, porn, work, adultery, other people's approval, screen time, or whatever.

I'm reminded of a proverb a coworker shared at the time, not knowing my struggles. She said, "A man takes a drink, the drink takes a drink, the drink takes the man." Those words are forever duct taped to my brain. It started with me freely taking the first dose. I had my free will in that sober moment. I had a choice when I reunited with that initial inhale of pot. And then my ability to choose was gone. Mary took a hit, the hit took a hit, the hit nearly destroyed Mary and her beautiful family. I'm told that relapses, no matter how much time in between, make recovery that much harder. I'm here to tell you, it's a fact, Jack.

What I really needed was sleep. I needed good self-care. I needed consistent exercise to repair my brain's faulty reward system. I needed my post-pregnancy hormones to settle down. I needed to address my past and faulty thought patterns. I needed my higher power. I needed to minimize my non-essential obligations. It never occurred to me to ask Jesus, Frank, or anyone for help, since I was used to doing everything myself.

I should have told Frank to PLEASE take the kids somewhere on Saturday morning and just let me sleep. I could have called my mom or girlfriends for help. I could have asked God for direction. I was stuck with the same thought patterns that I still struggle with, that *I must do everything. I must meet every commitment. I must give everything at work and at home. People are counting on me, and I can't let them down.*

I was always where I was supposed to be. And it was nowhere I wanted to be. There I was, living a life focused on meeting other people's expectations, or what I imagined them to be. I was an empty vessel efficiently completing tasks, trying to run from my past and gain approval. I wasn't concerning myself with important things like self-care and sanity.

Being bone-tired, hormonal, stressed, and having unaddressed trauma was a great recipe for depression, especially with someone like me who has those ruminating tendencies.

I later wondered if I was possessed for a moment. The Bible warns us against turning to mediums or spiritualists. (Leviticus 19:31 and 20:6). Don't mess with Reiki or drugs and invite a barrel full of sin and destruction into your life.

Around this time, I felt a scary shadow overcome me while lying half asleep in my bed several times. It felt like a night terror but without the fever. It frightened me so much that I curled up into a ball, squeezed my eyes shut, and hoped it would go away. I didn't think to pray or shout out to God.

During my commute to work I fantasized about driving my car into a ditch and making it look like an accident. Not a fatal wreck, just one that could give me at least a six-week hospital stay and some rest. I really should have taken some sick days or more time off. I didn't. I trudged on. I got promotions at work. I'd give my teammates great advice and tell them to take care of themselves. But I never took my own advice or gave myself permission to take mental health days off. I was drowning.

Instead of hopping off the hamster wheel, seeking help, and working on myself, I turned against Frank. Every bad feeling that I felt, I blamed Frank. Everything I loved about him I now hated and told him so. I nitpicked him to death. I told him that I wished he were a different man. That I regretted picking him as my life companion. I thought my despair was all his fault. I thought I should have married for money so I could stay at home with my kids and not be permanently exhausted. I had a bad case of "I wish I married someone-else-itis," and I wished for a man who would be more empathetic, read poetry to me, and tell me nice things all the time. No wonder God doesn't want us coveting. Nothing good comes from it.

Frank is not a poet. His spoken love language[5] is deeds. Mowing the lawn, playing catch with the kids, maintaining our cars, being honest and faithful to me, and quietly placing fresh-cut flowers in an empty McDonald's cup—that's who Frank is. He will never be the conversationalist I desperately thought I needed at the time. That's what girlfriends are for. I didn't recognize or verbalize my needs. He didn't read minds. It was ironic that I ended up marrying a man of few words when words of affirmation is *my* love language.

I remember as a young girl, hearing Mom constantly nitpicking Dad. I think most marriages go through this phase on the gameboard of life. The stress of young kids, jobs, bills, and exhaustion brings everyone's unresolved crap to the surface. On the gameboard, you either assign blame to anything other than yourself and chute directly to divorceville, or you begin the hard work of facing your demons and climb to the next level of unconditional love. For me, I chose divorceville with every turn on the gameboard. I've watched many people divorce at this part of the gameboard, and I was well on my way to repeating the pattern.

During this roaming in the desert period of my life, I remember clumsily praying a portion of Psalm 23, while sitting on the toilet crying, "The Lord is my shepherd; I shall not want." That's all I knew of the Psalm at the time. I wanted desperately out of hell, but I didn't have a map. It wasn't 40 years in the desert, but it sure felt like it. At my lowest, I was drinking, popping unprescribed pills, and smoking $400 worth of pot a month, and that's A LOT for 20 years ago.

I got down to 100 pounds, dramatically changed my hair, cutting it short. I flirted and bought a motorcycle. This generation of weed didn't give me the munchies like it did in my teenage years. It gave me energy, paranoia, and zero appetite.

---

5 Gary Chapman, *The 5 Love Languages: The Secret to Love That Lasts,* (Moody Publishers, 2015)

It's weird when I look back at photos from this period; I appeared well put together, happy and smiling, with expert makeup, perfect hair, and cute clothes. Although camera-ready, I was the most mentally unhealthy and unhappy I had ever been. All my issues came home to roost. I was back on the market again, searching for anyone who wasn't Frank. I became less committed to my sacred vows. I'd put on a good show for work and should win on Oscar for my acting skills, only to curl up in a ball at home sobbing like a baby and hate everything about myself, my husband, and my life. I wasn't my best at work, but at least my D game was better than some peoples' B game.

My poor kids had a shell of a mommy on autopilot and knew something was wrong. This period unfolded slowly after Joey was born and, by the time he hit three, I was at my worst. Joey even asked, "Are you leaving us, Mom?"

I had a slow-mo mental breakdown. I was unconsciously sabotaging my beautiful family and life. I was trying to gravitate back to what felt familiar—a life I thought I deserved—one full of pain and chaos. I was trying to move back into The House of Death.

My jacked-up brain couldn't see the blessings right in front of me. I had a great husband, healthy children, and a great career. I didn't recognize it, but life was good like the t-shirts said. I just didn't know how to handle it.

Unfortunately, there was no convincing my malfunctioning brain. According to current research from the *National Institute on Drug Abuse*[6] and the *Centers for Disease Control and Prevention*,[7] cannabis is associated and linked to schizophrenia and other psychoses, and early cannabis use increases that probability. With such

---

6   https://www.drugabuse.gov/publications/research-reports/marijuana/there-link-between-marijuana-use-psychiatric-disorders

7   https://www.cdc.gov/marijuana/nas/mental-health.html

frequent pot use, I believed I could read people's minds. Truth was, I was losing mine.

Heaven, Don't Make me Wait

Never travel faster than your guardian angel can fly.
— Mother Teresa

I DIDN'T GET the lightning-bolt answer to my prayers, but God was nudging me along the way. I just wasn't paying attention, due to my complete devotion to weed. A gal I was carpooling with at the time told me about the divorce she was going through and flippantly said, "Don't ever divorce, it's never what you think it is." She had no idea I was on the verge of divorce myself.

Another nudge was when I drove our minivan past the church and Joey asked from his car seat, "Momma, why don't we go to church anymore?" His question convicted me. The Lord was calling me back. Crazy how Satan comes after us, right when we're church-going Christians and getting stronger in our faith. And of course, he knows our weaknesses and prowls around like a lion, searching for someone to devour (1 Peter 5:8). My weaknesses are that I'm an addict, I don't ask for help, and often feel unworthy. And normal setbacks in life felt so painful that I didn't think I could bear them without drugs.

I got pulled over and ticketed three times within the same year by the highway patrol. One for riding my motorcycle on the sidewalk to hurry back to work from an appointment, and the other two for driving too fast and reckless. By the third ticket, I told the officer before he could say anything, "Just give me the damn ticket!" God was speaking louder, even during my dreams. I'd have this recurring dream of driving downtown where four major freeways intersect:

I'm going way too fast on the freeway. I can't see. My vision is blurred and it's dark. The breaks aren't working. I don't know which lane to be in to get to where I'm going. I don't know which freeway to choose. I'm panicked and about ready to crash. The car is going way too fast for me to think straight and inevitably I pick the wrong lane. I'm headed in the wrong direction, can't slow down and there's no exit in sight.

Desperate for some outlet and answers, but not stopping my addictions, I started journaling my thoughts, writing poems, sketching, and painting. My friend Naomi from work and I would take our breaks together and speed-write poems and share our dreams of being writers.

People had told me I was a good writer and communicator and asked me to write poems for special occasions. Frank often encouraged me to write a book. I didn't listen to him or anyone. I really didn't think much of myself; I didn't think I had any talents. Still, I made Frank and Naomi take me to a poetry recital where I could read my poetry to others in a downtown bookstore. There were a lot of single people filling the room, looking for some creative outlet, maybe more. The attendees included a few aging hippies and a dark-eyed guy in the corner wearing a charcoal beret, clutching his bongo drums. I remember going up to the podium and reading my poem to the onlookers, it went something like this:

One thing at a time,
So many thoughts racing in my mind,
I wish I could be fine,
And just do one thing at a time,
So many chores and tasks, making demands,
I want to escape and make other plans,
Maybe I'd read the paper or take a nap,
Or just sit still with my kids on my lap,
Lord, please help me find,

A way to do just one thing at a time.

I finally sought professional help at my husband's urging. The therapist looked like a former flower child and spoke like an airhead who took too much LSD. Guess what she concluded as I burst into a tearful litany of all my complaints?

"You need to leave your husband immediately," she said.

Her words shocked me. I knew it was reckless for her to suggest that I leave Frank after listening to me for fifteen minutes. But in all fairness, everything I said to her about my husband was negative. Even depressed me knew that a therapist shouldn't conclude something so drastic after one session. Frank wasn't perfect, but everyone bragged about how he's such a good man and father, even if I refused to see it.

After thirty minutes, the therapist concluded, "You have SEVERE DEPRESSION" as it was prominently displayed on her computer screen and on all screens during my subsequent doctor's appointments. She told me I had to take antidepressants. She sent me to an office down the hall.

The lady in charge of medicine gave me better advice than the therapist. "Stop smoking weed; it's not helping you." The prescription didn't either, but I still used both.

During my second therapy appointment, I happened to see a lady from work in the waiting room. I was absolutely mortified that my mental unwellness cover had been blown. My face must have turn beet red when I recognized her. I decided right then and there to not go back to my appointments, lest I get found out at work and be outed. My pride and concern for my career and what others thought about me outweighed my desire to follow through with my appointments and make my mental wellness a priority.

I should have sought out another therapist who I connected with and stuck it out. How sad that I felt ashamed for needing help.

I'm grateful that times have changed in the last twenty years, and many well-known people have come out to share their struggles. It took me years to even verbalize this journey to my best friends, let alone myself. I was great at keeping secrets.

Poolside Epiphany

A FRIEND TOLD me that we replay the trauma we lived through as children in our own lives. I later learned about research done on epigenetics[8] that tells us the effects of trauma can impact future generations.

Every generation gets their own pain. Grandma Lou lost two husbands and two sons. Grandpa lost his biological mom at birth and his dad shortly after. Mom grew up with an alcoholic father and lost two brothers. Dad's father stayed in his pajamas all day, so Dad got a paper route at the age of ten to pitch in to help his mom pay bills. Dad was embarrassed by his home too. They didn't have a backyard fence or curtains for the windows like the rest of the neighborhood, so Dad got another job to help save up to build the fence and buy curtains.

We're all broken in our own special way, and we have a choice in how we respond, even if we have present and previous generational crap to deal with.

Grace was seven at the pinnacle of my despair and pot-smoking addiction. Joey was nearly four. My husband and I were close to divorcing, with all the bickering, arguing, nitpicking and my self-hatred. And Frank was beyond done living with an active addict. We both threatened the D-word during our fights.

I was sitting by the pool watching Grace play in the water. I studied her. She looked like a spitting image of me at that age. It

---

8   Shui Jang, Lynne Postovit, Annamaria Cattaneo, Elisabeth B. Binder, Katherine J. Aitchison *Frontiers in Psychiatry*, 2019, https://www.frontiersin.org/articles/10.3389/fpsyt.2019.00808/full

was as if I were looking at my happy innocent self at age seven right before my parents divorced. Watching Grace, I imagined little Mary playing, blissfully unaware that her life would soon turn upside down and sufficient food, clothing and love would be a thing of the past. Soon Grace (Mary) will have a jacked-up childhood where people like Eddy and Misty will crush her spirit and severely delay her from becoming herself. In that moment by the pool, Grace and I were fused together…the same exact person. I was Grace. She was me. I realized in that instant that there's no freaking way I could do the same thing to my precious children what was done to me.

I realized my parents had no clue what they were about to set in motion with their divorce. Once Dad left, Mom started drinking and soon neglect, abuse, and horrible people came into our home. My parents could not have imagined the obstacles my siblings and I would have to overcome to begin to love and accept ourselves without the help of drugs and unhealthy coping devices. My parents may not have known what would come, but in that instant, I knew. And I knew I couldn't put Grace and Joey through any version of hell that my siblings and I went through. I knew right then and there I could not and would not divorce Frank. I had to break the cycle.

God smacked me upside the head in that moment and I am so grateful for his correction. I got up and picked up Grace and smothered her with tons of kisses on her chubby cheeks and said, "Mommy loves you so much!"

I found Frank inside and said, "Please give me time. I think all this mess is because of my childhood."

So yes, like my friend explained, I was literally replaying the situation I lived through with my parents. It was a template and timetable programmed deep inside of me. I was my mom, depressed, grumpy, and weary, dealing with unaddressed childhood trauma. I worked hard to get Frank to reject me so I wouldn't have to be the bad guy. I had already rejected myself.

I was also my dad, the one who wanted someone other than my spouse, and the one trying to start a new gameboard of life. The only difference between Mom and me was that I chose pot, pills, and alcohol to medicate. Mostly pot. Mom chose Coors. And instead of harming Leah, Chance, and me, I would harm Frank, Grace, and Joey. My two precious children would be the innocent victims caught up in the crossfire of their mom working through her childhood baggage, depression, and addictions. I came full circle.

I was on autopilot, reliving my parents' lives without questioning it. By the grace of God, that epiphanic moment by the pool helped me break the divorce cycle that was set in motion. The Lord IS my shepherd! I know, deep in my bones, that if I divorced, I would have regretted it and be living a sadder and more selfish version of life, piling on more trauma on my kids and on to the next generation. I would have lost the man that God picked just for me.

The other part of Psalm 23 says "...Even though I walk through the valley of the shadow of death, I will fear no evil, for you are with me. Your rod and your staff, they comfort me..." It occurred to me that the Psalm says, I'm *walking through* the valley of the shadow of death. I'm not pitching a tent and staying camped in the valley. I'm just walking through it, propped up by God's staff and corrected by his rod. Once I get through the valley, as I lean on the Lord to support me, I'll get back to the promised land of almond milk and honey-nut Cheerios, and out of that friggin' shadow.

So, what was I supposed to do while I was going through hell? Press on like "Lee Press on Nails." Or said better by Winston Churchill, "If you're going through hell, keep going."

I have since talked to many divorced women and the majority of them told me they could have and should have worked it out.

They have had to start over with the gameboard, replaying the same levels, only to get to the crossroads where they can either learn to weather the storms, grow, and get stronger, or decide to tap out and replay the levels again and again. Yes, some women and men should not stay with their abusive/addicted/adulterous spouses. That's a whole different gameboard.

They say marriage is work, but I found the real work is an inside job. Marriage just happens to be the primary backdrop and relationship where we root out selfishness, unfinished childhood, pride, entitlements, and all things ego as we go through life.

Marriage is like a long-term-self-discovery retreat. The trick is to stick with it, staying beside each other as we work through life's crap sandwiches, lifting one another up when the other one falls, and forgiving each other's trespasses. Hopefully we help each other to become a better version of ourselves. The gameboard gets really good when we hit the final level: unconditional love for ourselves, and our spouses, where we work hard to stay put. That's what Frank does for me and what I try to do for him—on our best days.

After my epiphany, my fog was beginning to lift. I wanted to fight for our marriage and stop smoking weed but hadn't quite committed to the latter. I was in too deep. At least Frank and I weren't racing towards the chute of divorceville and continued our gameboard, making slow progress. I'm thankful God answered my simple and inexperienced prayers and pulled me out of the pit. I'm thankful for the lessons as the tattered yarn of my past unraveled in my marriage and life. I'm grateful God prevented me from destroying another marriage and harming my precious children in the process.

I was about 75% through the valley when I got stuck. You know what the kicker was to completely lift the depression fog? It seems crazy, but it was something my old boss said to me. My boss, Dalton, was nothing like the saintly Cherise. Dalton was a mouth breather. He got on my last nerves, and it wasn't because of his facial hair or that he called me, "Kid". Kid, I didn't mind. What I did mind was that he didn't know how to lead a team, He would passively talk about what could be done, but in no way did he know how to plan, rally the troops, or execute. He was a good technician and in the wrong job match. He spoke in hypotheticals, which irritated the crap out of me.

"What we need to do is start thinking about how we're going to tackle the issue," he'd say.

I'd think, "Dude, just get on the whiteboard. We could map out a plan and tackle five issues in the time it would take you to think about what we're going to do for this one." Our team was stuck on perpetual pause. I should have found another job long ago.

I tried to make things better, but only got batted down and soon, I learned that my help was neither wanted nor respected, so I did what I could to work around Dalton. My work situation did not help my mental health. Yet Dalton's words were just what I needed. He told me that Norman, someone I considered a mentor who was looking out for me and my career, had said, "Mary's young and very immature."

That hurt, and I got as angry as one of my chin zits. Partially because it was true. I *was* immature. I tended to aim for a punchline to get a laugh and be silly. And I often didn't think *before* I spoke. I spoke to think. But one thing I AM NOT is a slacker or goof off. I am responsible and disciplined to a fault. OK, I knew he didn't say that I was a slacker, but I knew people could assume it by hearing his assessment of me. That's how my fragile self took it.

I thought Norman's careless words about me could harm my career and undermine all my hard work, especially coming from someone at his level. I thought he was my friend. Nope. He was nice to my face and talked crap about me.

Hearing what he had said jolted me back to reality and helped me to clearly see I was headed for destruction. Funny how ruining my marriage wasn't enough to completely snap me out of the fog. Potential career suicide did the trick. It revealed to me how much I attach my self-worth to my job and my ability to provide for myself. At the root of it was pride and my fear of living in poverty. I vowed never to be financially dependent on anyone. I thought Norman had ruined my career, my livelihood, and that the next day I'd be living with Eddy, subsisting on beans. I thought, "How dare Norman abuse my friendship and flippantly chip away at the track record that I had worked so friggin' hard to build?!"

I'm still immature, but my work ethic and ability to get results more than counterbalance that. I showed up every day despite my depression and put in an honest day's work, pretending to be OK. Guess what Norman? That shit wasn't easy, motherfucker! (Yes, I realize that last sentence confirms Norman's assessment.)

I'm glad God used my pride to help me get out of my self-imposed prison before going to prison for realsies. Shortly after that "immature" revelation, Frank and I prepared for a family trip to Hawaii. I didn't tell Frank, but I decided I would stop my antidepressants and weed habit on that trip. Cold turkey. That's how my mom quit booze. And my sister quit cocaine. And how I quit meth. There was no way I would be able to smuggle joints on the flight anyway, although I thought about it. I knew I wasn't supposed to stop my antidepressants cold turkey, but I also knew they weren't working for me. I'm sure they work for many, but not me. I shook like I had Parkinson's and was still sad. I had more of a thinking problem. Pills wouldn't fix that.

I ended up sleeping a lot in Maui, hardly leaving the hotel. I don't recall much of that trip, except for the incessant stomachache. The only food I craved was ramen noodles and they sat in my gut like a rock.

The Hawaiian trip was my turning point and rehab. The weed and pill habit that exacerbated my depression and postponed my recovery was now kicked to the curb. Praise the Lord! I have absolutely ZERO business reuniting with any form of cannabis EVER. Even though it's now legal in California. I have no business imbibing in any addictive substance for that matter, but I told myself it was OK to have cocktails. I started being nicer to myself and husband and began the process of inhabiting my body and life. It was still hard. I was exhausted and I would have crying fits, but they were fewer.

As I reflect, auto-pilot depressed me was doing her best back then, which wasn't awesome. I guess that must be true about my own mom and her eight-year bender. Drunk and depressed Mom was doing her best back then too, hanging on by a thread. And she didn't have a patient, helpful partner like I did. Somehow, we all managed. I'm thankful my postpartum, pot-smoking, motorcycle-riding days were behind me, and I prayed my kids would barely remember this period of our lives and remember the better times instead. Their mom will never forget them.

PART V – TRYING OUT NEW PRESCRIPTIONS

Nature does not hurry yet everything is accomplished. – Lao Tzu

SHORTLY AFTER WE returned from Hawaii, I did something I never do. I went to the mall all by myself after meeting with a new and improved therapist. After a good cry I just sat on the bench, eating my "Cheese on a Stick" corn dog, being present in the moment rather than a vessel that efficiently gets tasks done.

It was a nice change of pace. I'm usually in constant frenetic motion, approaching life like one long to do list with nothing to be enjoyed.

Efficiency is a hard habit to break for me. I have a profound respect for time. I get anxious if I feel like I'm taking up people's time, as if I don't have any right to occupy space on our shared planet. I'm not good at asking for anyone's help, or time. So, I speak fast, like a spaz, and do my best not to hold anyone up. There's too much to do! I feel my best when I'm using time wisely. Like doing two or three things at once, it makes me feel as if all is right in the universe. I worked full-time while going to school full-time, while also partying full-time. I won't take the time to put on my seatbelt until I'm driving so that I save a few seconds. I brush my teeth while peeing on the toilet. Why do I try to shave fractions of seconds off everything I do? I'm not an Olympic athlete.

I drive my friends crazy and say let's meet at 5:42 a.m. for a bike ride. I know precisely how much time things take. I can't help but take charge if the skating rink line has an improvement opportunity; I have been known to get the disclaimer forms and pass them out to the folks in line to help speed things along. I dressed my kids in their school clothes after their nightly baths so they could sleep in an extra five minutes. I eat my daily oatmeal and drink my first cup of coffee during my commute while answering emails and listening to an educational program so I can learn.

While grocery shopping, I have my headphones in so that I can listen to a book or podcast and learn while shopping. I have a mental catalogue of all the slow clerks and assess everyone's agility and speed before entering their checkout line. While in line, I'll plow through emails and do my physical therapy foot lifts. At my son's soccer practices and games, I'll get some of my runs in while craning my neck and cheering him on. I pray the rosary if I can't sleep. That way I'm getting some good prayers in while Mother Mary lulls me back to sleep. Playing Yahtzee, I hurry people along by calculating their best moves and the sum of their dice and tell them what they should do as I place the dice back in the cup by the next player. I'm super fun that way. I don't get professional pedicures since it's faster and cheaper if I do it. When I make a big Sunday breakfast, I also prepare my weekly yogurt culture, make homemade soup, and clean as I go.

No wonder I've had to chain myself to my laptop to get this book done. Conversely, I despise people wasting my time. Like, what's up with people walking slowly in a hallway two or three people wide with no regard to others? And why does it take people so much time to decide if it's safe to turn right on red while the traffic in the perpendicular lane traveling the opposite way take left-hand turns. Slow processors, slow drivers, and slow talkers drive me BONKERS.

I have more growing up to do and trust me, God's working on

it. He makes sure my checkout lines have a price check or some lady who wants to write an old-fashioned check.

Life isn't supposed to be a long list of chores we complete. It's meant to be enjoyed and lived. It's not a stream of frenetic motion on a hamster wheel going nowhere. Thank you for your prayers.

I find myself wanting to be more like Mr. Rogers, taking the time to do one thing at a time and leisurely hang up my pink cardigan in the closet where it belongs. I must remind myself of that quote by Kurt Vonnegut that says, "I am a human being, not a human doing."

Back at the mall, eating my deep-fried melted cheese, reminiscent of my beloved Government Cheese, I sat next to a guardian angel on a bench. She looked like a grandma with her white hair and polyester floral top. She broke our shared silence and said, "It sure is nice to take a moment for yourself."

Her words struck me like a lightning bolt. It felt like the roof of the mall had opened up, and a rainbow and doves appeared. I was fully present and said, "It sure is."

I was getting better at taking moments for myself. I've tried meth, alcohol, weed, and pills; they only destroy. I hoped I didn't have to relearn my lesson again. I still didn't call in sick for a mental health day like I should have when my hormones and mind went wonky. I should try that sometime. So many people call in sick for a hangnail, scratchy throat, beer flu or eye trouble. You know, they just can't "see" coming into work. I come in even when I'm on the verge of crapping my pants every hour (and sometimes do).

I got better at asking Frank for help with chores before getting to my breaking point and throwing a big-girl tantrum. He really doesn't mind doing chores. I was becoming myself, the person God intended me to be. But of course, I would screw up again.

Cheerleading Tryouts

I STILL STRUGGLED with doing too much and not setting healthy boundaries, a lifelong lesson of mine. My F-bomb-dropping therapist wisely prescribed two things: a calendar to mark my cycle and to go and do something fun. As if I needed a doctor's order to have fun. I did. I still approached life like one long to do list and didn't savor the journey.

I decided to take dancing classes. I always loved to dance and wanted to be a ballerina. I enrolled in a hip hop and jazz class at the local dance studio and brought some sunshine to my life. My classmates were 12-14 years old. I was the strange older lady in both classes.

After seeing a photo of myself, I was shocked to see how the weight had piled on. My fast metabolism had apparently slowed down, and I could no longer eat whatever I wanted. I'm super sensitive about my small eyes and the extra weight made them look even smaller, and we can't have that.

I stumbled on *The South Beach Diet* book by Arthur Agatston. It said to cut out the carbs for three weeks, so I did. In addition to dancing, I started to jog regularly. I had always loved running in my high school P.E. classes. I didn't realize it at the time, but exercise helped retrain my brain to generate the feel-good chemicals on their own rather than using unhealthy shortcuts. It was so nice to not think about the endless work and home chores when I jogged and danced. I even bought a dance costume and signed up for the recital. Our routine was set to Queen's, "I Want to Break Free." How apropos.

The dance recital happened to be at my church's social center. Many of the school moms saw me since they had their kids in the dance program. I wasn't even embarrassed; I felt proud. I had photos taken at the dance studio like the rest of the teenage girls and ordered a 4x6 for my mom's fridge.

The next week, when I walked in the dance studio to attend class, I saw a stack of flyers for the NBA cheerleader tryouts. I snuck one of the flyers and stuffed it in my gym bag, hoping nobody saw. I was so excited! I always wanted to be a cheerleader. And any time I attended a sporting event, I'd study the cheerleader's moves knowing I could do them too. I really wanted to join them, it looked like a blast.

After I got home and read over the flyer, I decided I would try out for the team. I prepared a routine for tryouts and practiced in my bedroom. I heard Britney Spears did 300 crunches a day for her chiseled abs, so I did that too. I sculpted my body to the best it had ever been, and without drugs this time. I developed a six pack, instead of drinking one.

I asked my crafty mom to bedazzle a red sports bra and black shorts for a uniform. I bought the nude-colored dance shoes, along with the proper stockings and showed up to the tryouts trying to blend in. I'm sure I was the only 35-year-old there and quickly regretted my heavy '80s eyeshadow.

I got the #1 spot, which meant I was the first one of the hundred or so girls to tryout. We all sat on the floor of the arena and stretched. I was so anxious, I decided to climb the stairs to burn off some of my nervous energy. After about twenty minutes, they asked us to line up in order of our numbers. We were told to state our names and something about ourselves. I was handed the microphone and confidently asked, "Can you hear me?" They nodded. I continued, "My name is Mary and I once shared strawberries with Ozzy Osbourne."

It was time for me to do my quick routine to whatever song they chose. They queued the music. I was surprised to hear Rhianna's "Pon de Replay." It caught me off guard by its irregular beat. I did my routine to the beat, best I could, and waited for the others to finish. And then we all sat in the bleachers waiting to see if we made it to the next round. They started dismissing girls by calling out our numbers. Many, who were much better than I, were sent home. Miraculously my number wasn't called. I made it past the first round of cuts and was absolutely thrilled with that outcome. Then it sunk in. There would be no way this working mother of two could commit to dancing at all those games and learn the choreography.

On the next round, we took five minutes to learn a routine that we would dance as a group. I didn't make it; I couldn't remember all the steps. I didn't care. I was so proud of myself for trying out to be a cheerleader and proving to myself that I could have made my junior high or high school team. I also proved to myself that I could add fun to my life by taking time to do things I enjoy, and I ended up having more energy to give to the ones I love. On the way home, I called Frank to brag about the results. I felt unmitigated happiness. I could get used to that.

Project from Heck Made Me Read the Bible

I have told you these things, that in me you may have peace. In the world you have trouble; but cheer up! I have overcome the world.
— John 16:33

I HAD JUST completed a large project from heck. The complex project had tons of issues. I worked many 18-hour days and I swear, those of us who persevered through that project got PTSD from it. There was this one colleague who was especially difficult, a bully. A version of Eddy, only better looking. At times he would wave his arms and make loud false statements as I asked about status, yelling, "We have bent over backwards to give you everything!"

"So you say." I calmly replied.

That made him storm out of the conference room and slam the door. Easily irritated, I'd inevitably mirror his anger and lash back during our exchanges. Of course, I didn't get anywhere with that approach and the whole project was a complete struggle. In retrospect I should have had him removed from the project. I kick myself for not doing that.

I remember sitting in many project meetings where I thought about all that needed to be done. It overwhelmed me. I became nauseous thinking about the enormity of the tasks. I literally wanted to vomit in the corner waste basket. It was all-consuming.

I'm proud to say I didn't lean on any substances during this challenging time. I leaned on the Lord. I prayed. I read parts and pieces of the Bible. The scripture that comforted me the most was John 16:33: "I have told you these things, that in me you may have peace. In the world you have trouble; but cheer up! I have overcome the world." I'd have blissful moments of comfort when I believed God's words.

I still worried constantly about the system. I listened to Dale Carnegie's, *How to Quit Worrying and Start Living* audio book several times on weekends. I enlisted the prayers of the patron saint for this technology. I called vendors on Christmas while lying on my couch with the flu because the system went down.

I fainted from exhaustion one Saturday. As I stood in my kitchen, with my coffee mug in hand, I heard ringing in my ears and the room went black. I fell with my face landing on the coffee mug as it smashed to pieces on the porcelain tile. Frank heard the noise and ran over to me. I was passed out cold on the floor with a sliced chin.

As I came to, I heard Frank yelling, "Dammit Mary, fuck!" He's not the type of guy who gets overly happy or mad. His emotions are usually flatlined, even though his wife has extreme highs and lows. The only strong emotion he ever displayed was anger, and then only in crisis situations, like when one of our kids got hurt. He didn't show fear or sadness. He went straight to anger. It's all he's got in his bag of emotions.

I called the advice nurse and they told us to go to the emergency room. Thankfully, I was fine. I was just doing three jobs at once. My day job, the project manager job, and filling in for a vacant supervisor position. Oh, and trying to be a wife and mom.

The project team members and I worked long days and nights. We got through it, and we still have the scars to prove it. I've got the permanent one on my chin.

After celebrating with my team, I felt like I deserved a reward. I often thought about what I would do with a large lottery jackpot and dreamt of buying a pink car and hiring a housekeeper. Then I thought, what's stopping me from doing it now? I knew immediately how to reward myself. I could legitimately afford a housekeeper to help me twice a month. And I could afford a car payment. Why not make it pink?

Frank found an older pink Mary Kay Cadillac on eBay and bought it for a great price. I dyed my hair pink. I hired a great housekeeper who came twice a month. Life was good. I may not have won the lottery, but I was starting to live my best life, speak up to bullies, and take care of some unfinished childhood business.

I realized it was never too late to give myself a good childhood. People might think it's weird for a grownup to drive a pink car, have pink hair, or wear sparkles and shoes that light up. And it probably is. But like my friend from work says, "Life's too short to not wear sparkles." I couldn't agree more.

Just recently I picked up a couple of shirts from Target in the little girls' section. One had a sparkly rainbow and the other had a sequined star. The girls' section has way cuter clothes at a much cheaper price. The shirts remind me of the sparkly shirts from the '70s and happier times.

I love it when I stumble across a yard sale with old stuff. When I saw a giant wooden spoon and fork at a sale, of course I bought it. Bright-colored vintage dresses? Yes please! Obnoxious glass lamps hanging from chains? Heck yes! I'm trying to redo the '70s and '80s in present time. It's like hitting Edit Undo or Control Z on the keyboard of life and removing the mildew from my past. It's no wonder people say I remind them of a hippy. I'm just catching up. Thanks for not judging me for living out my childhood in my later years.

After the project, I was asked to deliver a speech about retrospective project lessons. I made it fun, and I shared that, on every project, you will find people that you want to work with again, and others that you will want to avoid. That there are no shortcuts to completing a project. To succeed, it requires hard work and persistence over time.

I shared fictitious names for possible team members like, "Logistical Laura." She's the gal who will anticipate what needs to be done and make it happen. People like her are invaluable; they take care of the numerous details that need addressing. And then we have "Does nothing Dora" who works hard at looking busy but adds zero value to the project. And then there's "Trash-talking Tina," my least favorite. She's the one who is just like Does nothing Dora but throws everyone else under the bus to deflect the attention from her, so nobody figures out she's not doing anything.

After that project, anytime my work cell phone rang, my heart raced, I felt anxious, and I immediately thought the system was down again. I decided to change my ringtone so I wouldn't be so easily triggered. It helped.

I needed to regroup and take a moment to have my spirit catch up with my body. I had never taken three weeks off from work, but decided I earned it. And since I was in turbo-speed project mode, I decided to channel that energy and plan a European vacation for my family. Frank and I had already been to Germany a few times since his mom is a lovely German lady, and he has a lot of family back there, so it wasn't too hard to plan. We already had passports.

Before we left, I decided to paint our bedroom a soft shade of Shamrock Shake green to cover up the overpowering hot pink paint. That way I'd have a nice fresh room to come home to after the trip. I always loved that color. It reminded me of the times I spent at Grandma Penny's house when Mom and Dad loved each other. Grandma Penny's walls were painted that shade of green. It took me a solid three-day holiday weekend of non-stop painting, except to grab a quick bite and pass out at night.

We started our trip in Germany. Frank's kind-hearted father and brother met us there. We all stopped for a few days to hang out with Frank's Oma and Uncles. Frank's ability to speak German and translate always amazed me. I couldn't wait to dive in and eat schnitzel and desserts off Oma's fancy plates.

After Germany, we visited Rome, where we saw the Sistine Chapel and many of Michelangelo's works. I learned that Saint Peter, Jesus' rambunctious apostle and our first Pope, was buried under Saint Peter's Basilica. I had no clue.

We took the train to Florence to see Michelangelo's *David* sculpture. When I walked in and saw *David* in all his magnificent splendor, he took my breath away. He is ginormous and stunning, standing center stage in the gallery, with heart-shaped pupils. I loved that Michelangelo answered his call and became one of God's amazing artists. I loved that David was chosen as the anointed king even though he was the scrawny brother nobody ever thought was suitable to be a king. David was just like all of us who feel left out, and he ended up being one of God's favorites, even after he committed adultery. David's story gave me hope.

My family and I ended our trip in the beautiful Cinque Terra. I had always felt guilty for consuming so many books but not making time for the most important book in the universe. The Bible. Seeing all of civilization's rich history and Saint Peter's Basilica inspired me to stop thinking about it and do it. So, when I returned from our trip, I began to read the entire Bible, starting from Genesis. Since then, I've read it three times and counting.

I'm so glad I did. God's Word lives within me and every wise word that has ever been written or will be written is sourced from that holy book. Being closer to Him helps me be more resilient when life smacks me. Or when I smack myself.

After we returned, I interviewed for a promotion, but didn't get the job. I was bummed. I did the rounds and got feedback from key executives. There was this one who said, "Yes, I know you completed that project, but do it again." She continued, "And you're too nice." Huh. Too nice? That part hurt the most. It hurt because I knew there was some truth to it.

I was too nice. I never stood up to Eddy, Misty, or people like them. I wish I would have. I could have stood up more to that colleague and had him replaced, even though I did earn the name, "No-Holding-Back Hughes" during the project. There's always room for improvement. Bullies kept showing up in different sets of skin. God made me retake the class until I got it right.

Some might tell you I have gone a little too far in the speaking up department. I'm decent at it now. I speak my mind. I learned how to say no. I state the unpleasant facts when they need to be stated.

Finding My Passion

Pray as though everything depended on God. Work as though everything depended on you. – Saint Augustine

MY MENTAL STATE was in a much better place now that I had eliminated foreign and illegal substances, hung out with God, read positive books, exercised regularly, and danced. I hardly drank. I was learning how to do life well. My husband and I even liked each other. Things were going so well, I had to find a way to mess it up.

I still tended to not live in the moment and daydream, getting lost inside my head. I obsessed about the next thing I had to get done and only THEN could I relax and have peace. The only problem with that is there was always more to do. It was never ending. My chronic somewhere-else-itis and situational depression decided to pay me another damn visit, and I opened the door, let them in, and served them cocktails.

My husband and I decided to go to Sea Ranch for a week. It was a beautiful spot near the Pacific Coast. We rented a home during spring break and invited my mom and Lionel. After a few days of having fun and taking in the beautiful ocean views, Mom told me that she and Lionel were heading home. It made me sad that she cut the trip short by a few days and didn't plan to stay for Easter. I thought we were all having fun. Her sudden departure made me feel completely and suddenly depressed. I didn't know why.

I later realized it triggered my dormant childhood feelings of abandonment. Here I was with my beautiful family, in a beautiful ocean-view home, and I reverted to a younger Mary, abandoned by her mom and dad. My typical running routine couldn't snap me out of my funk. I decided to read a book. Books have helped my life journey tremendously, more than the sum of five appointments I've had with therapists by this point. And once Mom left, I needed some extra book-support.

I love reading about something that I'm feeling but haven't yet found the vocabulary to articulate. I am so grateful for authors sharing their stories and shooting giant truth darts directly to my heart so I can better understand myself and what I am going through.

This great book was, *Finding Your Own North Star*, by Martha

Beck. I remember feeling even more depressed after reading a few chapters about discovering your essential self and purpose. I slammed the book down and thought, "I don't know my friggin' purpose. I'm not Oprah or Warren Buffet, and I don't love my job." I loved the people I worked with, but this whole showing up to work every day while juggling a multitude of life tasks can just piss you off. The book struck a painful chord in me. Maybe I wasn't answering a call to do something else, but I wasn't ready to accept the call either.

As a Catholic, I pray the rosary and there are different parts of the Gospel we meditate on, depending on the day. No, we don't worship Mary like some people think, but we do ask her to pray for us, like we would ask any of our friends. On Fridays we meditate on the sorrowful mysteries: The Agony in the Garden, The Scourging at the Pillar, The Crowning of Thorns, The Carrying of the Cross, and The Crucifixion.

I made up my own version of the sorrowful mysteries based on my work life. The Agony in the Parking Lot as I coaxed myself out of the car and into the building. The Scourging/Ass-Whooping of unkind remarks during a meeting from a borderline sociopath or narcissist colleague. The Crowning of Middle-Management, where I have some power to make things better, but not enough. The Carrying of Poor-Performers' Burdens and Water along with my own because they're not poor enough in their performance to get fired. And the Crucifixion of all my Hopes and Dreams because I really didn't know if I was climbing the correct career ladder. Sometimes the drudgery of going to work every day could be just too much for this girl.

Mom leaving Sea Ranch early and my ungratefulness, brought on a miniature bout of depression and somewhere-else-itis. How ungrateful I could be sometimes. God gave me more than I ever hoped for, and this was how I thanked Him?

As the weeks passed, I pondered Martha's book. My poet friend Naomi and I reunited and picked up where we left off, dreaming about a different life. We wanted an artist's life, rather than the jobs we had. Surely there was more to life than this.

Naomi taught me the joys of making homemade soaps, lotions, and sugar scrubs. Soon obliging Frank and I were hitting the craft show circuit buying a booth for the local shows. I was trying to escape my 9 to 5 once again, but this time it wasn't Amway.

At the time, my informal therapist, Oprah, was talking about finding your passion. I lied to myself and others that *this* was my passion. It wasn't. Not working a 9 to 5 was my passion. At the time, being somewhere else and discontent was my north star.

The life of a craft show artisan was a ton of work for hardly any pay. I thought it was my ticket out of my job. Don't get me wrong, I was grateful to have benefits, job security, and a paycheck, but my restlessness fueled my fire to try to give this craft show gig a try. I can't believe how much time I spent making soap before dropping the kids off for school, which caused me to be extra grumpy and stressed. What the heck was I thinking? I should've been playing Barbies with Grace or catch with Joey rather than chasing this false passion and making soaps and lotions. I should've applied for a different job than the one I had.

The mornings of weekend craft shows would all feel the same. Every crafter had the look of hope and optimism on their faces. Each crafter silently sized one another up. By mid-day, it was clear who was having a good day and who wasn't by the downcast or elated facial expression. I remember walking a show and asking a fellow crafter about her beautiful figurines. She looked at me like I was a shoplifter and said, "I never give away my secrets." She thought I was going to go home and copy her work. I didn't want to do figurines; I was just the soap lady showing an interest in her lovely work.

I always felt bad for the crafters who didn't have a good show. I knew how much work it was to make your stuff. I knew the disappointment of people walking by without stopping. I knew it was better to not give off a vibe of desperation or hope for a sale; it was best to act aloof and disinterested. I knew that we rarely had an amazingly profitable day.

I folded that business in a year or two after realizing I got paid less than minimum wage for my time. I was better off at my crappy job. Maybe it wasn't so crappy after all. At least I learned how to make soap and still do it for fun.

I was living an incredible life that I should have been thoroughly grateful for. God was still working with the broken pieces of clay-Mary. My flesh wasn't quite there yet, but my spirit was willing.

My boss at the time did me a favor. He gave me thirty minutes to decide if I wanted to keep the job I had or move with a portion of my team to another part of the organization. If I stayed, I would be in the forefront of the hottest technology at the time, which appealed to my ego. If I went, I would take the older technology and move to a different bureau. I prayed about it and flipped a dime. Heads I would stay. Tails I would go.

As I flipped the coin, I heard a voice inside my heart that said, "Take a leap of faith." It was the same voice that told me Frank was marriage material. The coin landed on tails. Much to my surprise, and everyone else's, I took the leap of faith. I called my prospective new boss to get a feel for who he was. I loved him immediately. I took my quieter team members along, and we moved to the other side of the building.

Unbeknownst to me, this would set my career on another path I couldn't have master planned if I'd tried. Just like working for Cherise, I once again had a leadership chain that elevated my skills rather than stifle them. I had leaders who listened to my voice rather than muzzle it. Thanks to my new assignment, I was free to use my project management, people, and results-oriented skills. I wondered why I hadn't jumped ship sooner. I began to love my job.

Pinky Promise

Life is like a buffet, and most poor bastards are starving to death.
– Auntie Mame

I WAS LEARNING to approach life like a delicious buffet that deserved to be sampled. It had been a while since I had a dance class when I ran into a former coworker at Sam's Club. "Hey Rosemary, what are you up to?!"

She beamed with excitement and said, "You'll never believe it, I'm in roller derby." She told me all about her new adventure and showed me photos of her skating. It sounded like a total blast. I had to try it. My love of roller skating, plus the cute and fun outfits she showed me made it seem even better.

By then I was training for my first half marathon after asking one of the school moms about the 13.1 sticker on her car. She told me she trained for a half marathon and recently completed it. I told her there was no way I could run that far. She looked me in the eyes and said, "Mary, you can totally do it." I believed her, copied her training plan, and went for it. I did a triathlon shortly after. She was right, I *could* do it.

I took down Rosemary's information and the date of tryouts. When I got home, I approached Frank. "Honey, there's something fun I want to do, and I really need your support."

Frank got that look on his face like, "Oh no, what now?" He did not enjoy being the guy who had to drop off and pick up my bicycle or kayak, and then wait for me at the various athletic events. He preferred to spend his weekends restoring old cars.

"I really want to do roller derby and if I get on the team, I'll need more of your help at home so I can attend practices and games."

He agreed. He knows me. When I get fixated on something, there's no stopping me. He doesn't call me "Extreme Mary" for nothing.

In a few weeks it was time to show up to tryouts. I drove to the roller rink, thirty miles away from our house. A bunch of college girls and adventurous moms like me wore colorful clothes and used bandanas to hold back our hair. I wore bright blue shorts and a hot pink shirt, and my newly purchased knee and elbow pads. I borrowed skates and a helmet from the skating rink.

After skating a bunch of drills and laps, tryouts were done. The coaches had us gather in a circle and announced who made the team-in-training.

I got on the team!

OK, they took everyone. We were called, "fresh meat" since we were the new girls. The coaches told us, "It's like football on skates, and some of you will break a bone or two."

Team practices were 9 p.m. to 11 p.m. twice a week, a schedule great for college-aged girls, but not awesome for us thrill-seeking moms. I showed up to every damn one. The heavily tattooed coaches told me I showed promise as a Jammer with my fast and nimble skating abilities. A Jammer is the one who wears a star on her helmet, and skates fast to avoid the opposite team who wants to knock us down. The goal is to earn points by lapping the "pack" of the other team.

A few months later, as I was skating warmup laps before my graduation bout, a referee flailed out of control behind me. I didn't see him coming. I hit the floor hard, face and arm first. His ginormous body landed on top of me. He must have been six feet something and two hundred pounds. The worst part was he didn't even say SORRY or help me up. The coward just skated away.

I got up and knew something was wrong with my arm. I tried to find some ice at the snack bar, but the coaches asked us to line up and prepare for our bout to see if we could earn our place on an official game roster. So much for the ice.

I lined up and did my graduation bout trying to pass girls who wanted to pummel me while protecting my aching arm. I fell a couple more times thanks to some skilled blocks.

After our bout, they gathered us around to share our results. I passed! I was so happy to graduate from fresh meat to a real team. I couldn't wait to wear my official uniform. I picked my derby name, "Pinky Promise" and chose the number 3:16 as in John 3:16. Pinky Swears was my first choice but it was already taken.

I couldn't sleep that whole night from the pain in my right arm. I lay in bed waiting for morning to come so I could get an appointment. There was no way I'd sit in the emergency room for four hours.

The x-ray showed my arm was broken in two places. They put my arm in a hot pink cast and gave me a sling.

After nine months of spending way too much time attending practices, games, and charitable events without being put on a roster, I decided I was better off doing sports that didn't routinely break players' bones. And roller derby politics were more complicated than office politics.

Actor's Studio

I STILL HAD a nagging dream to become an actress. I squashed that dream long ago, thinking there was no way I would succeed.

I didn't want to have unfinished business before I left earth, so I signed up for classes through a Groupon. I wasn't as good as I remembered, and I hadn't used that muscle that was so effortless when I was a kid. Plus, it was awkward trying to pretend to be the wife of a 70-year-old dude from class. The worst part was sitting in class waiting for my turn way past bedtime. Once my Groupon expired, it was going to cost me $220 a month. I was too frugal to keep paying to lose more sleep.

My itch for acting got scratched and I realized it required too much waiting around. That was pure torture for me. Maybe in an alternate universe I would have been an actress. My doppelganger Renee Zellweger is amazing, and the industry doesn't need two of us. God made a good life for me despite me not realizing my dreams of being an actress or ballerina.

I sometimes wonder if Dad hadn't left, what life I might be living now. Would I be the actress or dancer that I dreamt of being? Or would I work in technology? Would I have children and a good husband? Who knows? I'm glad I can pick my nose, have cellulite and existential crises, and not end up on the front page of *The Enquirer*.

Maybe if I realized those dreams, I would've had more nervous breakdowns, and shaved off my eyebrows in a Kmart bathroom, or got a forehead tattoo. I'm glad my slow-mo breakdowns didn't make headlines. I'm glad I have a husband who sticks with me rather than romping with his gorgeous co-stars. I'm not sure I would have handled bigtime success well.

What I do know is that I am grateful for my now simple and happy life. I'm thankful I keep showing up to my everyday obligations and continue to learn lessons despite my depressive detours. It certainly has given me peace and happiness making myself useful and doing some good in this world.

Auntie Raven Came Back

AROUND THE TIME of my acting adventure, Auntie Raven left her husband for good. She showed up at Grandma Lou's house claiming that it was her turn to help.

Mom had taken care of Grandma's finances, doctor's appointments, TV remote issues, and any confusing paperwork. I was in charge of Grandma's benefit paperwork, Darlene's finances, and keeping Grandma supplied with audio books. Uncle Bruce, Auntie Eleanor, and the rest of us helped maintain Grandma's yard. I was appointed Darlene's official guardian according to the Veteran's Affairs, even though she still lived with Grandma.

We knew that, at some point, Grandma wouldn't be around, and someone would need to take care of Darlene. Frank and I were prepared to do that. Grace, Joey, and I often visited Grandma Lou and Darlene, taking them shopping at Walmart and Kmart. Grandma always kept us well fed with her homemade soups and her famous "Grandma's Crappy Goulash." It tasted heavenly.

When Auntie showed up out of the blue, the whole family was suspicious of her motives, but we let her move in with Grandma and Aunt Darlene. Auntie Raven didn't have a car and looked sober from the outside.

I took Auntie Raven out for an ice cream cone one day. She repeated several times how much she really wanted to help Grandma, that it was her turn to help. She shared that she had recently kicked an OxyContin habit. Always skeptical of Auntie, I hoped she meant what she said.

A couple weeks later, Auntie called, "Hey, can you spare $10 bucks? I want to take a break and go shoot some pool."

"Sure, I'll be right over!" I happily drove to Grandma's and handed her the money. It seemed innocent enough.

While there, I noticed Auntie was ignoring our instructions for Grandma's diet requirements. "Here, try this." Auntie generously dipped a salty cracker in a tub of flavored cream cheese and fed it to Grandma. Grandma didn't mind the snacks. Problem was, Grandma had diabetes and congestive heart failure. Salt and sugar were a no-no.

Before Auntie Raven arrived back on the scene, we took turns taking Grandma shopping. We carefully read the labels and made sure Grandma had healthy choices.

I peeked in Grandma's cupboards and saw high sodium canned goods, chips, and cookies.

"Auntie, we really need to watch what Grandma eats. No salt or sugar. OK?"

"Yeah, yeah, I know."

Soon, Auntie started going to the grocery store by herself. Grandma let her take her ATM card and pick up whatever cravings they had. I had online access to Grandma's bank account to help her pay bills and watched her funds dwindle after Auntie Raven showed up. I told Mom, "Auntie is going to the store a couple of times a day. I think she's taking cash withdrawals each time."

After meeting a new boyfriend at the local bar, Auntie Raven started using meth in addition to her usual pot. Her volatile moods and her uncontrollable screaming and yelling gave her away. I heard it for myself when I called Grandma on the phone one Sunday. It sounded like there was a maniac in the house. Auntie Raven regressed to her usual drug abusing, thieving self.

Darlene ended up so ill from the stress of Auntie's "caretaking" that she was hospitalized and had to be placed in a nursing home. Auntie Darlene could no longer go to the bathroom by herself and had uncontrollable diarrhea. The hospital tried to put her in a facility a hundred miles away. Leah fought hard to get Darlene in a local nursing home so we could all easily visit.

Grandma was distraught. Mom and I knew Auntie Raven had to go. Immediately. We should have made her leave sooner and we were mad at ourselves for allowing Auntie back in. Auntie had proven many times she couldn't be trusted. Why would this time have been any different? She needed rehab and therapy.

The next morning, Mom and I showed up to Grandma Lou's house and Mom ordered Auntie Raven out. To help get rid of her without police, we signed over Grandma's Toyota to Auntie. Grandma Lou couldn't drive any longer due to her failing eyesight and didn't need a car anymore. With Darlene in the nursing home, Grandma Lou wasn't doing well either. Shortly after Auntie Raven left, Grandma Lou got sick and ended up in the hospital.

A couple weeks later, Grandma Lou was improving, and the doctors suggested a pacemaker. I remember visiting Grandma Lou in the hospital before her procedure. It was the Fall of 2009. For some reason, I couldn't stop sobbing as I snuggled with her on her hospital bed. The nurses came in and saw me sobbing and told me, "Don't worry honey, everything will be fine. It's a routine procedure."

My soul knew something the nurses didn't. Grandma quickly deteriorated after that procedure and died five days later while Auntie Eleanor, Uncle Bruce and I were at her bedside. My favorite lady was gone. She was my faithful buffer during the worst times of my life. I could easily have been like Auntie Raven if I hadn't had Grandma's positive influence.

I went into project mode and planned Grandma's funeral. It was a graveside service with close family and friends, with a Catholic priest. Auntie Raven didn't attend; it would be years before we heard from her again. I wrote and read a poem for Grandma's funeral.

Chance and his wife hosted the family after the service. Chance made a lovely slideshow tribute to our family matriarch and rock.

I made sure Darlene could leave her nursing home to attend the funeral. That meant I had to help her use the restroom and call on my brother's three handsome strapping young boys to help, since I couldn't lift her myself.

I returned to work and carried my sadness with me. As Frank and I drove home from work one day, it was raining. We noticed a car just like Grandma's old gray 1985 Ford Taurus. We were surprised that jalopy could still run. A rainbow appeared in the sky. Grandma was saying hello and letting us know she was fine. Rainbows now always mean Grandma's saying hi.

Job from Heck

ONE OF MY dear colleagues whom I adore got a promotion and her job from heck became vacant. Hillary liked a challenge and could handle tough assignments. She warned me, "YOU DO NOT WANT THAT JOB!" I could trust what she said so there was no way I'd apply.

That week my boss asked me to take her job. He told me that it would make me competitive for the next level. I politely told him no. He pleaded. I told him I'd pray about it.

I prayed about it and my initial answer was confirmed. The next day I called my boss. "Thanks for thinking of me, I appreciate the opportunity. But it's still a no."

A couple days later, it was no longer a request. I had a new job.

It was nearly three years of heck. Truly the hardest assignment of my entire career. I experienced stranger-than-fiction situations that I cannot put in writing. For my troubles, I was recognized with an exceptional leadership award, and a handsome glass statue.

The night before the leadership-award ceremony, I got body aches, a fever, and chills. I really thought I should power through and show up to collect my award. I thought people would think I was a slacker if I were a no-show for the ceremony. I deliriously tossed and turned and kept changing my mind. I didn't get out of bed and felt guilty for weeks that I didn't show up. In retrospect, I'm certain nobody cared.

The assignment was extremely frustrating and did not make my home life great. I had no energy to give to my husband or children. I was running on fumes once again, and we know that's not a good recipe for anyone, especially me.

I still allowed myself cocktails after I kicked my weed habit.

My drink of choice was now a lemon drop martini. Only on the weekends, and just a couple. Or four. Then it became Thursdays through Sundays. Thursday was almost the weekend, right? Then it became just vodka with a capful of cranberry juice. I knew I was in dangerous territory with alcohol. I'd been down that road before. I made a mental note to give it up for Lent. That was four months away.

I finally put my foot down at home. I told my husband he could not wake me up at 4 a.m. to make sure his three times a week marital embrace quota was met. He's got a lot of great qualities but like everyone, he's not perfect. Truth is, he can be a real a-hole when he doesn't get enough. Being a working mom, that duty was a low priority for me. But I was excellent at completing all the things on my to-do lists.

Through the years, I thought Frank's needs trumped my need for sleep. And I didn't want to deal with cranky Franky. I was fed up with work and fed up with Frank's voracious appetite. Most of all, I was angry at myself for not implementing reasonable sleep boundaries on day one of our marriage.

Why didn't I? On some level I still felt like he would leave me if I didn't meet my quota. It's what I figured happened to Mom. I thought unconditional love didn't really exist unless I was giving my body to my man. After seventeen years of marriage and sleep deprivation, I understood why Lorena Bobbitt cut off her husband's penis.

Frank proved my hypothesis correct one morning. After drawing my sleep boundaries, he woke up before I did on a workday. Likely insane from his unsatisfied morning wood, Frank woke me up and said, "I think we should divorce so at least we can still be friends."

I went from half asleep to shell-shocked. I thought, "Um, what in the actual hell, did he just say that? Where did that come from? I knew it. Everyone leaves. Of course, he would too."

My long-held theory was proven correct. He only loved me if I was achieving his metrics. He had never been the type of guy who expressed his feelings and it always made me suspicious. Like he was keeping secrets from me. I thought the years of him not vocalizing his feelings might backfire one day. I hadn't yet read, *Men are from Mars, Women Are from Venus* by John Gray. This was it. I said nothing to Frank, but thought, "OK, now what?"

We both showered and did our pre-work routine. We carpooled to work in silence. My mind went into project management mode. We'll need to sell the house, get our own places, divide the contents and assets, and tell the kids. I got through my workday. That night I researched what to do when your husband wants a divorce. My search results told me to not beg for him to come back. To accept it. Maybe he would come to his senses and maybe he wouldn't. But if you beg, chances were that it wasn't going to work out. Kind of like selling soap at a craft fair. Act nonchalant.

A funny thing happened. I didn't need to act nonchalant. I accepted it. My worst fears were here, and I was still alive. I thought, "I'm a pretty good catch. A little crazy, yes, but worth it. Maybe I'll stay single and enjoy my quieter life. I'll get some more peace and the best sleep of my life. This might not be so bad."

That night as I got ready for bed, I asked Frank, "How do you want to deal with the house?"

"I don't know what you're talking about."

"Remember, we're getting a divorce?"

"Don't be silly. I didn't mean it."

"WHAT THE FUCK!!!! HOW COULD YOU SAY THAT, AND LET ME GO THE WHOLE DAY THINKING THIS WAS IT? YOU MUST HAVE MEANT IT DEEP DOWN!"

He brushed the whole thing off. I was beyond livid and stayed that way.

As the weeks followed, I kept bringing it up, trying to get this man of few words to share his innermost thoughts. He insisted he didn't mean it. Each time I brought it up, I got fired up like it was yesterday. He maintained he didn't mean it. That's when I said, "If you're going to ultimately leave, GO!"

After going around this mountain a few times, he finally admitted, "Someone needed a wake-up call."

"Oh really!? You're trying to teach me a lesson, like you're my parent? So, you're saying your love is conditional. That you'll only stay married as long as you are getting enough?!"

He tried to calm me down. "No. I don't need it. We don't have to do it anymore."

"All I ever thought I had to offer a man was my body, and you're no different." I started convulsing and sobbing and couldn't stop.

He hugged me. I've trained him that it's best to just hug me during my meltdowns.

I know healthy marriages have a healthy sex life. I know libidos never match up. His was much stronger when we were younger. And mine is finally catching up. Real funny, God. Frank's happiness ingredients consist of food, classic cars, and sex. It pissed me off when I surveyed other ladies for their stats, and it was like one or two times a month. Why did I have to be an overachiever in everything? OK, who am I kidding? I barely cook.

Usually, Frank's needs are taken care of and so are mine. But it's no longer an anxious let me check the box and make sure I met my quota for the week. And yes, he has too many cars and often cooks.

After 28 years with Frank, I know real love isn't a feeling, otherwise nobody would stay married. Real love is extending oneself for the benefit of the other, even when you don't feel like it. Love is patient, kind, true, unselfish and bears all things (Corinthians 13:4-7).

I don't have a pretty bow to tie on this story. Life is messy and so is marriage. I know I'm supposed to forgive completely. And I have more work to do on this particular matter. I've always had this cloud of divorce hanging over, and this certainly didn't help. Sometimes we slide back several spaces on the marriage gameboard. But I'm in it for the long game. I think he is too.

Mom's Back in the Hospital

MOM HAD BEEN near death's door several times. She was a fighter and always got better. I got used to driving to the hospital when my mom couldn't breathe. This time, I was chatting on the phone with Lionel when I heard her yell in the background, "Call 911!" She couldn't breathe again because of her COPD. I had a hunch I couldn't trust Lionel to dial 911 correctly. I was right. He called 411. Thankfully, Mom made it to the hospital that time and got back on track.

A couple months later, Mom got the flu, and it wasn't good. She was admitted to the hospital to get her heart and lungs stable. Unknown to everyone but Mom and Lionel, she swapped her unlimited Vicodin prescription for two bottles of red wine each night. She reunited with her old addiction, and it was not going well.

Over the years, I had thought it was okay to offer wine when I hosted Easter or Thanksgiving. She seemed to have a healthy relationship with alcohol. Mom had decreased her visits and didn't want to stay long at family events. She was more of a recluse than ever. I hadn't realized it was because she needed her alcohol fix.

I can't believe how naïve I was. Intellectually I knew once an alcoholic, always an alcoholic. I knew that alcoholism is a progressive disease. Those words had never sunk in before, but soon made sense. Once she took the first drink, she progressively got worse like any addict. It was a ticking time bomb.

I found Mom's hospital room. She seemed OK, wearing oxygen tubes in her nostrils.

"Hi Mom!"

"Hi honey."

"You doing OK?"

"Fine."

After a few minutes of me chatting about work, kids, the weather—anything to avoid uncomfortable silence, her eyes narrowed and darkened. The mean alcoholic version of Mom appeared. She launched surprisingly cruel words my way and I felt so small and helpless. I can't recall what she said, but I'll never forget the look in her eyes. I regressed to my scared eight-year-old self. Thoughts raced through my head. I thought that version of Mom was long gone. Now 40, I didn't have to stick around and put up with this bullshit.

I didn't realize she was experiencing delirium tremens from alcohol withdrawals. I didn't realize she was on death's door. I just couldn't deal with that nightmare version of Mom. I left the hospital as soon as I could, shocked by what happened.

After I got home, she became unresponsive. She couldn't breathe on her own and was intubated. Alcoholism + COPD + Crohn's + Chronic Depression = NOT GOOD.

Lionel and I traveled to the hospital together each day. I had stopped drinking during Lent like I promised myself and God. To calm my nerves, I munched on my beloved hard-shelled Cadbury milk chocolate eggs on the drive over. Mom was non-responsive for several days and we kept vigil and watched the skilled nurse suction out her lungs. It looked like she was hurting mom; my body cringed in discomfort.

After five days, the doctors told us the longer Mom was intubated, the less likely she would be able to breathe on her own. They said we needed to try and extubate her. Uncle Bruce, Auntie Eleanor, Lionel, and I were there. We said our prayers.

They gently pulled the tube out. We watched Mom's heart and

oxygen monitor. Mom took a breath. And another. We held ours. The hospital staff seemed satisfied. Mom pulled through! When she finally got the energy to speak, Mom told me that while she was intubated, the nurse was trying to kill her. I went along with it, knowing Mom was probably hallucinating.

After a couple more days, Mom left the ICU. Monica and I came to visit her after work. I snuggled with Mom in her hospital bed and approached the elephant in the room, staring straight ahead and said, "I'm never drinking again." I wanted to see what she'd say.

"I'm not either."

That was the end of our conversation.

Mom got well enough to attend our Easter celebration. She still needed her oxygen tank, but that was expected. I was like Martha from the Bible frantically preparing the meal, working in the kitchen when I really should have savored being with Mom, kneeling beside her, and just being with her like Mary did with Jesus. Mom was happy to eat my cheesy, mayonnaise-laden artichoke dip and I was happy to nourish her 80-pound body. Mom asked me to plan a future visit and give her a haircut.

A few days later, Mom was back in the hospital with breathing trouble. I visited her. The doctor at the time came in and said, "I'm sorry. There's nothing we can do." And walked out, leaving me there holding a live grenade.

I wished he would've said something that gave us hope. I sat on Mom's bed with her. She had her TV on. She received her hourly breathing treatments. I sobbed. My soul knew something I didn't want to fully admit. I texted Chance and Leah telling them they should come visit Mom soon. Stupid me decided to leave and get my grocery shopping done, always trying to squeeze in another chore. As I got up to leave, Mom said, "Grampa is going to get paranoid. Help him with the bills, you know where my passwords are. And be nice to Frank."

I didn't think much of her words at the time. Lionel aka Grampa often thinks people are out to get him and is prone to conspiracy theories. A few years earlier, he stopped talking to Frank. He had it in his mind that Frank said, "Lionel is stupid," while they worked on a cement-pour project. Frank would never say anything like that. So, Lionel, once Frank's best friend, abruptly stopped talking to him.

I planned to visit Mom the next morning, thinking my brother and sister would soon visit. That night Lionel called. He sounded like he was crying. "The hospital called. She's refusing her breathing treatments."

"I'm leaving now. You coming with me?"

"I can't see her like that."

I hung up and rushed to get my purse and keys and said to my family, "I gotta go!"

"Mom, I want to go," Grace insisted.

"Honey, I don't want you to see Grandma like this."

"Mom, I can take it, I'm old enough."

Remembering I hadn't been allowed to see my grandpa or Uncle John on their deathbeds but wished I had been, I relented. Grace was almost 14. Frank and Joey stayed home.

I sped to the hospital while Grace helped me call Chance and Leah to tell them to meet us there. I dialed my priest. He didn't answer. I felt like such an idiot for not calling him earlier. If anyone needed the anointing of the sick months ago, it was Mom.

Once parked, Grace and I ran to the ICU and found Mom. I wondered where Chance and Leah were; they lived much closer to the hospital than me. There was Mom, sitting up in the hospital bed, convulsing and gasping for air, unable to talk, her whole body desperately fighting to get oxygen. I yelled towards the nursing station, "Get her treatment now!"

Mom couldn't respond, but I felt her yell a resounding, "NO!" telling me she didn't want to be saved.

A minute later, her body stopped trying to breathe.

Mom died.

My tears wouldn't stop. I couldn't catch my breath. The weight of everything hit. She's freaking gone!

I felt the sorrow of losing the many versions of Mom. The one before Dad left, the mean one and the one after she got sober. I was also sad for losing the mom I wished I had, the one who would have put me in ballet classes, made sure I tried out for cheerleading and protected me from bullies.

It's indescribable the pain of losing Mom. She was my life-support in and out of utero, even when it wasn't ideal. She was my mom. The one I bitched to about Leah and life.

Leah and Chance walked in seconds later and joined Grace and me in our convulsive sobbing. They had the extra heartbreak of not making it in time.

Chance was waiting for Leah in the parking lot, and to this day, he beats himself up for not visiting Mom earlier that day or making it to her room in time. My efficiency paid off that evening.

I must've asked because a local priest came and anointed Mom's dead body. She was wearing the brown scapular I gave her. The scapular necklace is supposed to give us heavenly help. Mom died on the eve of Divine Mercy Sunday, a week after Easter. I repeatedly prayed, "God, please make sure she's in heaven with Grandma. In Jesus' name, Amen." Dang, I miss my mom.

A few days later, I sat in my backyard alone with my broken heart, praying that Mom was in heaven with Grandma Lou, and regretting that I hadn't cut her hair like she'd asked. Suddenly two large yellow butterflies flew so close to my nose they freaked me out. I instinctively shooed them away with my hands.

And then I remembered that Mom's favorite color was yellow, and I knew that she and Grandma were letting me know that all was well. I wished I had let the butterflies land on me. Leah and I planned Mom's funeral and I read the poem I wrote for her.

Everyone came to my house after her graveside service. Jimmy pointed out the yellow butterfly hanging out by the yellow rose bush Auntie Eleanor and Uncle Bruce brought for me. I decided yellow butterflies meant Mom was saying hi.

I replayed the day mom died, and I beat myself up for going grocery shopping. I remembered her last words to me, "Be nice to Frank." She must've seen herself in me and how I treat Frank. I think she didn't want me to replay her life, driving a decent man away, inviting future pain into everyone's lives. Good parting advice, Mom. Frank's the guy God picked out for me. God knows what he's doing and can pick a way better marriage partner, even though it took too long for me to realize that.

I was listening to an artist's interview when I had an epiphany. He said that artists need their alone time before creativity kicks in and visits. I realized how fitting it was that I married a man who allows me so much of that. At first, I broke up with him when he wasn't "enthusiastic enough about this relationship," then got over it. Then seven years into marriage I cursed him again for not being a conversationalist or poet. But God knew what I needed in a life partner all along. Frank tinkers on his cars while I do my creativity thing and often live inside my head.

In the hustle of raising children and running on the treadmill of life, it's hard to get in touch with your true self. But Lord willing, there's time for that later. I didn't think I liked to be alone. I was always on the go, hanging with friends when I was younger, escaping The House of Death, running away from being still and allowing my feelings to catch up with me.

Now I treasure my alone time. I get plenty of social activity at work. Too much really. I remember having a job where I trained people on how to build websites and would basically collapse at home after teaching all day and pouring myself out. Who knew this outgoing girl was a severe introvert and required space to think and create rather than a hubby who was all up in her lime-flavored Kool-Aid?

I remembered telling Mom I was no longer drinking while she lay in the hospital. I didn't realize it at the time, but I made a deathbed promise. I decided I'd better break the alcoholism cycle too and not tempt fate. It was easier that way. I am my mom on so many levels. My siblings say I look and sound like her. Sometimes when I say words out loud, I hear her voice coming out of me.

Watching Mom's life was like hitching a ride in a time machine for mine. It's a 23-year advance look into my future if I make the same choices she did. I've already followed a portion of her path, with similar results. That realization helped me to forgive her because I too need forgiveness. I can be exactly like Mom.

I knew my future if I kept up my unhealthy vodka routine. I am an addict. Mom was an addict. And a ton more of my relatives are addicts. Heck, I'm sure 80% of us are addicted to something. I drank more than I should, and not for the right reasons. I drank to make my difficult feelings and days go away.

Mom's lack of sobriety near the end of her life sealed the deal for my complete sobriety. Her example and self-inflicted alcohol imprisonment led me to my freedom. Her death helped me live. I hope this serves as a warning for my children and future grandchildren to not lean on chemicals of any kind, but to take care of oneself, and press through the pains of life by leaning on the Lord, breathing, and finding joy in the simple things. If I can do it, anyone can.

I wondered if Mom wanted to die alone like a cat does. She loved her cats. I had no idea she had declined her breathing treatments after I left the hospital to go grocery shopping. She must have decided she was done fighting. She was stubborn like that.

I'm glad I told her, "I love you on earth and I love you in heaven" that day. I had no clue I was saying goodbye when I hurried out of the hospital to do my shopping. I had no idea how big that moment was until later. I wish I would have stayed by her side, knowing that groceries and chores could wait. What a dumb ass.

Mom probably wanted it that way—to die alone. She didn't want to trouble anyone. When sober, she knew how to give so much that she ended up hastening her death. I remember her hosting Thanksgiving for the last time, ending up in the hospital and nearly dying from her Crohn's. She said she wasn't feeling well but I brushed it off and didn't offer to host. It finally made me realize that I needed to take over hosting Thanksgiving and Easter and to believe Mom when she said she wasn't feeling well.

For years, Mom still watched my kids after school despite her pain. She told me many times that I needed to slow down, or I was going to burn out. She was speaking from experience and could see herself in me.

Mom wasn't good at receiving, and she felt like she wasn't enough. I learned from her example. When we'd stay at the Ritz during my sister's abundance, I'd watch my mom walk through the crowds saying, "Excuse me. Pardon me. Sorry," every five seconds as if she too didn't feel like she had the right to occupy any space on the sidewalk, let alone in this world. When did our apologies for living begin? When did it become an issue to exist in this world and think we were always in the way of other people living their lives? Why didn't we feel that we had value and a right to take up space on earth? Why were we overly concerned with the comfort of others at the expense of our own? When did we demote ourselves to less than human?

I realized we should all make space for one another and be kind as we intersect with each other. A simple smile will do, or "Pardon," is all we need. Every single one of us was breathed into existence by Our heavenly Father. He knitted every one of us and loves us as His all-time favorite kid. We all have a God-given right to take our place in this world along with our brothers and sisters.

I'm sad that Mom won't get to see her grandchildren marry. I'm sad I didn't have a better childhood. I'm sad that she was sad about her choices. She replayed her dad's life patterns. He drank too much, and he died at 64 too. At least she doesn't have to struggle anymore.

I fully intend to make good on my promise to not drink. I saw how easily that slippery slope could lead to bad things. I believe weed is the devil's lettuce and alcohol is the devil's nectar. At first, I missed alcohol. After a hard week, during vacations and holidays. But I never missed the bad sleep or getting up multiple times to pee. I didn't miss waking up with swollen eyes and a stuffy nose and feeling lousy. I'd rather have healthier organs and take my excess calories in homemade baked goods anyway. This is my 10th year of alcohol sobriety and I'm planning on living beyond 64, Lord willing.

I Guess I'm a Thief

Mom was right. Lionel was paranoid. I didn't realize how bad it was until a few weeks after Mom died.

I offered to help Lionel take care of the bills. He never trusted computers. I walked him through every computer screen narrating what I was doing. The bills got paid and I thought we were cool. A few days later I heard from Chance.

"Grampa says you stole a bottle of bourbon from the house while you paid the bills."

"Why would I do that? Mom probably drank it."

A few weeks later Leah called, "Grampa thinks you stole $40,000."

"What the hell?! Where does he come up with this stuff?"

I was now public enemy number one and Lionel was so convinced, that for a moment, Chance believed it might be true. Soon Leah was public enemy number two for trying to talk some sense into Lionel. I'm guessing Lionel thought he had more money in the bank. Mom had been in charge of paying the bills and was never great with money. But somehow, I was the scapegoat.

Lionel decided to move into a retirement community and have more of a social life. Pissed at Leah and me, Lionel decided Chance would now inherit his home and property rather than split it three ways. Chance began to make plans to sell his current home and move in.

Shortly after my alleged thieving, my family and I returned from a trip. I was greeted with a pile of Mom's clothes left on my kitchen table. Lionel must've placed it there. I loved the smell of that pile and I kept some of it so I could remember Mom. Leah and I were not allowed to go through Mom's belongings or retrieve our kids' favorite toys.

Chance and his wife helped Lionel move his belongings to his new neighborhood where all the attractive widows lived. Right before moving in, Lionel manufactured another story and accused Chance and his wife of stealing a box of paperwork from him. So now Chance and his wife were on the outs. Lionel stopped talking to all of us. I think his grief made his brain go into overdrive with conspiracy theories.

One of Lionel's friends, Igor, bought the house for a song and kept my mom's hummingbird feeder even though he overheard me requesting it. I instantly disliked Igor because of it.

I mailed Lionel a Christmas card that year and he returned the card. I kept sending cards every year along with recent school photos of the kids.

A few years went by, and Lionel reached out to Chance. He asked if he was in jail. Chance didn't understand the question, but Lionel said that the police had called, and he wired $10K to make sure Chance could get out of jail. Chance told him that he wasn't in jail, nor was he in trouble.

Chance realized Lionel had been the victim of one of those telephone scams. The perpetrators make you think they're the police and put someone pretending to be your kid on the phone for confirmation. It puts the victim in the fight or flight part of their brain which makes them not think clearly and do something stupid like wire $10K.

Chance and Lionel set aside the past and rekindled their relationship. I started to call Lionel and give him updates on Grace and Joey. He was kind to me and never said anything about the purported bourbon or the $40k theft. He'd save that for his conversations with everyone else.

Auntie Raven Visits

I WAS HOSTING a backyard barbeque for my son's friends and their parents. One of my friends came up to me with a look of concern saying, "There's a lady out front here to see you." I put away my plate of tri-tip and walked out front and saw a tiny woman. It took me a moment to process who I was seeing.

Auntie Raven had been driven to my house by her former coworker who felt sorry for her. Auntie Raven spoke rapidly and said, "You look just like your mother—I have so much to tell you. I've been going in deep to save women from human trafficking.

You wouldn't believe it Mary." She started sobbing and pointed to her teeth "Look, I even lost all of my teeth and some of my hair."

She took off her bandana and showed a large bald spot on the top of her head. "I'm saving women from human trafficking. It's worth it if I save even one of them." She handed me a note written on binder paper folded like a middle school note and said, "I will talk to you later; you have a party to get back to."

I was shocked by her appearance. It all happened so fast, I believed what she said. After she left, logic kicked in. I knew intimately what prolonged meth use looked like and it looked like Auntie Raven. I read the note and it was a bunch of nonsense. I saw one of my church friends out front who happened to witness the whole encounter. He was also a police officer. "What just happened?" I asked.

"That's called drug-induced psychosis," he said.

Once all my guests left and I got my kitchen clean, I reached out to my cousin to let her know of her mom's recent visit. She explained that her mom did too many drugs one night and thought she was getting chased by a werewolf and got herself booked on a 5150. At some point during that night, she lost her teeth and her hair caught on fire, causing second degree burns. My cousin said she was limiting her contact with her mom since she threatened her and her children. I decided not to call the phone number on the note Auntie Raven handed me. But darn, Auntie remembered where I lived.

Several months later Auntie Raven showed up at my house again. I pulled into my driveway with my family. We noticed a small girl in our front yard. Upon closer inspection, I realized it was Auntie Raven, with grocery bags full of her belongings. I said, "Hi Auntie."

"Can I jump in your pool and sleep in your yard?"

My people-pleasing tendencies almost got the better of me. I wanted to say yes. Instead, I said, "You can take a shower and I'll make you a plate of food and get you some clean clothes."

My family and I watched Auntie Raven pace inside our house and listened to her unwell monologue, "You hear that airplane? They're following me. I'm going to meet with the Governor tomorrow. I'm going to fly to Philadelphia to rewrite the constitution. I have a large gold nugget and I'm setting up a conservancy for the family."

My wide-eyed kids watched her pace back and forth and listened to her nonsensical monologue.

As she showered, I asked Frank, "What are we going to do?"

"She's not staying here. We can drive her to the motel and pay for a night."

After she ate her plate of macaroni and cheese and meatloaf, I said, "I'll be happy to take you to the motel a few miles away and pay for a night's stay."

She agreed and walked out front to put her things in my trunk. As she waited out front, I didn't realize Frank told her, "I don't know what kind of lifestyle you're living, but we have kids and you're not welcome to ever come back here."

Auntie Raven had been smart, gorgeous and a voracious reader. She preferred to take shortcuts in life and not follow through on her responsibilities. Being the last of six children, there wasn't much parenting left in my grandparents and she was permitted to drop out of school at 16 and get married. The marriage lasted a month or so. I thought back to the time she visited Mom's house when Grandpa was dying. She and Mom were having such a good time as I got ready for school. I'm glad Mom knew better than to let me play hooky.

Later, seeing how Auntie Raven's life ended up, I realized that staying home and partying instead of fulfilling your obligations and keeping a job does not make for a happy life. Delaying gratification and being disciplined does.

On the drive over, I asked, "Are you getting any help?"

She started to get agitated, and I could feel the mood shift in the car. She was on the verge of getting violent. I drove faster. She was defensive and shot back, "I'm fine!"

At the motel's front desk Auntie Raven paced behind me. I'm guessing she needed more of her drug. I paid cash at the front desk because I had no idea what she might do to the room and didn't want my name traced to it. She yelled something at me as I drove away. I was relieved to get the heck out of there.

When I got home, Frank told me what he had said. I'm sure that played into her sudden mood shift. I was sad to see Auntie so far gone, but also grateful that my teenage kids got to see firsthand how drugs destroy a life and an intelligent mind. Auntie Raven's visit was better than any "Don't do drugs" lecture I could have given. I pray they don't choose that route and often warn them of the addict gene their mom and family have.

Part VI – Grow Up Already

Thank God for Having to Show up to a Job

For even when we were with you, we commanded you this:
'If anyone is not willing to work, don't let him eat'
– Thessalonians 3:10

I RECALL FROM my high-school psychology class that we need something to do, someone to love, and something to look forward to for our mental health. None of us are exempt from that and nobody should sit back and live the life of luxury, even if we win the lottery. We need to make ourselves useful.

Sometimes I've subscribed to the opposite of what psychology teaches. Sometimes I think I need some job to lament, someone to nitpick, and a future obligation I wished I hadn't agreed to and now dreaded.

I've gotten to the place where I'm so thankful for having to show up to work. I've been on this career path for 30 years now, earning government gouda. Because of me dragging my butt out of bed when I didn't feel like it, I've learned so much more about myself than I would have if I had married a rich man and didn't have to work. Plus, to be a trophy wife requires more beauty and boobs than I was given.

Work has been my ego refinery and talent fitness center. Thanks to having to show up to work, I discovered I'm a decent speaker and writer, and I can easily plan and visualize all the tasks that need to be done to get to success. And I don't get on peoples' nerves too bad. Thanks to work, I'm no longer that timid girl who wouldn't speak her truth or confront the Eddy's of the world. I've learned how to deal with difficult personalities and stick up for myself and others. When I put that stuff on my resume, I call it strong planning, organizational, communication, and emotional intelligence skills.

The stress of life and work have removed so many impurities and gunk that needed sloughing. Doing 30 years of the daily grind has shown me I can bounce back from setbacks and failures. I'm more resilient because I kept showing up even after screwing up. Like when I try to give feedback and it goes off the rails, or when my speech gets tongue-tied, I don't beat myself up as much as I used to.

Thanks to my career, I'm becoming more of who God intended me to be. If I didn't have to work, I probably would not have evolved much and spent my time focusing on my outsides, like going to collagen and blowout appointments and personal trainer sessions. This way I was forced to focus on the innermost me where true treasure lies, not the outward which quickly fades.

I've worked since I was at least ten years old, and I am looking forward to tapping out of my career once I hit the magic age and get to collect the best Government Cheese ever, a pension! It's been very tempting to tap out sooner. After the mistakes I have made, I'm surprised I haven't been shown the door. All I ever wanted was a job that would allow me to pay for groceries without having a panic attack. I'm proud to be a civil servant, and I love the security blanket of knowing where my next paycheck will come from.

Auntie Raven's former best friend and my prior babysitter, Barbara, works at the same place I do. We often share updates about our families. As part of a leadership program, Barbara and I were paired up in a mentoring relationship which is another glimpse into how God works. Barbara has been a great sounding board for me as I sort out my life and work problems.

I guess I'll go back to work tomorrow. I always do.

Lionel

Lionel got cancer. Still thinking I stole $40K and a bottle of bourbon, he told Chance when he died, I would get $1, Leah and Chance would get a few thousand, and the rest should go to the diabetes foundation. He was a Type 1 Diabetic.

It didn't take me long to decide to visit. I knew what Jesus would want me to do, even though it still hurt that I was wrongfully accused. I called him.

"Hi Lionel, I'm going to pay you a visit today. Is there anything you need? Do you need a haircut?"

"Yes, and I could use a shave, and can you trim my toenails? And could you pick up some root beer?"

"You bet. I'll grab my scissors and clippers. See you soon!"

I wheeled him outside to get fresh air and take care of his grooming needs. He had a friend from his neighborhood visiting too. I handed Lionel his root beer. I didn't like that his friend was smoking a cigarette nearby while I tended to Lionel. The smell of cigarettes makes me feel rage since it reminds me of my days of living at The House of Death. I set aside my auto-pilot rage knowing this is exactly what I should be doing, taking care of a dying man who wanted his hair and nails trimmed before meeting his maker.

Later that evening Lionel became unresponsive. Chance, his family, and I visited Lionel the next day. He was allowed morphine every hour. My brother was too scared to give it to him. I told Chance I'd do it and gave it to Lionel on the prescribed hourly schedule.

I didn't know if Lionel really needed it and second guessed my motives. Was I hastening his death because the bedside vigil made me uncomfortable? Or was I doing the right thing, making sure he got his morphine on time?

As Lionel took his last breaths, Chance's wife, the nurse, and I cried and sang, "Come Holy Spirit, Come…"

I know Lionel must have had something wrong with his brain that caused him to think so poorly of me. I know that I remind many people, including him, of Mom. My voice is similar and I'm starting to look more like her. I think I was a proxy for the real source of his pain. He projected his unaddressed anger or sadness with Mom towards me.

Being the most trusted, Chance and his wife took care of Lionel's finances and liquidated everything. Chance and his wife took the bulk of the estate and gave us some of Lionel's gun collection and his fishing boat, and a couple thousand to Leah. I hadn't expected anything, let alone $1. And no, I never took $40K. Thanks for not thinking I did.

I ran into Igor at a local restaurant. The one who scored Lionel's beautiful property and Mom's hummingbird feeder. My sweet husband arrived in the restaurant's waiting area before me, and I saw him chatting it up with Igor and his friends. I thought, "Oh shit. There's that guy. I can't be fake and be nice. What do I do?"

I approached my husband and the huddle of Igor and friends. Frank said, "Mary, you remember Igor, right?" I'm usually bubbly and cheerful in greeting people but this time I restrained myself. I stood there stiff, my face fixed in a cold emotionless stare and said three words: "I remember you."

Perspective

When we judge others, we leave no room to love them.
– Mother Teresa

NOT TOO LONG ago, Jimmy visited Summer and Misty. He told me how they all reminisced about the "good old days" of going to softball games and living with Eddy at my mom's house. His words rocked my world. I thought, "The *good old days*? Oh my freaking gosh—their *best days* were my *worst days*!" Back then, I would have traded anything to be treated as well as Misty. Now, I know better. My heart goes out to them knowing one of my lowest points in life was their highest. How much lower did things get? According to the photos, Summer and Misty have the wisdom and skin well beyond their chronological years.

What was it that made Eddy and Misty target me says more about them than it does me. Now that I closely examine the bong resin of my life, Eddy is getting smaller and less powerful. And when he shows up in other people, triggering my hard-coded responses, I have better governance over my old thought patterns. I see these perceived assaults for what they are. No more (or shall we say much less) clenched jaw, upset tummy, or tight fists as I go about my day. I'm inhabiting my whole self. Mostly. I have a voice. Usually. I still over-explain myself to help prevent perceived judgments. Or I crack stupid jokes, and spontaneously dance. I'm working on that—my comedy material and dance moves, that is.

Eddy is like the Scooby Doo villain who has been unmasked and is no longer scary. I'm sad for his choices. It's safe to say he did not live his best life. Neither did his children. Or maybe they did, and it could have been much worse. Who am I to say?

I have fewer recurring dreams where I'm living in The House of Death. Each dream varies a little, yet the same. Mom has left to live with her new husband, and I'm there alone. The house is always in its dilapidated shape. Sometimes it's damaged from a fire. I'm usually in the process of selling it and know that it needs a remodel and I consider selling it as is, just to be done with it, even though I'll take a loss and my siblings will be disappointed. Usually Eddy and his brother are squatting in the house and Mom won't help me make them leave. I don't know exactly what this means, but I really don't want them taking up space in my subconscious and showing up in my dreams. I'd much rather fly or see Grandma, Mom, and Grandpa during my dreams.

I heard Eddy died of cirrhosis of the liver. I'm surprised he lasted so long. I often wonder why God lets mean people live so long and sometimes takes the nicer ones early. It's like my cat Princess. She's the one-eyed mean kitty of the litter and is outliving her younger siblings. Here's a quote I read somewhere that reminded me of Eddy, Summer, and Misty, from the wise words of Thich Nhat Hanh:

"When you plant lettuce, if it does not grow well, you don't blame the lettuce. You look for reasons it is not doing well. It may need fertilizer, or more water, or less sun. You never blame the lettuce."

They were like a bunch of wilted lettuce that wasn't nourished well. May their lettuce be thriving now. May Eddy's rest in peace. I'll try to love and not judge because love is the greatest commandment. (Matt 22:36-40).

Gardens grow better with fertilizer. And crap makes a good fertilizer. Too much crap, and it's not healthy for the garden. Just enough and your garden will thrive. I'm grateful for my crap sandwiches. It helped this Mary's Garden grow.

Jimmy said, "You should call Misty, I have her phone number." I didn't want to, but I felt like God gave me a hint through Jimmy. Obediently, I reached out to her social media account, extending an olive branch to my past, here's what I wrote:

"Hey Misty, it's Mary! Happy almost Bday. I just got a msg from Jimmy (love him!) saying you guys just had a get together with your uncles and him. So glad to hear you are alive and well. He gave me a ph number, I called it and got some lady. Guess he made a typo. Anyway, just reaching out to say hi, hope you and your family are well. I bet a lot has happened since I last saw you. Sorry to hear about your dad. In looking back, I know he had his demons and want to believe he was doing the best he could. That's all any one of us can do here. How's your kids? How's Summer. I live in Northern Californa; I do see Monica and Denise and Shelly when life doesn't get in the way. Even Monica and I work at the same place, but I still get too busy at work to have lunch with her. I should get my priorities straight. They're doing well. Don't think Monica's on f/b, but Denise is. I have two kids and they're the joy of my life. Jimmy said your kids are great, I'm sure you make a great mom. I remember when you had your first. Anyway, hope to hear back from you."

She read my message that day and never responded.

Jailtime

IT WAS TIME for me to find a new ministry. I've taught children's confirmation classes, cleaned up after events, and served Holy Communion. I don't like cleaning my own house, let alone events. I nearly dropped an F-bomb while teaching the kids when a loud noise startled me. I had a grumpy old man complain that I wasn't reverent enough around the body of Christ. And if there's too much blood of Christ left over after communion, I'm expected to chug it. I started hoping there would be plenty leftover whenever I served. None of these ministries were a good match.

God flicked my ear to become a jail minister. He whispered that idea to me for a couple of years. I thought He was crazy and didn't know what He was asking. I heard it said, "God doesn't call the qualified, he qualifies the called." God knew the girls in jail are more my speed, and they would be more forgiving if I curse or don't seem reverent enough.

After going through the lengthy background check, and pairing up with my amazing minister mentor Ray, it was time to teach solo. I studied the sermon on the mount scripture for my first session. The elevator took me to a series of doors where I had to get buzzed in. I arranged the chairs in a half circle and acted like I knew what I was doing with the CD player, trying to get a worship song ready.

I read through my notes and waited for my first group of girls. I was nervous and sweating, pleading with God, "Help me!"

I saw a crowd of girls wearing orange jumpsuits congregating by the glass door. Soon they were buzzed in. I smiled as they grabbed their chairs and said, "Hi!"

Like Ray taught, we started with an opening prayer, a worship song, introductions, and prayer intentions. I told the girls my brief resume. "Hi I'm Mary. I've been addicted to boys, pills, weed, meth, and alcohol. Now I'm addicted to Jesus, exercise, and homemade baked goods."

I offered up their prayer intentions to the Lord. "Please help Annabelle's court appointment go well. Please help Nancy get her kids back. Please help Clare and all of us stay sober. And for all the intentions on our heart, we ask this in Your name. Your will be done. Amen."

A funny thing happens when I beg God to help me. He does! Words flew out of my mouth. Funny analogies came to me. I spoke from my knowledge bank of scripture, self-help books, and life, powered by the Holy Spirit Himself. During the two-hour class I said, "When life gives you a crap sandwich, don't smoke the rock, grab onto the rock." We all laughed at that one. I could only tell them that with conviction because I did exactly what they were doing, except I never got caught and forced to wear orange.

I've seen so much love and kindness in jail. And they're smart and fearless. In one class, a dark-haired beauty, Marla, startled me when she dove quickly out of her chair. I didn't realize one of the girls was fainting. Marla saved the girl from smacking her head on the cold tiles. The girls might be facing serious charges, but they still have plenty of love and kindness to give. I found my ministry.

Auntie Raven's Back

ONE OCTOBER, AUNTIE Raven showed up at my job. I was typing away at my computer when my desk phone rang. Caller ID showed it was the lobby's security desk. It was our wedding anniversary and I thought maybe Frank had a bouquet of flowers delivered. I picked up. The security guard said, "We have a Raven Marie here to see you." I was puzzled. Then I realized it was Auntie Raven. Marie was her middle name.

I immediately decided that I would not go out to meet her in the front entrance of my office that houses thousands of employees. I called Frank, second-guessing myself, "Should I go out there? Maybe she is clean?" We decided against it.

An hour later I called the security desk. "Is Raven still there?"

"Yes, and she said she's cold."

"I'll come down soon. But can you please observe and be ready to escort her out if she starts acting crazy."

I grabbed a drink, an apple, and a public transportation ticket. I hurried to the locker room I use when I cycle to work and retrieved a pair of my clean underwear and socks. I knew better from my Al-Anon meetings and reading than to give an addict money.

When I approached Auntie in the lunchroom, I saw the security personnel nearby waiting and observing. I noticed a few people from work looking at us, wondering what was going on.

Auntie Raven turned around, took a look at me, and said, "You look just like your mom!" I thanked her.

"How are you doing?" I asked.

She rambled some nonsense.

"I have some snacks, clean socks, and underwear for you."

She raised her voice, "I don't want your damn underwear, it would be like I'm in your pants!"

I interrupted several times and calmly repeated, "Auntie, I can give you a ride to the hospital or a train pass to go to the local shelter." She did not take me up on my repeated offers. She got belligerent and even louder.

I waived at the security guard to come help and said to Auntie, "You need to leave and not come back!"

She started screaming, "MARY! WHAT DID YOU AND FRANK DO WITH THE MONEY!???"

I had no idea what she was talking about. What's with everyone accusing me of taking money? I swiftly walked away from the lunchroom scene as she continued to follow behind me and yell crazy incoherent sentences.

I yelled back, "YOU NEED MENTAL HELP!" The security guard escorted her out the door as all lunchroom eyeballs watched.

I walked through the security turnstile and back to my desk. I called Uncle Bruce and Auntie Eleanor to let them know what happened and vent. That put them on alert that she might show up to their house next.

Auntie Raven showed up at my work the following year, also in October. My buddy Ray says that's when the jails get full because it's cold outside. My homeless Auntie must get cold in October too. This time I didn't wonder if she was clean. I didn't go out to greet her. I often wondered if she was still alive. This visit confirmed she was.

The following summer, her kind former coworker once again drove Auntie Raven to my house on a Saturday afternoon. I was in my front yard sitting in a chair enjoying a book. I was home alone since my husband stepped out to run an errand. I heard a car drive up and thought it was the neighbors. I heard footsteps walking through my gravel and someone talking to one of my cats. My heart dropped. I knew it was Auntie Raven.

I stood up and took one look at her. Her gaunt face and wild eyes indicated she was still active in her addiction. Thankfully, the Holy Spirit took over. I told her, "Raven, you are not clean. You need help. You need to leave now, or I am calling the cops."

She lucidly said, "Well, I've done a little but not that much." She then spoke her typical nonsense and began yelling at me.

This time, I loudly repeated. "RAVEN, YOU ARE NOT CLEAN, I'M CALLING THE COPS IF YOU DON'T LEAVE!" I started walking to get my phone. She walked the other way and left with her former coworker, who I'm sure isn't thrilled Raven keeps showing up at her doorstep.

I pray Raven gets clean and well. She has beautiful children and grandchildren. I heard she's currently living in a homeless encampment.

There's a famous marshmallow study[9] where kids were put in a room with a lone marshmallow and told to not eat it. And that if they obey, they will be rewarded with two marshmallows. Some kids get impatient and eat the marshmallow, lick it, or smell it. And some obey and delay their gratification for a greater reward. The kids who knew how to delay gratification were more successful later in life, as defined by education, economic status, and other measures.

I wondered what Auntie might have done in that study. I guessed she would have eaten the marshmallow, located the stash of all the remaining marshmallows and gobbled those too. Then

---

[9] The delayed gratification study, "The Stanford Marshmallow Experiment" in 1972 was led by Walter Mischel, a psychologist and professor at Stanford University.

the staff would come in the room, and she'd make up a compelling story, with crocodile tears streaming down her face, telling the study facilitators that they didn't explain the rules correctly and that she misunderstood. It wasn't her fault!

Codependent A Little Less

THANKS TO THE help of 12 Steps, Al-Anon, much prayer, and the fact that my sister wiped out Aunt Darlene's burial fund without telling me, I stopped giving my sister money for her routine emergencies. I really thought she would bounce back. Weren't we made from the same tough stuff?

Instead of giving her more money, I gave her unsolicited advice. I thought the thousands of loaned dollars gave me that right. I repeatedly suggested she get her government job back. I suggested that she and her family take whatever jobs they could find, pool the money and work towards getting back on track. Showing up to my job every day worked for me and millions of others. Surely, we're not wrong?

My advice was not welcomed. Leah sent me a strongly worded email admonishing me. I had to do the 12 steps on my sister starting with, "I am powerless over my sister's life decisions and my life became unmanageable." I detached with love. I let go and let God. I let the crisis happen. That wasn't easy. It was freaking hard. I was so consumed with her life; I was unable to participate in my own.

I'm thankful for the day when I opened up the bank statement for Darlene's burial fund and saw that the balance was now $0.00. This was money from the sale of Grandma's mobile home, after she died. I thought I was the victim of identity theft when I saw all those zeros.

I called the bank. After several minutes of them telling me a withdrawal was made in Texas, they finally mentioned my sister's name. "Wait, what?! Was the withdrawal in Texas or what?"

The telephone agent said, "It was a withdrawal by a Leah...."

I was PISSED beyond measure. How could she wipe out all of Darlene's burial fund money? I made the mistake of allowing Leah to borrow a little from the account thinking she was going to pay it right back. How could Leah let her life get this far off track?! How did she go from millions, to not having a pot to piss in, or a window to throw it out of? I thought she would be like the pig who built his house out of bricks.

With help from Melody Beattie's masterpiece, *Codependent No More*, I released Leah to God. I needed to mind my own damn business and stop trying to ram advice down my sister's throat when she didn't want it. Unfortunately, this lesson cost thousands and tons of self-inflicted torture. I wasn't addicted to drugs anymore. I was addicted to fear and worry. I gave Leah's status in life absolute power over mine. If her life was off the rails, I was unable to enjoy mine.

My unsolicited lectures, telephone seminars, and emails didn't work. What I really needed to do was let God run the universe and stay out of his business. I needed to, "Be still and know that He is God" (Psalm 46:10). <u>And you're not, Mary!</u> It wasn't my job to run around trying to fix everyone's life or insert myself into God's lesson plan for everybody else.

Less *is* more and I didn't have to work that hard. I can only be in charge of my own life, really. If anyone wants to make dumb decisions, it's not my job to make sure they learn their lessons in a timeframe that makes me comfortable. If folks haven't figured out that getting a job and paying your damn bills is a good formula to have some peace, food, and shelter, well, I formally resign as the instructor.

A therapist wisely told me, "Everybody gets to do their own

life, that's how this thing works." I'm on my path, Leah's on hers. I cannot jump into her skin and live her life while also trying to live my own.

Six months after I started my jail ministry, I learned why God insisted I join that ministry. My sister went to jail, and not as a visitor. I was thankful Mom had already died by the time my sister's life hit a new low. I'm certain it would have hurt her more than it hurt me. And that's saying a lot.

Thanks to serving as a jail minister, I knew about the love and support Leah would receive from her roommates. I saw it with my own two eyeballs, and I desperately needed that reassurance.

Shortly after I learned Leah was in jail, my family of four got on a plane to France. I wanted to have one last big vacation before the kids started to leave the nest.

I planned the trip a year in advance and couldn't fully enjoy it knowing Leah was in jail. My heart ached. I was distracted. I felt guilty that I had a great life and Leah didn't. My family visited many beautiful churches, including Notre Dame before it caught fire. I got on my knees and prayed for Leah and her family in every church.

Leah served her sentence for driving several pounds of green stuff across state lines. I guess it was to help dig herself out of a financial hole. I wondered why I hadn't heard from Leah in months, and my life was more peaceful because of it. Leah was pissed at me and already stopped talking to our dad, brother, and finally me. I hoped she must have taken some of my advice and started earning an income.

I didn't want to reach out to Leah. I was so angry that she let her life come to this. It took me a few weeks after returning from France before I wrote the first of 19 letters to Leah, but that's another book.

Near the end of her incarceration, I learned all about probation and adding money to a commissary account. I made dozens of calls to transfer her probation to California and got her a plane ticket to return home. I was happy she was free. I didn't plan on handing out money for her next crisis and she knew that.

A few months after her release, she incessantly called my work phone. I couldn't take the calls but checked the messages. She said, "I really hate to ask, but I need $350 to pay for storage, otherwise I won't be able to get the kids' photos." I didn't want to call back and start this cycle again. It's a simple answer. Yes or no. I wanted to say no.

I finally called her back after she continued to robo-call me during work. I went into teacher mode. "Look, your priorities are food and shelter….in no way should you be paying for a storage fee. Let that stuff go."

She responded, "But I got the first month free and I was in a hurry…and I just need to get the pictures out, and in order to do that, I have to pay $350 by 10 p.m., otherwise it's lost forever." She's skilled at backing me in a corner.

I relented and paid for the storage. Thankfully, she hasn't asked for any more financial assistance since then.

Months later, I learned she lost her storage when she called and asked if Frank and I could take her to the storage facility and pick up some boxes. She admitted she lost the storage and said the storage facility set aside her boxes of family photos.

Darlene's health was deteriorating. She was getting all sorts of infections at her nursing home and was in and out of the hospital. It was time for her to join Grandma and Mom. Near the end, she barely knew I visited. I was sad and relieved when she passed. Dealing with Health and Human services to annually renew her benefits was a larger chore than it should've been.

I resented that I was the only regular visitor. I know it's hard going to the nursing home. It smells like a porta-potty and it's depressing. I tried to encourage family members, but they had their reasons for not visiting.

It was time to plan another funeral, without the cushion of Darlene's burial fund. In a burst of anger, I told the family that Leah helped herself to what was left of the burial fund. I was thankful Auntie Eleanor and Uncle Bruce contributed to the costs. But my tattling on Leah added more strife to our broken family relationships. I instantly regretted my tattling.

I chose a silver casket since Darlene loved the Raiders football team. At Darlene's funeral, I read my poem tribute to her life.

From Helicoptering to Gallivanting

Do not confine your children to your own learning, for they were born in another time. – Hebrew Proverb

AFTER DARLENE DIED, I joined a biker gang. Some of us have tattoos. We're called "Gallivanting Gals." We're a hodgepodge of nine distinct personalities who would never have become friends if we hadn't bonded over bicycling. And I just love us. God put these ladies in my path at the right time. Most are ahead of me in being empty nesters and menopause. They are a wealth of advice, kindness, and fun. One of them is Monica. We've cycled around Tahoe and rode a century (that's 100 miles) in one day. A few of us hiked 100 miles in eight days in Ireland. During each mile, we laugh, chat, and learn. I'm grateful God picks my friends because nobody else would have put us together. God makes sure we find our squad.

Like my friends warned, my kids started to be real jerks before they left for college. It was their way of breaking up with me and forming their independence. Everything I did annoyed them. Every comment that came out of their mouths was marked with irritation.

"Mom, why do you pick at your food like that."

"Mom, why are you so oblivious?"

"Mom, why do you make that weird face."

They ganged up on me which caused me to mock them with a cheer, "One, two, three… MOM SUCKS!"

Once Grace and Joey were both away at college, I couldn't help but think of all the things I did wrong and could have done differently.

I dug out our dusty video cassettes and took them to Costco to convert to DVDs. It was money well spent.

I watched several hours of home videos from when the kids were babies to about nine. I saw evidence of a good mom taking time to patiently feed her babies, read books to them, teach them how to ride bikes, watch their school plays, snuggle, and give them elaborate birthday parties.

Those videos put me at peace and helped me stop beating myself up for my darkest period. I was a better mom than I remembered.

Like my gallivanting friends said, being an empty nester isn't horrible. It's peaceful at home and there are less clothes on the floor and groceries to buy.

It's wonderful when the kids come and visit. I load up on their favorite snacks and look forward to their visits. I'm so proud of them. They're kind, smart, and hard-working. But sometimes I over-worry about their journey. I know that worrying means I'm lacking faith.

To comfort me, I often ponder the great poem by Khalil Gibran. He wrote, "Our children are not ours. They come through us but they're not from us." My favorite part is, "You are the bows from which your children as living arrows are sent forth." Only sometimes I feel like a defective bow and didn't launch my kids as far as I should've. Like my faulty bow launched them only a few feet in front of me and I need a redo. What I really need to do is trust that their launch was what it was supposed to be, and that God will guide my children as he guides all of us. Surely, He won't help everyone else and forget about my kids. He's the archer, I'm just the bow.

My repeat lesson is about control. A gallivanting girlfriend told me that people who are controlling usually had little to no control growing up, so they try to make up for that by controlling their lives and the lives of others. It makes sense why I did so many weird rituals when I was little. Like when I held my breath for 30 seconds when I saw the number six. Or I cracked my knuckles and toes constantly. I wish I would have met her sooner.

Being a tad controlling, I'm an experienced backseat driver in my kids' lives. I sometimes reach over for their steering wheel, brake, and gas pedal and try to take over. They say I make a life lesson out of everything, and they're tired of my sermons. I can't help it; I want to make sure they don't make the same mistakes as I did.

Another gallivanting girlfriend told me that my new job description is to just listen and not give advice unless asked. And when I'm listening, know that my kids are hearing their own words during that time, which is more powerful than mine at this point in their lives.

I occasionally receive parental paychecks from my kids, confirming I didn't screw them up too bad. Joey texted me at 4 a.m. from his college dorm, "I love u so much. Mom. Ur the sweetest most kind person I know and I'm happy to call u my mom <red heart emoji>"

I wrote back the next day when I woke up, "Wow, I sure do love u too! I'm overwhelmingly happy to call you son, Joey. <Kiss emoji x2, 2 pink hearts, prayers, large pink heart.>"

I asked him later if it was a drunk text and he said no. He had been up all night talking to a friend about life. She had broken up with her boyfriend. She's a good girl and she makes my son food.

Grace recently gave me a sizable parental paycheck I'll never forget. She called on her way home from the dentist and told me, "The new hygienist was nice. She asked me what I was up to. I told her I graduated from Cal Poly and have a job helping people with disability benefits. She asked me all about my job and how I had my act together at such a young age. I told her I get my work ethic from my mom."

Grace made my soul burst with joy. She knew I'd appreciate hearing that story.

If I don't get another compliment from my kids, I don't care. I'll be more than happy with these two.

Just Say Nope

The trees, the plants, the flowers grow in silence. The stars, the sun, the moon move in silence. Silence gives us a new perspective.
– Mother Teresa

WHEN I GET invited to do too many events, several of the invitations make me immediately say, "Nope" loudly in my head. Spending three hours doing a painting on my precious weekend does not sound like fun. Hitting happy hour after work to eat greasy appetizers and take time from my vital decompress time is not happiness. Yes, I love people, but I also require significant alone time. I don't have much energy after work. Any introvert who works in technology knows what I am talking about. After work, I'd much rather get a workout in, eat, and have a clean kitchen before I wind down, and read a good book.

Too often, I'll go along with the crowd and come home irritable because I neglected my much-needed time of respite. But lately I've been getting more and more comfortable with saying no. And just recently I responded 100% authentically to an invitation for the first time in my life. But before I tell you how that went down, let me tell you some of the mistakes I have made.

As an eager to please teenager, I'd say yes to everyone even though I made prior commitments, only having to cancel on everyone but my favorite invitation. That earned me the nickname, "Flake" by Monica. I didn't have the nerve to say, "I made other plans" or, "I'm going dancing with Violet."

Fast forward 30+ years and it's a similar but more mature battle. When friends text "Let's get together for some happy hour appetizers after work." Everyone quickly responds affirmatively while I'm wishing I had the courage to say, "Nope." But time and time again, I'll go along, despite my mind and body protesting. I end up enjoying everyone's company and the mozzarella sticks.

Driving home I think to myself; it was fun and maybe I *can* do things after work. By the time I get home, with my face greasy from the day, mascara now dripping down my cheeks, all I want to do is shower and go to bed. Of course, I'm greeted with shoes and socks all over the floor and tools or car parts scattered on the kitchen counter. Frank is unbothered by clutter. That mess is the tipping point that sends my frazzled ass off the cliff, and I'm just not nice.

I take out my frustration and anger on the people I love the most. All because I didn't want to say nope to people who don't have to live with the worst version of me when I don't get my required decompress time. I mean there's yelling and an occasional threat of moving out on my own. You know me by now, I'm not kidding. I have done this repeatedly and you think I'd finally learn. Nope.

Thinking way back to reading through Dad's *Playboy* magazines, I wonder, what are my Turn-Ons and Turn-Offs? Today if I were interviewed, I would say my Turn Ons are: Cancelled plans so I can be by myself. Wearing pajamas all day on Sunday. A clean and quiet house with lit candles. A well-manicured yard. A good book. Sparkles. Jogging outside. Jesus. Kind words. Turn Offs: Inefficiency. Having to do something twice due to incompetence. Slow walkers and customer service representatives. Car parts on my kitchen counter. And single-use appliances that take up space. Yes, I realize I'm contradicting myself.

I've made progress, you wouldn't even recognize me! Monica asked if any of us girls would be willing to ride around Tahoe again. We did this ride a couple years ago to honor her beautiful Angelica who was tragically murdered by an ex-boyfriend. We wanted to get Monica focused on physical exercise to help her, and it would be a beautiful ride to honor her precious daughter whose life was cut short.

That ride almost literally knocked me out after I dropped a water bottle, stopped abruptly, and a cyclist rammed into me causing me to get air born and slam into the concrete. Monica saw the whole thing in slow motion and watched me get vertical with the front tire on the ground and the other directly above in the air as I flipped. Once we got pedaling again, Queen's "Another One Bites the Dust" started playing on Monica's phone. We agreed it was Angelica being her silly self as she helped us finish the ride that honored her.

I got a flat tire on the last two miles of the 70+ mile ride. The only flat out of eight of us. Even with all of that, I really didn't feel like spending a whole weekend up there when I'd rather do my recluse-recharging routine. Guess what my first thought was? You are correct. So, after seeing one of the more mature/no-nonsense girls respond with, "I can't," sans excuses, I was inspired to write back for the first time in my life that one authentic Mary word…. "*Nope!*" I am making progress! I hope to continue this trend.

Cure for Somewhere-Else-Itis

I'M A LIVING miracle. I could've easily ended up in the gutter with a needle hanging out of my arm while my pimp looked after me. But God is hilarious, patient, kind, and merciful. Instead, I have a legit job and I get to work with smart people. He took this Government-Cheese eating, red-headed stepchild and shaped me from my flawed upbringing, numerous addictions and transformed me into a God-fearing, law-abiding, tax-paying, sober, decent wife, and mom. Still half crazy, but a miracle.

I will forever be a work in progress, until I die. I have plenty more lessons to learn and hopefully fewer to relearn.

I hope I'm in complete remission of somewhere-else-itis. I found the only cure is being grateful and content in all circumstances, cuddling closer to God and following through on His divine ear flicks. When I heed His suggestions, I have this immense and profound sense of peace and synchronicity, and that I am one with creation. His heavenly cues lead me to what I'm supposed to do next. He told me to read the Bible. I did. He told me to write. So, I'm writing. He told me to visit prisoners. I've never been so fulfilled.

I learned when my life is congruent with His will, that is where real peace lies. I don't need to numb myself with meth, alcohol, opiates, soda, cupcakes, whatever. Ok, maybe cupcakes, but not all 24 at one time.

I often think about the wise words I read from Myles Munroe's book, *Understanding Your Potential*. He said the wealthiest place on earth is the cemetery, "…There lie buried companies that were never started, inventions that were never made, bestselling books that were never written, and masterpieces that were never painted. In the cemetery is buried the greatest treasure of untapped potential." I don't want to be the non-writing author or non-serving jail minister who Myles wrote about.

Imagine a world where we all knew that we had God-given talents and used them to benefit the world. The prisons would be empty, there would be no addictions, no envy, or pride, just each of us doing our thing, making this planet even more beautiful. Deathbeds would have no regrets, but satisfaction of a life well-lived.

A former coworker reminded me that I used to say, long before I met Frank, "I'm going to graduate from college. Then I'm going to get married. After being married for two years, I will have two kids. I want to be a good example for my future children."

I wanted to be the kind of mom a kid wants to be born to. With me sober and still married, I guess I did break the addiction and divorce cycle. Joey and Grace are becoming more of who they're supposed to be, discovering their talents and purpose. God heard my heart's desires and made them a reality. He blessed me more than I could have ever imagined.

Mother Teresa said, "I am a little pencil in God's hands. He does the thinking. He does the writing. He does everything and sometimes it is really hard because it is a broken pencil, and He has to sharpen it a little more." And "Spread love everywhere you go. Let no one ever come to you without leaving happier." I'm no saint, but I sure would like to be the best Mary. I'll be God's disco ball, shining specks of light, color, and love.

Mom Visits from the Grave

MOM OFTEN HELPED Frank and me with the kids during the elementary school years. I'm so grateful the kids got to see the best parts of Mom. While Frank and I finished up our workdays, she was first in the car line to pick up the kids. She'd drive them to the gas station so they could pick out their favorite candy. Then she'd take them back to our house and wait for us to get home from work. It was a huge help.

I think I showed Mom how to love. Over the years, she watched me hug and love on my kids, bake cookies with them, scream for them during sports games, and take them on fun family vacations every year.

One day after work, the kids were seated at the kitchen table doing their homework and Mom sat on my comfy green couch solving one of her sudoku puzzles. Out of the blue she said, "I wish you were my mom so I could be a little girl again and feel a mom's arms love me."

I didn't realize how profound this moment was until much later. I took a brief pause, sat down next to her, and gave her a hug and said, "Oh Mom, I love you so much!"

I wish I would have hugged her longer and savored the moment more. I wish I would have asked her more about her upbringing. I wish I had realized that Mom was verbalizing one of her biggest compliments. She was telling me I was a good mom, and she was proud of me. Maybe she was even approaching an apology, telling me she wished she could have been better at the mom thing.

My siblings and I got the best version of Grandma Lou and Grandpa. They were different people by the time we came along. Mom didn't get the love she wanted either. Grandma Lou was busy with six kids, one with special needs, and an alcoholic husband. Mom had no idea how to receive or give love in healthy ways. Why should I fault her?

Yes, I wished Mom didn't succumb to her addiction and allow her boyfriend to terrorize her children. When I try to rationalize it, I come up with a couple answers. She had serious baggage of her own from her upbringing and alcoholic father. And being rejected by anyone is devastating, let alone your spouse.

I had dinner with Leah and told her about some of the stories I was writing and the book title. She reminded me of other stories I blocked. Leah reminded me that it took a long time for me to agree that Mom did not like her.

We never got an apology from Mom, and she got defensive whenever we'd bring up the past. When Mom and Grandma Lou were still alive, at every Thanksgiving, Easter, or kids' birthday party, Leah, Chance, and I would inevitably have a therapy session, laughing about the crazy stories when really, we were crying inside and still trying to process what happened. We *had* to talk about it.

If I'm honest, I was more disappointed with Mom than Dad. She was present in my life, contributed to my pain and witnessed my daily disappointments. She had the power to kick Eddy out, be nicer to her kids, and stop drinking. She didn't use her power. Dad was conveniently absent most of the time, always having money for a new 280 Z every few years while we had holes in our shoes, minimal clothing, and intermittent food.

Being the charming one, Dad gave better apologies later and claimed, "I had no idea what was going on in that house!"

To which I answered, "You're right, you *weren't* there" with crystal clear un-passive aggression.

Mom did many things right. She put fear in us which turned out to be a blessing. She tried to make up for lost time once she got sober. The cast of characters coming in and out of our house and struggles made us stronger. We know how to overcome adversities and think on our feet. My brother and I turned out surprisingly well. My sister has her struggles and is on her own path. Leah says incarceration saved her life, but that's another book.

I got a little moment of courage during one family event and asked Mom to apologize. It didn't go how I envisioned. She defensively said, "I did the best I could."

I thought, but didn't dare say, "Really, Mom? That was your best?" A part of me knows she could and should have done better.

A more evolved part of me believes that she did her best. She was hanging on by a thread. I've been there too.

Sitting at The Old Spaghetti Factory with Leah, I decided to pretend I was Mom and Leah would be herself, and I would give her the apology she deserved. It went like this:

"Leah. Honey. I love you. I should have been a better mother to you. I made some huge mistakes and I'm so sorry. I was a broken person myself trying to get through the days and I chose alcohol to numb my pain. The attention and love I gave to Summer and Misty should have been also given to you. I put booze, Eddy, Summer, and Misty above you. I didn't love you like you deserved to be loved. I wasn't there for you when you needed a training bra, started your period, and I know I physically and verbally abused you and allowed others to do the same. While alive, I couldn't bear to face what I had done and fully admit it to myself, let alone you, and give you, Mary, or Chance the apology you deserved. Instead, I stuffed it down and ended up deteriorating my health both physically and mentally. I ended up drinking again near the end of my life, just to cope. I'm sorry honey. Now that I'm in heaven I know the love our Lord has for all of us, and I should have given that to you, my daughter, and my children. I messed up the most important job I had while on the planet. I ask that you please forgive me. I know you are a loving mother and are learning from my mistakes and I take comfort in that. Plus remember your dad was the asshole who ended the marriage. I wanted to work things out, but he didn't. I regret so much and wish I gave you the mom you deserved for all your years. Be strong daughter, I love you. I'll see you in heaven."

We both teared up and I wish I had recorded it. It just came to me, and I think it's what Mom would have said if she could. Better late than never. If you don't get the apology you deserve…ask a sibling or loving friend to serve as a proxy. The Holy Spirit will give you the words and the healing.

That's it for Now

My upbringing, life experiences, and stupid choices put layers upon layers of crap that I have worked to slough off with a truth loofa. All my corrupt thought patterns were rooted in the crap sandwiches I was first served by others, then handcrafted my own, toasted on whole grain bread.

I thought I was fine after I dug myself out of poverty and shameful environment. That was only step one. Life's pressures had a way of making me reveal, deal, heal and complete all the steps.

I numbed these tough feelings until I realized it only made things worse. Until I faced my issues head on, with a sober mind, I kept repeating my lessons. I learned to get used to difficult feelings, cuddle up with them, thank them, and Febreze my garbage thinking with fresh and healthy thought patterns, one step at a time.

I want to live my best life. I don't want anyone else to make similar mistakes. I hope my story helps you too. No amount of victimhood, shame or blame is going to move any of us forward. Every one of us needs to air out our dirty laundry, take our dusty bones out of the closet, high-five them for the lessons, and drop 'em off at the thrift store or dumpster. That way our past doesn't have any power over us once it's out there. (Please note dear reader, some of us may need to face our painful past with the help of a professional. And remember, I'm not a doctor. This stuff ain't easy!)

I'm much better at standing up for myself and not permitting disrespect thrown my way. Most days. I had a recent altercation that may or may not demonstrate my growth. You be the judge.

I popped by Walmart to pick up a few things. I noticed that if I wanted to buy a cosmetic item, I had to pay for it in the secure cosmetic part of the store. I picked up a couple lemons, bag of flour, grabbed eye makeup and headed to the makeup counter. A lady in front of me was having issues with her credit card and took a long time. The line started to queue up. I was next and as the cashier was ringing up my items, I heard a lady say, "This is for makeup only."

She was talking to me. I turned around, looked her in the eyes and said, "Why don't you believe the best in me?"

She snottily said, "That's a lemon I see in your hand."

I grabbed my makeup items and flatly replied, "Yes, and here's my makeup."

"Well, I buy my makeup here and my groceries in the other line," she said.

I thought for a half a second and cheerfully said, "Well…you deserve a blue ribbon."

She slammed her black eyeliner on the counter and left.

I guess she showed me. I'm sure she's an Eddy in someone's life. Not in mine. Not today.

One More Thing

Yesterday is gone. Tomorrow has not yet come.
We have only today. Let us begin. – Mother Teresa

I DON'T HAVE a perfect ending that ties all these stories in a fancy package like the ending of *Fast Times at Ridgemont High* did so brilliantly for us. You heard my sister went to jail and now she's out. Jimmy is still in my life and is full of wisdom. Like when 911 happened, I asked how he was doing and he answered, "It's a good day. A plane hasn't hit my building!"

Auntie Raven is still alive. I pray she gets sober.

Chance has intermittent contact with Misty. She asked her friends to pray for Summer because she was facing jail time for allegedly participating in a robbery. Misty earned her degree. I hope their children and grandchildren are doing well.

My pedophile boyfriend Dudley moved back to his hometown. His life was cut short when he confronted a man who allegedly owed him money and ended up killing him with a gun and fled the scene. As the cops chased him down, Dudley pulled over and shot himself before the cops could take him. May he rest in peace. Dang, I'm glad I found Frank.

My elementary school friend Fay ended up dating the hottest guy in high school. While in college I heard she incurred a mountain of debt trying to sustain her fashion icon image. I hope she climbed out of debt. She looked great at our high school reunion.

I usually host Thanksgiving and Easter for my entire family. We have a great time, even though Mom, Grandma Lou, and Aunt Darlene are in heaven, and my sister's family no longer joins us. I pray they will someday.

I can buy all the groceries I want without having a panic attack at the cash register. I still compare prices and don't go buck wild, but I'm finally realizing I'm no longer destitute. Although I still cut Frank's hair.

One thing I know is this. Life is better understood in retrospect. God knows our paths, our choices and the choices imposed on us. He sees the long game on this chessboard. And He always makes it right for His kids. After writing down and processing my past it makes more sense. I feel more sincere forgiveness towards the people who hurt me. It wasn't about me; it was about their pain. And although I can't confidently say they did the best they could. They did a decent job considering the amount of alcohol consumed.

I'm imperfect like the rest of us; but trying to do good in this world. I still have meltdowns when I'm doing too much and forget to say no and take time for myself. I pray I stay on this path and don't reunite with old addictions. I've seen how that plays out in so many lives, including my own. I don't want to live Satan's version of my life and regress to becoming his chew toy. Been there, done that, got the bite marks. I want to live out God's version of my life and tap into His presence and have Him guide me through the rest of the journey. He gives me nudges and sometimes I'm alert and disciplined enough to respond.

And guess what? I found a bag of weed in my car. I thought my car hit a skunk. I hate throwing away food or wasting anything and for a hot second, I actually thought, "Hmmmm, that probably cost $25, should I?" And I immediately threw it in the garbage after quickly texting my family a photo asking, "Why is this bag of weed in my Subaru? P.S. I threw that evil <poop emoji> in the garbage." The devil prowls around like a lion and he's patient. (1 Peter 5:8) Not me, not today, not tomorrow. After all, I'm God's disco ball. And disco balls don't shine brightly when they're stoned.

As I'm reading through the Old Testament again, I noticed how simple life was. Make wine, bread, and have barbeques for God. He loves the smell. There weren't too many expectations. All He ever wanted from his creation was for us to follow a few rules, love Him and each other. And don't make stupid idols. It seemed simple. Why do I think I have to be constantly doing, producing, creating, striving? As I think about my next chapter in life, what's my purpose, what's God want me to do? Maybe all He wants from me is to follow the rules and love. Maybe I don't have to produce so much, like fill up my calendar so there's no white space. Maybe I'm just supposed to live one day at a time. Just let it happen without me being anxious and trying so hard. Just breathe and do the next thing, whatever that is, He'll tell me. There's no need to be a spaz.

The Bible doesn't talk about how Abraham was trying to find his purpose or how Moses dreamt of being a motivational speaker or that Paul wanted his story to go viral. What the heck is wrong with us people today? For now, I guess my point is to share my story like Anne Lamott suggests, "Tell your stories. If people wanted you to write warmly about them, they should have behaved better." I hope sharing my journey has helped you.

P.S. If I get my hands on the Government Cheese recipe, I'll label it Gub'ment Cheese, it could be an amazing business venture with many people like me who would happily pay for it now. Who's with me?

Acknowledgements

THANKS TO ALL my siblings for loving me and helping me remember some stories. Thanks to Mom and Dad for giving me life, love, and a childhood crappy enough to make things interesting and keep me humble. Thanks Grandma Lou for being the best role model. Thanks to my children for being kind humans and loving your momma. Thanks to my hubby, for being the calm to my crazy and making me the best lattes. And to my entire family, BFFs, the GGs, my peeps from the neighborhood and parish, all my home girls and boys, and everyone depicted in the book. Thanks to Dover, Tomi, and Nicole for your strong artistic shoulders to lean on. Thank you, Jesus, for being my light, rock, and salvation. And thanks to all my unwitting therapists and teachers, especially: Oprah and her guests, Joyce Meyer, Dr. Laura, M. Scott Peck, David D. Burns, Myles Munroe, Anne Lamott, Melody Beattie, Viktor Frankl, Saint Teresa of Calcutta, Sr. Ann Shields, Byron Katie, Dax Shepard & Monica Padman, Marc Maron, Tim Ferriss, Monsignor Kidder, the Father, Son, and Holy Spirit. And a special shout out to my hard-working beloved colleagues who give government workers a good name. And of course, to Government Cheese. You ooey-gooey-yellow-orange goodness, thanks for keeping me fed.

About the Author

M.K. Hughes is a writer, wisdom seeker and sees herself as God's disco ball trying to shine specks of light, color, and love wherever she goes. She is a recovering addict, worrywart, and helicopter parent of two. M.K. serves as a Technology Director in the public sector and ministers at her local jail. She and her husband live in Northern California.

i *Grandma Lou's Poem*

I don't have to tell you that Grandma Lou was an incredible woman,
She survived two husbands, two sons, and still managed to be fun,
She was a gifted painter, historian, deck builder, gardener, and decorator,
She loved her family, good food, steamy romance novels, and lots of silk flowers,
You wouldn't want to make Grandma mad, it wasn't a pretty sight,
Even Bruce knows, he said, "I'm going to tell my MOM!" after a school fight,
When you hugged her, you could get a whiff of White Shoulders with your nose,
Not that long ago, you didn't even need to be in the same room to smell her Tea Rose,
Our Mom made sure we often visited, as their house was like Disneyland for us,
The wood floors, the swimming pool, and the bottle shop sodas were a plus,
The beautiful bathroom with soap shaped like miniature flowers,
Which Leah insisted on me eating the "candy" because she once had the power,
Her Paradise house was a summer vacation home for us kids,
We'd stack wood, walk to the sign with Darlene, and hang out in Darlene's crib,
While driving in Paradise, Grandpa would speed up at this certain hill,
Grandma would say, "<blank>-Dammit Joe!" and we were all thrilled,

We remember eating SOS by the buckets, Grandma's crappy goulash, and Albertson's Cheetos,
Drinking a warm soda from under Darlene's bed, maybe swiss mocha or a hot cocoa,
The best meal of all, we remember tasted so divine,
Until we discovered it was bug soup, she said, "Eat it, it's fine!"
Then Grandma moved to town, she wanted to be closer to all of us,
So, we all descended at Paradise, and packed up her stuff,
It was awesome, having Grandma and Darlene a lot closer,
To ask for advice on a recipe, listen to her stories and be there for her,
Grandma and Darlene were frequent shoppers at the Grocery Store and Kmart,
Where everyone knew them by name as each of them pushed their own cart,
If you went shopping with her, one thing's for sure,
She'd holler out your name louder than any store speakers,
We all made sure at family events we'd all get together,
As Grandma would boss us around stirring the gravy, being our center,
I know she's happy that we enjoyed each other's company while we were at her bedside,
While heaven prepared her colorful room, and the angels were at her side,
And at our next family gathering, she won't be around to put extra salt in the gravy,
But she'll be happy to look down at us eating, laughing, and continuing as her family,
We love you Grandma Lou!

ii *Mom's Poem*

Mom was an adorable child with blue eyes and blonde curly hair,
The third child of six, you bet she learned how to share
Grampa was in the service, so they moved a lot,
Maybe that's why she didn't travel; she wanted to stay in one spot,
From Japan to Huntington Beach and eventually home,
Mom did more than her share of chores as the family would grow,
She loved her siblings, her horse Snooky, and the outdoors,
Soon she'd marry, have us three kids, who knew what was in store,
Mom made sure we were baptized, and the Holy Spirit is in us,
The best gift she ever gave was ensuring we have Jesus,
As a young one I remember us having fun, hanging out at Grandma Lou's
Drinking sodas from the bottle shop and swimming in the pool,
Leah would boss me around like nobody could (and still does),
Chance became a healthy boy despite his rough entry into this world,
I remember when my school day was done, I'd scurry to get out of that place,
I'd run outside, look for the white Datsun and hope to see a smile on my mom's face,
She kept a watchful eye on all that went on,
The way she called your name would get your attention,
The "scary mom look" she had down pat,
Don't mess with mom, 'cause she'd bite back,
Mom taught me to be practical and get clothes a size larger,
And how a pot of beans could stretch out farther,
Life took a turn and mom did the best she could with what she had,
Her cross was heavy, and she often felt bad,

But then she met Lionel, and married the sweetest man ever,
We are his family and thank him for making mom's life better,
She was so happy with Lionel, her new love, life was good,
They watched over Chance and rode motorcycles around the neighborhood,
Mom loved peace and quiet and juicy red meat,
Her family, her shows, and cats at her feet,
She had an uncanny ability to sniff out BS,
Everyone soon learned to not put that to the test,
I wish things were different and mom was still here,
So I can pick up the phone and bend her ear,
I'd ask her how to make her fried chicken, and how was Japan,
And why didn't I get blessed with her skin that could tan?
She's probably laughing with John, or holding her brother Larry's hand,
Or shooting a game of pool with Grandma or playing Rummy with her dad,
Mom wouldn't want us to fuss or be sad and blue,
But like her favorite song would say, it's her party and we can cry if we want to!

iii *Darlene's Poem*

Darlene's entry into this world was not what we'd all expect,
She started off blind in one eye with injuries caused by forceps,
Her limits did not stop her from trying her best with her mom as her guide,
She never gave up and was able to walk and talk by the time she was 5,
She was the oldest girl, second born out of six little ones,
It was loud and crazy family with lots of drama and fun,
Darlene graduated from High School and would retain everything she took in,
Always able to recite facts on command and all trivia games she would win,
Her brain was like a database, remembering all birthdays, and events; nothing was lost,
She wasn't quiet or shy, raising her voice and index finger to get her point across,
Darlene enjoyed her music, K.D. Lang, Clay Aiken, and especially Patsy Cline
She loved watching her Raiders play, Jay Leno and Days of Our Lives,
All her nieces and nephews remember how cool it was to visit her room,
She'd have a stash of sodas under the bed and we'd guzzle them while she'd listen to her tunes,
We'd also watch the Price Is Right, The Barbara Mandrel show or Lawrence Welk,

During commercials, she'd do her own and moisturize herself with Rose Milk,
She loved a wine cooler, Bartle's and James was her favorite,
She usually asked for two and her cheeks got rosy from drinking it,
In Paradise, we would walk up the road with her, to the sign and back,
Grandpa would force her to do it and she would give him some flack,
When Grandpa died, Grandma and Darlene moved closer to make a fresh start,
They could be seen most days strolling the aisles of Dollar Tree, Lucky or Kmart,
When shopping, Grandma would yell to make sure Darlene was close,
And Darlene would yell back just as loud in her unique voice,
Her health took a turn and she ended up in a nursing home,
Soon she was a favorite, making fast friends with everyone,
Darlene was a friend to all, full of love and light that brightly shined,
It's no mistake that she was born on the day of St Valentine,
We know she quickly entered heaven since she was without sin,
We'll miss her dearly but happy she's with the Lord, her parents some of her siblings again!